MARGARET FULTON'S
FAVOURITE RECIPES

Pork and Veal Terrine, Chicken in Wine and Burgundy Pears

MARGARET FULTON'S
FAVOURITE RECIPES

COOKERY EDITOR "WOMAN'S DAY"
PHOTOGRAPHY WAL EASTON

PAUL HAMLYN
SYDNEY LONDON NEW YORK TORONTO

Published by Paul Hamlyn Pty. Ltd., 176 South Creek Road,
Dee Why West, New South Wales, 2099
First Published 1971 as Entertaining with Margaret Fulton
Reprinted 1973
Copyright © Paul Hamlyn Pty. Ltd. 1971
Printed by Lee Fung, Hong Kong
ISBN 0 600 04146 8

Contents

Acknowledgements

I'm a lucky person, because my work is also my hobby. Also, for many years as cookery editor of 'Woman's Day', I've had the pleasure of working side by side with people who love good food and cooking as much as I do.

Entertaining is something most good cooks love to do and the 'Woman's Day' team is no exception. Cooking is such a pleasure to them that they consider it a joy to prepare a special meal for friends. They delight in trying out new recipes not only at work, but at home, and the next day they'll discuss the results, sharing particularly successful ideas.

Like many cooks I am forever on the lookout for new and interesting recipes. My friends, who over the years have entertained me and my family so generously, will recognise many of their recipes and their party themes throughout this book.

To all of these people I would like to express my sincerest thanks and appreciation.

Finally, I want to say a special thank you to three people who made this book possible. Firstly to my husband Denis, whose belief in my work has cost him many a comfortable and relaxed evening at home, more often than not preparing his own meal, while I worked in complete ignorance of his discomforts. Then June Hattenfels, who worked side by side with me, chapter by chapter, testing and re-typing recipes into the wee small hours of the morning. Lastly, Wal Easton, whose great skill as a photographer has brought life and interest to the dishes pictured in this book.

Thank you, thank you all.

M.F.

Introduction

What is a party? It can be many things, a celebration, a family gathering, a crowd of casual acquaintances or just a few friends meeting for drinks and food and conversation. Most of all, a party is a gathering of happy people. From earliest times men have met together to share their simple bread and herbs. Fellowship and companionship represent man's finer feelings toward mankind and the opening of your home to friends, the trouble taken to please them, is a practical expression of 'love thy neighbour'.

Very important to a successful party is special food. It must be something out of the ordinary. Not necessarily expensive or elaborate, but prepared with care and served with a flourish.

Planning a party menu gives me, and I am sure you too, great pleasure. I am aware of the need, not only to provide good food, but to choose the kind of recipe that enables me to be a hostess, not just a cook. This book is full of such recipes.

I am repeating the system which proved such a success in my first book, the 'Margaret Fulton Cookbook'. All recipes have been given a one, two or three spot rating.

- A simple and quick recipe that a beginner could accomplish with ease.

●● Dishes for the average cook with a knowledge of basic techniques but requiring a little more time.

●●● A special dish, requiring more skill and probably taking some time to prepare.

Beginners should not be discouraged from trying out three spot recipes, just be prepared to give them more time and concentration.

One word of advice, don't let your duties as hostess get you down. With planning and those indispensable lists that all good hostesses rely on, you should be able to enjoy your own parties just as much as your guests do. You will work harder, of course, but seeing everyone relax and have a wonderful time will be reward enough.

In this book the main concern is good food to serve your guests, but no amount of elaborate preparation can take the place of your genuine pleasure in their company.

You will find menus and suggestions for all kinds of parties in this book . . . from intimate gatherings with a few friends to large and lavish celebrations. Whichever you plan, I have just one wish for you, have a lovely party!

Margaret Fulton

To my daughter
Suzanne
who shares my joy
and love of
cooking

The Big Party

Gourmet Buffet for Grand Occasions
for ten or twenty people

Has it happened to you? Have you wanted to give a party for a very special person or a very special reason, an absolutely super party? Can you do it? Perhaps more to the point, can you afford it? Once you have made this last and most important decision, be assured that this is a menu to set you up as the 'Hostess with the mostest'. This is a foolproof menu, one I have used many times. Practice makes perfect, but even with no time to practise you will be able to cope with this one.

The soup comes from a can and the final additions only take minutes. For easy service pour the soup from a large jug and if you are very busy the guests will find it easy to help themselves. If you own a trolley, wheel it into the buffet room complete with soup and soup cups. As guests finish, it is easy to collect the cups and just wheel them out of sight.

Pastry cases and custard for the quiche may be made days ahead and stored in the refrigerator. Just before the party, pour custard into pastry, top with salmon and bake for the required 25 minutes.

Glazed Fillet of Beef, because it is covered with aspic, will keep in top condition even when prepared a day before. The savarins freeze well so can be made weeks, even months in advance. All in all, a very workable if extravagant extravaganza of a menu.

Wines: The wines must be the best you can provide for this special meal. A good wine merchant will be your best adviser but look for a flor sherry to serve with the soup, a light riesling or white burgundy with the quiche and a full flavoured cabernet sauvignon or claret-type red wine for the beef. With the savarins there is really no need to serve a wine but a rich aromatic sauterne could be offered.

Lady Curzon Soup
Smoked Salmon Quiche
Glazed Fillet of Beef
Hearts of Palm Salad
Tomato and Cucumber Salad
Strawberry Savarins

Lady Curzon Soup •

2 x 10 oz. cans clear
   turtle soup
¾ cup cream

¾ cup brandy
3 teaspoons curry powder

If using concentrated turtle soup heat with 2 cans of water according to directions on can. Mix cream, brandy and curry powder and heat gently. Add to hot soup, bring just to the boil and serve immediately. Serves 8-10, double for larger party. Serve in small soup cups. Failing sufficient soup cups, fine porcelain tea cups may be used, or Japanese lacquer bowls with lids.

Note: If turtle soup is not the concentrated variety, it will be necessary to make up the quantity (2 pints) with an extra 2 cans soup.

Glazed Fillet of Beef, Hearts of Palm Salad (soup bowls for Lady Curzon Soup in background)

11

Smoked Salmon Quiche ••

1 quantity short crust
  pastry (see page 25)
3 eggs, lightly beaten
2 cups cream
1 egg yolk

pinch ground nutmeg
salt and pepper
8 oz. smoked salmon,
  finely sliced

Prepare pastry as described on page 25. Place flan ring on a greased baking tray. On lightly floured board roll out pastry about 1-inch larger than flan ring. Place over and ease into ring, pressing into fluted sides. Take care not to stretch pastry or it will shrink away from the sides. Trim off pastry by rolling a rolling pin over top. There should be little surplus pastry.

The flan case may be brushed with a little egg white if desired, as a precaution against filling seeping through.

Combine eggs, cream, egg yolk, nutmeg, salt and pepper. Strain into flan case. Cover custard with slices of smoked salmon and spoon a little of the custard over them. Bake in a hot oven (400°F.) for 10 minutes, reduce temperature to moderate (350°F.) and bake a further 15 minutes or until custard is set and golden. Serves 6-8. Make 3 quiches for a larger buffet.

Glazed Fillet of Beef •••

1 x 3 lb. fillet of beef
salt and pepper
3 oz. butter
¼ cup brandy
1 x 10 oz. can clear turtle
  soup
2 tablespoons dry sherry

1 tablespoon gelatine
1 x 4½ oz. can devilled ham
  paste
1 hard-boiled egg
1 shallot
black pickled walnut
  (optional)

Trim fillet, remove all tissue and skin with a sharp knife. Rub meat with salt and pepper. Heat butter in shallow pan and sauté fillet until brown on all sides for about 10 minutes, turning constantly with two spoons. Warm brandy, ignite and pour over fillet, shake pan and cook until flame dies down. Baste with juices and cook a further 1 minute. Place fillet in a shallow roasting pan. Pour pan juices over and bake for a further 15-20 minutes in a hot oven (400°F.).

Allow beef to cool. Chill in refrigerator. Mix turtle soup with equal quantity of water, bring to the boil. Add dry sherry. Sprinkle gelatine over 2 tablespoons cold water, when sponge forms stir into hot soup. Allow to cool. Take out ¾ cup mixture. Set remainder in a flat tin in refrigerator.

Spread cold beef with ham paste. Halve hard-boiled egg and remove yolk. Cut slices of white to form petals of a flower, arrange on beef, sieve egg yolk and use for centres. Drop green shallot into boiling water for 1 minute, cut stem and leaves from green and arrange on beef. A pickled walnut cut in fancy shapes may be used to add contrast to decoration.

Spoon gelatine glaze, which should be nearly set, over beef. Chill well.

Arrange beef on a platter and surround with chopped turtle aspic. Serves 8-10. Prepare 2 fillets for larger buffet.

If it is difficult to obtain a 3 lb. fillet, 2 smaller fillets may be used. The cooking time is still the same. Decorate one of the pieces of fillet, mask the other with ham paste and glaze, and cut into slices and arrange on platter. Beef should be carved into ½-inch slices.

Note: If serving on a silver salver, it is wise to arrange beef on a croûte of bread. Cut a slice of bread lengthwise, 1-inch thick and the length of the beef. Brush with melted butter and bake in a moderate oven (350°F.) for 20 minutes or until golden. This protects tray when beef is carved.

Hearts of Palm Salad •

3 x 14 oz. cans hearts
  of palm
¾ cup French dressing
  (see page 16)
1 small bunch curly endive,
  lettuce or watercress

canned red pimiento
  and chopped parsley
  to garnish

Drain hearts of palm, add French dressing and chill in refrigerator. Wash salad greens, dry well and chill. Arrange on platter with hearts of palm on top. Cut pimiento into shapes with small decorative cutters or into strips and use to garnish hearts of palm. Sprinkle with chopped parsley. Serves 8-10. For larger buffet make 2 salads.

Alternate Method: Cut palm hearts into 1-inch slices and proceed with recipe as above.

Tomato and Cucumber Salad •

1 small white onion
6 medium sized tomatoes
1 tablespoon finely
  chopped parsley
2 cucumbers, peeled and
  sliced

½ cup French dressing
  (see page 16)
½ teaspoon sugar
fresh dill or parsley
  for garnish

Chop onion finely, put into pan with cold water to cover. Bring to the boil. Drain and rinse in cold water.

Peel tomatoes and cut each into 4 slices. Combine parsley and onion and sprinkle over tomatoes. Cover and chill. Combine cucumber slices, French dressing and sugar, chill. To serve, drain cucumber slices and arrange in the centre of a platter. Sprinkle with snipped dill. Place tomato slices around edge. Serves 8-10. For a larger buffet make 2 salads.

Strawberry Savarins •••

Prepare Savarin au Rhum as described on page 16. Do not decorate with preserved fruit, instead, fill each savarin with lightly sugared fresh strawberries.

The quantity given for savarins will serve 16-20. Have an extra bowl of sugared strawberries for those who may prefer strawberries and cream without the savarin.

Cold Buffet Party

for fifteen or thirty people

Nothing makes a party go like good food, good company and good drinks. The right music will make it swing or set a mellow, romantic mood. Flowers, balloons, mistletoe all have their place and each has its time to star on the party scene.

Don't get carried away thinking that impromptu parties are the best, as the most successful parties are the result of good planning. This buffet is an example of careful planning. The soup and chicken dish may be prepared days ahead. The ham is sliced before baking,

therefore making it easy for guests to help themsleves. Savarins freeze well, so make them months ahead if it is going to help on the day.

Wines: Two bowls of punch—each different—are a good idea, especially in the summertime. Keep the punch bowls filled. Sangria is a good summer party drink. Should you prefer wines, a light rosé wine would go well with the soup and chicken and a light aromatic red wine with the ham.

*Consult index for recipe

Iced Curry Soup
Chicken Indienne
Macaroni Salad
Apricot Glazed Ham
Spiced Apricots
Snow Capped Tomatoes
Green Salad
Cauliflower Salad *
Savarin au Rhum

*Consult index for recipe.

Iced Curry Soup •

Prepare soup and creamy topping well ahead and chill both in refrigerator until required. The chicken stock comes from simmering the chicken for the main dish.

½ bunch shallots	3 pints chicken stock
2 oz. butter	1 strip lemon rind
1 tablespoon curry paste or powder	1 bay leaf
2 tablespoons (1 oz.) plain flour	2 tablespoons arrowroot
	2 tablespoons cold water
Cream Topping:	
¼ pint port	¼ pint cream
1 teaspoon curry paste or powder	

Leave about 3-inches of green on shallots, chop finely. Cook in butter until soft. Add curry paste and cook 4-5 minutes. Stir in flour, cook for a few minutes, then pour in the stock. Bring to the boil, add lemon rind and bay leaf and simmer for 20 minutes. Strain, return to pan. Mix arrowroot with cold water, add to soup and bring to the boil, stirring continously, simmer 2-3 minutes. Chill soup, and serve in cups topped with spoonfuls of cream topping. Serves 15.

For Cream Topping: Mix port and curry paste together and simmer until reduced to half. Leave until cold. Whip cream, then stir in curry mixture.

For 30 guests prepare a double quantity of this recipe.

Apricot Glazed Ham ••

1 x 6-8 lb. canned ham	1 tablespoon honey
¾ cup apricot conserve	½ teaspoon ground ginger
1½ tablespoons white vinegar	watercress or parsley to garnish

Cut ham into ¼-inch thick slices. Re-shape and tie two separate strands of string around sides of ham and one strand over top, sides and base to keep ham intact. Put into a shallow roasting pan. Combine apricot conserve, vinegar, honey and ginger. Heat 5 minutes and sieve. Brush this glaze over ham and bake in a hot oven (400°F.) for 20 minutes, reduce to moderate (350°F.) and bake for a further 1-1½ hours. Brush with remaining glaze every 20-30 minutes. Place ham on serving platter, remove string and garnish with watercress. Serve with Spiced Apricots. May be served warm or cold. Serves 25-30.

For fewer guests use a slightly smaller ham.

Mayonnaise ••

2 egg yolks	½ pint olive oil
½ teaspoon salt	2 teaspoons boiling water,
little white pepper	optional
½ teaspoon dry mustard	
2 teaspoons lemon juice	
or white vinegar	

Put egg yolks, salt, pepper, mustard and 1 teaspoon lemon juice into a bowl. Beat vigorously with a whisk and add oil drop by drop, until a little more than ¼ cup has been added. As mixture thickens, add remaining oil in a thin stream while beating continually and stopping now and then to check that the mixture is well blended. When all oil has been added, stir in remaining lemon juice. Add boiling water to mayonnaise that is to be kept briefly. Makes approximately ½ pint.

Chicken Indienne ••

If chicken pieces are available use 4-5 lb. pieces (legs and breasts) or buy 2 whole chickens each weighing about 2½ lb. The main dish can be prepared days ahead, which is ideal for Christmas entertaining when there are so many parties to attend that you could be socially involved just before your own party.

4-5 lb. chicken pieces	salt
½ cup white wine	5 peppercorns
bouquet garni (bunch	2 teaspoons dried
of fresh herbs)	tarragon
1 carrot	4 oz. toasted cashew nuts
2 onions, halved	
Sauce Indienne:	
3 tablespoons oil	2-3 slices lemon
2 onions, finely chopped	pepper and salt
2 cloves garlic, crushed	3 tablespoons apricot
1-2 tablespoons curry	or other fruit
powder	chutney
2-3 teaspoons tomato	1 pint mayonnaise
paste	¼ pint cream

Put chicken pieces (or whole chickens) into a large boiler and pour in enough water to cover. Add wine, bouquet garni, scraped carrot, onions, 2 teaspoons salt, peppercorns and tarragon. Cover and slowly bring to the boil and simmer very gently for 20-35 minutes or until tender. During cooking, taste stock and add more salt if necessary. Remove from heat and allow chicken to cool in stock.

When cold remove skin and bones. Cut chicken into large pieces and put into a bowl. Add Sauce Indienne, cover and chill for 2 hours, or overnight. Spoon into a serving dish and garnish with chopped toasted cashew nuts.

For Sauce Indienne: Heat oil, add onions and garlic.

Cook gently until onion is transparent. Add curry powder and cook, stirring for a few minutes. Blend in tomato paste. Add lemon slices and seasoning. Cook gently for 1-2 minutes. Allow to cool. Remove lemon slices. When cold add chutney, mayonnaise and cream. Mix well. Taste and add more seasoning if necessary. Serves 12-15 people.

Note: If commercial mayonnaise is used, whip cream slightly before adding to mixture.

For 30 guests prepare this recipe twice rather than double quantities, although the sauce, being simple to prepare, may be doubled.

Macaroni Salad •

1 lb. macaroni	1 lb. frozen peas, cooked
3 tablespoons oil	2 red peppers, cut into
1 tablespoon paprika	fine strips
pepper	½ cup sliced, stuffed
½ cup French dressing	olives
(see page 16)	

Cook macaroni in plenty of boiling salted water in a large boiler for 15-20 minutes until tender. Drain and rinse well. Sprinkle with oil, toss well to prevent macaroni sticking. Cool. Add paprika pepper to French dressing. Stir through cold macaroni. Add peas, red peppers and olives, cover and chill 2 hours or until required. Toss again before serving. Serves 12-15.

Prepare two quantities for a larger party.

Spiced Apricots •

2 x 28 oz. cans apricot	¼ cup white vinegar
halves	½ cup (4 oz.) sugar
8 whole cloves	1 small orange, sliced
1-inch stick cinnamon	extra cloves
8 whole allspice (pimento)	

Drain apricots, reserve 1 cup syrup. Tie whole cloves, cinnamon and allspice in a piece of muslin or cheesecloth and put into saucepan with reserved apricot syrup, vinegar, sugar and orange slices. Bring to the boil, add apricot halves and simmer 5 minutes. Cover and allow to cool at room temperature. Remove spice bag. Serve warm or chilled. If liked, stud some apricot halves with extra whole cloves. Spiced Apricots improve on keeping, after 1 week they are at their best.

Glazed Leg of Ham, Spiced Fruits, Asparagus Mousse, Saffron Rice Salad with Stuffed Eggs and Brandied Fruit Cake

Green Salad •

2 large lettuce
1 bunch endive
1 bunch watercress

1 cucumber (optional)
1 cup French dressing

Wash salad greens and dry thoroughly, chill. About 4 hours before serving, tear salad greens into bite-size pieces and thinly slice cucumber. Arrange in salad bowls. Cover and chill. Sprinkle French dressing over salad greens just before serving and toss well until each leaf glistens. Serves 15-20. Increase lettuce to 4 for 30 guests.

French Dressing •

¾ cup olive or other salad oil
¼ cup vinegar
1 teaspoon salt

1 teaspoon freshly ground pepper
2 cloves garlic, crushed

Combine all ingredients in a bowl and beat with a fork, or whisk until well combined. Strain before using.

Snow Capped Tomatoes •

This unusual way of serving a popular vegetable adds colour to any table. Stack them in a pyramid and top each with sour cream dressing. If small tomatoes are not available use larger ones cut into wedges. Serve in a bowl with sauce spooned over.

15 small ripe tomatoes
1 cucumber
½ teaspoon salt
1 small onion
1 small clove garlic

½ pint sour cream
few drops hot pepper sauce
salt and pepper
1 teaspoon lemon juice

Pour boiling water over tomatoes in a bowl. Quickly transfer tomatoes into iced water, peel off skins and remove cores. Chill. Peel cucumber, halve lengthwise and remove seeds. Chop the flesh finely. Sprinkle with salt and press lightly. Stand for about 30 minutes. Drain. Grate onion and crush garlic, mix with cucumber, sour cream, hot pepper sauce, salt and pepper to taste, and lemon juice. Chill.

About 1 hour before serving, assemble tomatoes on serving plate in a pyramid, spoon sour cream sauce over tomatoes.

Note: If sour cream mixture thickens, add a little cream.

For more guests increase tomatoes to allow 1 whole small or ½ large tomato per person.

(a) The ham for Apricot Glazed Ham is sliced before baking then re-shaped and tied with string to keep the ham intact.

Savarin au Rhum • •

4 cups (1 lb.) plain flour
½ teaspoon salt
1 oz. compressed yeast
1½ tablespoons (1½ oz.) sugar

½ pint warm milk
4 eggs
8 oz. softened butter

Syrup:
1 pint water
2 cups (1 lb.) sugar

1-inch vanilla bean
6 tablespoons rum

Apricot Glaze:
1½ cups apricot jam
2 tablespoons water

2 tablespoons kirsch or rum

Sift flour and salt into a large warmed mixing bowl. Cream yeast, sugar and milk in a small bowl. Make a well in centre of flour and add dissolved yeast mixture. Sprinkle a little of the flour from sides over the top, cover with a cloth and leave in a warm place for 15 minutes. Beat eggs, add to the yeast mixture with softened butter. Mix to a smooth elastic dough, beating vigorously with hand. Cover with a cloth and allow to double in bulk in warm place, approximately 30 minutes.

Place mixture into two well-greased 9-inch savarin moulds or ring tins and allow to stand in a warm place until mixture rises to top of moulds. Bake in a hot oven (400°F.) for approximately 20 minutes. While still hot, spoon over syrup. Allow to stand for about 30 minutes until syrup has been absorbed. Turn on to serving plate and brush with Apricot Glaze. Before serving, fill centre with whipped cream. Decorate with glacé fruits and blanched almonds. Makes 2 savarins, each serving 8-10.

For Syrup: Combine water, sugar and vanilla bean. Stir over heat until sugar dissolves. Bring to the boil and boil for 10 minutes. Add rum.

For Apricot Glaze: Heat jam with water, stirring until boiling. Add kirsch, then press through a sieve.

Note: Savarins may be cooked several weeks before the party and frozen. (Do not pour the syrup over before freezing). Wrap the cooled savarins completely in foil, then freeze. To thaw, remove from freezer the night before the party. At serving time, heat in a moderately hot oven (375°F.) for 15 minutes. Pour hot syrup over and glaze. Or take straight from freezer and put into a hot oven (400°F.) (still wrapped in foil) for 30 minutes.

For a small party or dinner the recipe may be halved and baked in one tin. Or make the quantity given here and store one savarin in the freezer for a later date. Savarins freeze well for 3 months at 0°F.

(b) Remove string and serve ham with Spiced Apricots.

Wine and Cheese Party

Plan a wine and cheese party. All you need is a selection of cheeses and wines set out for sampling and you have the basis of a party that can be great fun.

Breads are important. Look for the unusual—a round cottage loaf, crusty French or black and rye for variety. Biscuits, too, add interest. Buy plain water biscuits, a new shape or flavour in crackers or those wafer thin crispbreads imported from Scandinavian countries.

Setting the Scene

Half the fun of going to a wine and cheese party is being free to wander and taste at will. With this in mind, arrange the wines and cheese buffet style so that guests can easily cut a cube or slice of cheese, select their bread, then move on to the wine. For a large number of people two or three smaller tables is better than a large one. Wooden boards, even kitchen chopping boards can be brought into service, with a knife for each cheese. Name tags will help identify the cheeses.

Consider hiring wine glasses from a catering firm, allowing, if possible, 2-3 wine glasses per person, otherwise 1 glass per person and provide a bowl of water and a tea towel for guests to rinse and wipe their glasses. Paper napkins come in attractive colours and designs, so why not use them for this kind of party.

A final word, perhaps unnecessary. It is a good idea to provide a 'slop' bucket for wines that are rejected. All too often favourite pot plants and bowls of flowers collect unwanted glasses of wine!

Wine Selection

It is usual to allow half a bottle of all wines combined per person. You will find it a distinct economy to buy wine in a jar or flagon whenever possible. A half gallon jar of wine is almost equal to three ordinary bottles. Sherry is also obtainable in jars or flagons. Flagons come into their own for larger parties. For smaller parties you may want to be more selective in the choice of quality wines.

How Much Wine to Buy?

Having worked out how much wine you will need (half a 26 fl. oz. bottle per person), plan for variety. The order of tasting is usually white before red and within each group from light bodied to full bodied. Most wine advisors suggest a variety of six to eight wines.

In setting up the wine tasting area, arrange wines in order of tasting, say from left to right, even go as far as labelling bottles 1, 2, 3, etc.

What to Buy

Whites ranging from a light fresh young hock or medium dry in the moselle style and a very dry white wine in the hock or chablis style. Allow for the sweet-tooths with a moselle or sauterne. Also consider the full flavoured white burgundy-style wines. Serve well-chilled—two hours in the refrigerator, or one hour in crushed ice, is ample.

Rosé wines also have their place at a wine tasting, they go well with the milder cheeses. Chill as for white wine.

Red wines should be opened about 45 minutes before serving to allow the bouquet and flavour to breathe and develop and so complement the full flavour of the cheese.

Select from a light astringent claret to a full flavoured red wine and older burgundy or claret.

A bottle of tawny port, Madeira and dry sherry can be placed on a sideboard for those who fancy fortified wine.

A good rule to remember when giving a Wine and Cheese Party is to serve a suitable quality wine which will correspond with the quality of your cheese. You can team a milder wine with the mellow and milder cheeses.

However, if you are to serve cheese and wine after dinner, always serve your best wines with a small variety of cheeses, chosen with care.

Claret can be served with most cheeses, but for your strong cheeses oloroso sherry goes very well. With the mellow and mild cheeses, a good dry red wine may also be served.

Now on to the very mild cheeses—in the summertime serve a chilled fresh, young white wine in the hock style, or moselle or sauterne if your tooth is sweet. In winter you could make a hot spiced punch. Make your choice from the punch and cup recipes given. All go well at a Wine and Cheese Party.

A wine master?

When the professionals throw a wine tasting, the wine master assumes the role of a master of ceremonies. You may find you have a dedicated amateur in your midst who is willing to conduct the tasting. In any case it is as well to know something about wine and this is what the professionals look for.

1. Appearance: The glass is held by the stem and raised to the light to check on clarity and colour. Candles set around the room make the ideal light for this. All wines should be brilliantly clear.

2. Aroma: Swirl the wine gently in the glass, this releases the bouquet. Take a sniff and try to remember the aroma. This is an important part of wine tasting because taste is very closely related to what we smell.

3. Taste: Take a sip but do not swallow the wine. Let the wine rest in your mouth, then roll it around your tongue. This allows time to register the various tastes present in the wine.

To identify what you taste

Once you start tasting wine it follows that you will be interested enough to know what you are looking for in a wine. Discussing the wines with other guests helps form opinions. It is surprising, with a little practice, how soon one learns to evaluate a wine. Learning a few terms is certainly a help.

Bouquet: Describes the delicate fragrances and aromas which the wine assumes as its alcohol and fruit acids oxidise. It is the subtle essence, the very spirit of wine.

Full Bodied: Describes a wine that has substance which seems to fill the mouth. A good red wine or white burgundy should have this quality.

Harsh: Used to describe a rough, biting, sharp taste that is certainly discordant, often found in young wines. It is easy to recognise.

Mellow: On the palate a soft, rich and mellow taste, sometimes with just a little sweetness. Indicates a ripe,

17

mature wine, usually well made.

Acidity: Too much, of course, will give you a 'vinegarish' sour taste but, when light, it gives a pleasant tartness to the wine that can be most refreshing.

Astringency: Some wines that have not had time to mature have this quality. It is not necessarily a sign of an inferior wine, merely too young. It is easy to detect, for you find it makes the lips pucker.

Choosing the cheese

Allow 1 lb. cheese for every four guests, or a little more if the party takes place at a time when they might be expected to forego a meal. Make a balanced selection of at least four or more fine cheeses, including strong, mellow and mild and, for some tastes, a very mild cheese.

In each category you can choose from a wide selection of Australian, English and imported cheeses.

Strong Cheese: The strong Australian cheeses include Crackerbarrel, Coon, Kameruka, Australian blue vein, Mil-lel, and some Cheddars. The English strong cheeses include Stilton, Double Gloucester and Lancashire.

Unusual and Potted Cheese: If you are interested in venturing into unusual imported cheeses, Canadian old wine, Canadian Cheddar, Port Salut, Camembert and Danish Tilsit are always popular. Included in this bracket also are the Potted Cheeses which are easy to make at home.

Mellow and Mild Cheese: In the category of mellow and mild cheeses of medium strength, choose mild Cheddars, Swiss, Philadelphia and cottage cheese. Leicester, Wensleydale, Caerphilly and Cheshire cheeses are available at leading city cheese counters.

From the imported Continental cheeses, the following are mild but interesting: Gouda and Edam (both Dutch), Danish Esrom, Danbo and Samsoe.

When to Buy: Buy your cheeses on the day of the party if possible, as they are at their best when absolutely fresh. If not, store them in plastic containers or aluminium foil until required. Do not use greaseproof paper as this causes the cheese to sweat. If you put cheese in a refrigerator take it out at least an hour before the party starts so that it can mellow.

Bread and biscuits

Allow plenty of bread and biscuits, buying the most delectable assortment possible. Twists and plaits, Vienna loaves or long French sticks are easy for guests to break into pieces themselves. An old fashioned cottage loaf is worth ordering because it looks and tastes so good. Miniature brown loaves are also delicious with cheese. So are breadsticks of the Italian type, crispbreads, crackers, and wholemeal biscuits.

Bread, biscuits and crispbreads should be as fresh as possible and bread should not be sliced in advance as it dries so quickly. Place bread knives next to loaves which require cutting, or let guests break pieces off long French sticks. Biscuits and crispbreads that are not quite fresh can be crisped in a hot oven (400°F.) for a few minutes. Bread, if brushed with milk and wrapped in aluminium foil, can be improved in the same way.

As for butter, serve some unsalted and some salted to suit all tastes. 1 lb. butter makes about 40 pats, so you will need at least 1 lb. to serve 20 guests.

Relishes and Pickles

Although nothing could be nicer than cheese 'straight' with buttered bread or biscuits, the extras you serve add a party look and taste to the buffet: little dishes of mixed sweet pickles, tiny pickled onions, walnuts, gherkins and containers of cocktail sticks placed nearby. Radish roses and celery curls can also be served.

Potted Cheese •

While providing a variety of natural cheese is often all that is necessary at a wine and cheese tasting, potted cheeses add interest. Also, after the party, remember this is a good way to use up leftover cheese! If you expect guests to stay over the time they would normally have a meal, consider one hot dish like Pissaladiere or Pizzas (see index for recipes).

Liptauer Cheese Mould •

8 oz. cottage cheese
4 oz. butter, well creamed
2 anchovy fillets, well drained of oil and finely chopped
1 tablespoon caraway seeds
1 tablespoon chopped capers
2 teaspoons chopped chives
1 tablespoon paprika pepper
1 teaspoon prepared English mustard
½ teaspoon salt
pinch celery salt
capers for garnish

Sieve the cottage cheese and gradually beat into the creamed butter. When whipped add remaining ingredients and combine thoroughly. Pile on a plate, forming a cone shape. Gently press capers for garnish into a pattern from top to bottom.

This is a highly flavoured cheese and is suitable for cocktail savouries and spreading on thin slices of pumpernickel or rye bread.

French Potted Cheese in Sauterne •

1½ lb. Cheddar cheese
½ cup thick sour cream
salt
pinch cayenne pepper
pinch mace
4 oz. unsalted butter
¼ cup sauterne
melted butter

Grate cheese using finest grating edge. Add cream and mix to a thick paste. Season with salt, cayenne and mace, then gradually beat in the softened butter and wine. When mixture is well blended, pack tightly into small pots. Coat surface with melted butter and cover pots with a round of buttered white paper and secure with string. Refrigerate until required.

Savarin au Rhum

Celebration Buffet

for twenty people

An annual party can almost become an institution. Christmas is a time for sharing, the New Year deserves to be brought in in style, and we all have an anniversary worthy of celebration.

Throughout the years I have collected what must by now be recognised by my friends as 'party pieces'. This year a few new dishes were added to my repertoire. Asparagus Mousse, light and delicate, was first served to me in London by an international food writer. Like many good recipes created by good cooks, it is surprisingly easy to prepare. Another newcomer following a visit to

Dublin, home of fine hams and Guinness (the combination proves formidable), is Glazed Leg of Ham. The ham is equally good served warm or cold and is such a dazzler, you will probably find it worth repeating during the year for dinner parties for smaller numbers.

Wines: Select one or two punches from the drinks chapter. Allow guests to help themselves from the bowls and keep the bowls well filled. If toasts are to be drunk, champagne is the only adequate drink when an engagement is to be announced, an anniversary remembered — or when you have sold your first book!

Asparagus Mousse
Glazed Leg of Ham
Spiced Fruits
Saffron Rice Salad
with Stuffed Eggs
Green Salad
Sherry Soufflé*
Brandied Fruit Cake

*Consult index for recipe.

Asparagus Mousse ••

2 x 16 oz. cans asparagus
  spears
2 tablespoons gelatine
6 tablespoons water
¾ pint cream
salt and pepper

3 egg whites
few drops green food
  colouring, optional
extra asparagus spears
  and pimiento strips
  to garnish

Drain asparagus and rub the spears through a sieve, or purée in a blender, then rub through a sieve to remove any stringy stalk. Sprinkle gelatine over water, when soft, stand in boiling water until gelatine is dissolved. Add dissolved gelatine to asparagus purée, stirring continuously. Cool, then chill until mixture begins to thicken around the edges. Whip cream lightly and gradually stir into the asparagus until smooth. Season to taste with salt and white pepper. Fold in stiffly beaten egg whites and tint a delicate green with food colouring. Pour into a 3-pint mould which has been rinsed with cold water. Chill.

Before serving turn out on to a plate and garnish with extra green asparagus spears and strips of pimiento. Serve very cold. Serves 8.

Prepare double quantity for 20 serves. Set the mixture in two moulds. The mousse may be prepared a day or

two before serving. Cover moulds with aluminium foil or clear plastic wrap before refrigerating.

Glazed Leg of Ham ••

1 x 15 lb. cooked leg
  of ham
1½ cups Guinness stout
1 cup (8 oz.) sugar
2 teaspoons dry mustard
1 teaspoon ground ginger

1 teaspoon ground
  cardamom
extra 2-3 tablespoons
  stout
watercress or parsley to
  garnish

Peel skin off ham, leaving portion around bone. Place ham, fat side up, in a roasting pan and pour 1½ cups stout over. Bake in a moderately slow oven (325°F.) for 3 hours, basting occasionally with stout.

Remove ham from oven and baste with drippings. Score fat diagonally to form diamond pattern. Mix sugar, mustard, ginger and cardamom and add enough stout to moisten. Spread over ham. Increase oven temperature to hot (400°F.) and bake ham a further 35 minutes. Serve hot, garnished with watercress. Accompany with Spiced Fruits. Serves 20-30.

Spiced Fruits •

1 x 16 oz. jar brandied apricots
1 x 1 lb. 13 oz. can peach halves
1 x 1 lb. 13 oz. can pear halves
½ teaspoon whole cloves
1-inch stick cinnamon
8 whole allspice
¼ cup white vinegar
½ cup (4 oz.) sugar
2 oranges, sliced
extra cloves

Drain apricots and reserve syrup. Measure and add enough peach syrup to make 1 cup. Drain peaches and pears. Put cloves, cinnamon, allspice, reserved 1 cup syrup, vinegar, sugar and orange slices into saucepan. Bring to the boil, add fruit and simmer for 5 minutes. Cover and allow to cool. Chill. Remove spices before serving with ham. If liked, stud fruit with extra whole cloves.
Note: The flavour of fruit will improve if made 4-5 days in advance and kept in the refrigerator.

Saffron Rice Salad with Stuffed Eggs •

3 lb. long grain rice
1 cup oil
4 pints chicken stock or water and chicken stock cubes
6 teaspoons salt
2 good pinches saffron
4 teaspoons curry powder
Dressing:
⅓ cup white vinegar
1 cup olive oil
½ teaspoon paprika pepper
1 bunch shallots, sliced
2 red and 2 green peppers, diced
Stuffed Eggs (see page 29)
watercress or parsley to garnish

2 cloves garlic, crushed (optional)

Use two large saucepans to cook the rice—it's easier this way. In one of the pans, heat ½ cup oil and sauté 1½ lb. rice for a few minutes, stirring. Add half the stock, salt, saffron and curry powder. Bring to the boil, stir once, then reduce heat to very low, cover and cook for 20-25 minutes, without stirring. When cooked, fluff up with a fork and leave uncovered until cold. Repeat with remaining oil, stock, salt, saffron and curry powder in other pan.

Beat dressing ingredients until combined and add to rice a little at a time, tossing lightly but thoroughly to distribute evenly. Lastly add shallots and peppers. Chill until ready to serve. Toss again and pile rice on serving platter. Surround with Stuffed Eggs and garnish with watercress. Serves 20.

Stuffed Eggs •

Prepare Stuffed Eggs according to recipe on page 29, using 12 eggs.

Green Salad •

See recipe for Green Salad (for 20) on page 16.

Brandied Fruit Cake •

8 oz. raisins
1 cup coarsely chopped walnuts
½ cup glacé cherries, halved
3½ cups (14 oz.) plain flour
8 oz. butter
1½ cups (12 oz.) castor sugar
2 teaspoons grated orange rind
5 eggs
½ teaspoon salt
1½ teaspoons baking powder
1 tablespoon orange juice
½ cup brandy

Grease and flour a 10-inch ring tin. Set oven temperature at slow (300°F.).

Combine raisins, walnuts and cherries with ½ cup of the measured flour. Cream butter, sugar and orange rind in a large mixing bowl. Add eggs one at a time, beating well after each. Sift remaining 3 cups flour with salt and baking powder. Fold into creamed mixture alternately with orange juice or brandy. Place in prepared tin and bake in a slow oven (300°F.) for 2 hours and 10 minutes, turn out and cool on a wire cooling rack. Store in an airtight container. Cut into thin slices to serve.
Note: Store cake in an airtight container at least 2 days before serving to allow flavours to develop. This is a flavoursome cake with a fine, close texture that goes well with sherry or a Madeira wine.

To prepare Glazed Fillet of Beef spread the cooked and cooled beef with devilled ham paste.

The prepared turtle soup, which has been chilled until almost on the point of setting is spooned over the decorated beef.

A Large Cocktail Buffet

for thirty or more people

The cocktail party is, to my way of thinking, a much-maligned social event. Trouble seems to stem from the fact that many a hostess takes the invitation hours seriously, expecting guests to arrive and leave on time. Unless it is a very formal invitation for very formal reasons this never seems to happen.

Experience has taught me that when the food is up to the standard and quantity of the drinks a cocktail party is a most agreeable affair.

There are times when a cocktail party is the best way to entertain a large group of people. Social obligations have to be taken care of, returning hospitality, entertaining people you have only met once or twice but feel you should like to know better, casual acquaintances, business associates, 'characters' whom you have found fascinating, celebrations when you want to invite just about everyone you know, interstate or overseas visitors who should meet as many people as possible—the answer every time seems to be a cocktail party.

I have planned 3 cocktail parties, each one including at least one dish a little more substantial than the usual cocktail food. All too often the food seems to run out before the drinks, and the results are disastrous.

The recipes in each party are all interchangeable but try and include at least one hot dish. Cocktail pizzas, Pissaladiere and other pastry based dishes are easy for they can be made ahead and reheated as required.

What to Drink

When having a cocktail party and catering for a large number of people with individual preferences, making drinks can be quite a business. The best solution is to provide the basic spirits—Scotch, brandy, rum, gin and perhaps vodka which is becoming more popular. Everybody likes at least one of these. Provide plenty of ice and the 'mixers' like soda water, tonic, dry ginger and the important etceteras like lemon slices and olives. It's fun to make one or two cocktails that you know you can handle with ease, but do not attempt to pander to every whim and fancy, this requires the experience of a professional bartender. In the chapter on drinks you will find a selection of short and long drinks. Punches which can be a wonderful aid to a busy host are also included. Remember, too, the guests who prefer non-alcoholic drinks. They deserve more than just tonic or soda water, so include one of the non-alcoholic cocktails or coolers.

Carafes of wine, both red and white, are a good idea, especially as an accompaniment to the main hot dishes.

I wish you a gay and civilized cocktail party.

Cold dishes—
Smoked Salmon Dip
Sambal Dip
Gorgonzola Dip
Curried Walnuts or Cashews
Stuffed Eggs∗
Ham Canapés
Cigarettes
Seafood Tricorns
Hot dishes—
Pissaladiere
Swedish Meatballs
Bourekakia
or
Tiropetes

∗Consult index for recipe.

22

Cigarettes, Stuffed Eggs, Seafood Tricorns and Ham Canapés

Smoked Salmon Dip •

4 oz. smoked salmon
½ teaspoon capers
1 cup sour cream

pinch freshly ground
black pepper

Drain off excess oil from salmon. Chop the salmon and capers finely. Whip the cream (if sour cream is thick, this is unnecessary) and fold in salmon and capers. Place in a bowl and grind pepper over the top. Serve with fried prawn crisps, potato crisps or fresh crisp vegetables such as celery, carrot straws, radish roses.
Note: Shredded smoked salmon is available in glass jars. is less expensive than sliced salmon and perfectly suitable for this dip.

Sambal Dip •

½ large cucumber
½ green pepper
1 small white onion
1 clove garlic
4 radishes
2 sticks celery
½ teaspoon salt

½ teaspoon turmeric
½ teaspoon ground ginger
pinch chilli powder
pinch ground cumin
3 teaspoons tomato paste
1 cup thick sour cream

Peel cucumber, cut into halves lengthwise and remove seeds. Wash pepper and remove seeds. Finely chop cucumber, pepper, onion, garlic, radishes and celery. Season with salt, turmeric, ginger, chilli powder and cumin. Mix thoroughly. Blend in tomato paste, then stir in the sour cream, mixing thoroughly. Place in a bowl and chill until ready to serve. Serve as a dip with potato crisps, crackers or fried prawn crisps.

Ham Canapés •

Cut thinly sliced rye or black bread into rounds using a 2-inch biscuit cutter. Cut thinly sliced ham the same size. Mix butter with a little prepared mustard to give a mild flavour and spread on bread rounds. Place ham on bread and top each with a little cranberry sauce, lingonberry preserves or horseradish relish.
Note: Cranberry sauce and lingonberry preserves can be purchased from delicatessens and supermarkets which specialise in imported foods.

Curried Walnuts or Cashews •

Heat 2 tablespoons olive oil in a frying pan, add 2 teaspoons each of curry powder and Worcestershire sauce and a pinch of chilli powder. Stir mixture and when it is hot add 12 oz. (or 2 cups) walnuts or cashews. Remove from heat and stir until nuts are coated, then spread on a baking tray lined with aluminium foil. Bake in a slow oven (300°F.) for 10 minutes, until walnuts are crisp. Cook and store airtight until ready to serve.

Gorgonzola Dip •

4 oz. Gorgonzola or
other blue cheese
4 oz. cream cheese

2 tablespoons brandy or
cream

Mash the Gorgonzola, add cream cheese and beat until smooth. Stir in brandy, mixing until a soft and smooth consistency. Serve with sliced apples, pears or crackers.

Cigarettes •

8 oz. cream cheese
1 teaspoon dried tarragon
salt and pepper
lemon juice

6 oz. sliced prosciutto
(smoked raw ham)
2-3 oz. softened butter
paprika pepper

Beat cream cheese and tarragon well together. Season to taste with salt, pepper and a little lemon juice. Spread on prosciutto and roll up. Cover and chill. Before serving, cut rolls in halves and dip one end into softened butter, then into paprika pepper. Serve on platter. Makes 16-20.
Note: Any thinly sliced sausage such as teawurst or ham may be used for cigarettes. The thinner the sausage is sliced the more cigarettes this recipe makes.

Seafood Tricorns •

Pastry:
1½ cups (6 oz.) plain flour
½ teaspoon salt
pinch cayenne pepper
4 oz. butter

6 oz. Cheddar cheese,
finely grated
2 egg yolks
1 teaspoon lemon juice

Filling:
1 large cucumber
2 shallots, finely chopped
1 x 6½ oz. can king crab
meat

¼ pint thick sour cream
salt and pepper

Pastry: Sift flour, salt and cayenne pepper into a bowl. Rub in butter until mixture resembles breadcrumbs, then mix in cheese. Make a well in the centre and add egg yolks which have been beaten with lemon juice. Stir with a round bladed knife, adding a little iced water if necessary, to make a dough. Knead lightly, form into a ball and chill for at least 1 hour.

Roll pastry on a lightly floured surface to ⅛-inch thickness. Cut into 4-inch rounds and place each round on a circle of aluminium foil cut the same size as pastry. Prick pastry with a fork. Form each into a triangular-shaped shell by pinching foil together tightly at 3 equal intervals to form corners. Bake in a moderate oven (350°F.) for 10 minutes until pale golden brown. Cool.
For Filling: Peel cucumber, halve lengthwise and scoop out seeds. Finely chop enough cucumber to measure 1 cup. Sprinkle with salt and press lightly. Stand for 1 hour. Drain and press to extract all juices. Combine with

shallots, flaked crab meat and sour cream. Season to taste with salt and pepper.

Spoon the filling into tricorns just before serving. Makes 16-18.

Note: Thick home-made mayonnaise may be used in place of thick sour cream.

Swedish Meatballs •

12 oz. lean minced steak (or a mixture of beef, veal and pork)	butter for frying
	1 egg, slightly beaten
¾ cup soft white breadcrumbs	1 teaspoon salt
	freshly ground pepper
¼ cup cream	pinch ground ginger
¼ cup milk	pinch ground nutmeg
1 small onion	cornflour
	½ pint sour cream

Place finely minced meat in a bowl. Soak breadcrumbs in a mixture of cream and milk. Finely chop onion and fry gently in 1 oz. butter until tender, but not brown. Add to meat with soaked breadcrumbs, egg, salt, pepper, ginger and nutmeg. Beat vigorously until fluffy, chill for 30 minutes. Roll into 1-inch balls in a little cornflour.

Melt 2 oz. butter in a frying pan and cook meatballs, one layer at a time, shaking pan until brown on all sides and cooked through. Add more butter if necessary. Pierce meatballs with cocktail sticks and serve hot with a bowl of sour cream for dipping. Makes about 25.

Pissaladiere ••

You can bake Pissaladiere the day you need it or a day in advance. It is best not to refrigerate it. Reheat it in a slow oven (300°F.) for 10 minutes before serving. As well as being good with drinks this also makes an excellent luncheon dish or light meal when accompanied by a salad.

1 quantity short crust pastry (recipe follows)	salt and pepper
	½ cup grated parmesan cheese
3 tablespoons olive oil	
1 lb. onions, thinly sliced	1 x 1½ oz. can flat anchovy fillets
1 clove garlic, optional	
4 large ripe tomatoes, peeled and sliced	few black olives, halved and stoned
¼ teaspoon dried rosemary	

Prepare pastry and roll out on a lightly floured surface to fit a greased 8-inch pie plate or flan ring. Prick the base, line with greasproof paper or aluminium foil and weight with dried beans. Bake blind in a hot oven (400°F.) for 15 minutes, then remove and allow to cool. Remove paper and beans.

Meanwhile, heat oil in a heavy, shallow pan and gently cook onions covered, stirring occasionally, until soft and golden. This will take about 20 minutes. Add crushed garlic (if used), sliced tomato and rosemary. Season to taste with salt and freshly ground pepper. Cook, stirring constantly, until liquid has evaporated and mixture is fairly stiff. Sprinkle half the cheese in the flan case, then spoon in tomato filling, spreading evenly. Sprinkle with remaining cheese. Arrange anchovies on top in lattice pattern and place olives in the spaces. Sprinkle with a

little olive oil and return to oven for a further 25-30 minutes. Serve hot.

Note: 2 cups canned, drained tomatoes may replace tomatoes. Remove seeds from the tomatoes and slice.

Miniature Pissaladiere ••

Line 12 small greased tartlet pans with short crust pastry. If cases are large you will require double quantity of pastry. Chill the tart shells on a baking tray. Cover the bottom of the tart shells with grated parmesan cheese and fill with prepared filling (recipe above). Top each tart with crossed anchovies and a slice of pitted black olive. Bake in a moderate oven (350°F.) for about 25 minutes or until the shells are golden. Carefully remove from the pans and serve hot.

Short Crust Pastry •

Use this pastry for making savoury flans and tartlets. Enough pastry to line an 8 or 9-inch flan ring.

1 cup (4 oz.) plain flour	about 2 tablespoons iced water
¼ teaspoon salt	
2 oz. firm butter	

Sift flour and salt into a cold mixing bowl. Rub butter in until mixture resembles breadcrumbs. Make a well in the centre and add enough water to mix to a dough, using a round bladed knife. Do not knead. Form into a ball. Wrap and chill until required.

Note: The amount of pastry may seem rather small but is the right quantity to allow for a crisp pastry case.

Bourekakia ••

8 oz. filo pastry	8 oz. feta cheese, chopped
1 x 10 oz. packet frozen spinach	
	1 teaspoon ground nutmeg
2 onions	
1 oz. butter	½ cup finely chopped parsley
3 eggs, beaten	
½ cup finely chopped shallots including 1-inch of green end	salt and freshly ground black pepper
	4 oz. unsalted butter

Lay filo pastry flat on a damp tea towel and cover with a second damp tea towel so pastry will not dry out. Cook spinach according to packet directions but omit the butter and drain thoroughly. Remove all excess liquid by pressing lightly with a wooden spoon. Finely chop onions and fry in butter until golden brown. Combine eggs, shallots, cheese, nutmeg and parsley. Add onions, spinach and season with salt and pepper to taste.

Melt unsalted butter and brush a little over two shallow 8-inch square tins. Fold one sheet of the filo pastry in half and place in the tin. Trim pastry to fit. Brush with butter. Repeat this process in both tins until half pastry is used. Spread filling over the pastry and cover with remaining filo pastry, each layer folded and brushed with butter as before. Trim pastry edges to fit tin neatly. Cut into 1½-inch squares. Bake in a moderately hot oven (375°F.) for about 1 hour or until pastry is golden brown and puffed. Cut through squares while still hot and serve immediately. Makes about 40.

Note: Filo pastry comes in tissue-thin sheets and is available at speciality Greek delicatessens. It is difficult to make at home.

Tiropetes ••

The ingredients for this recipe are exactly the same as for Bourekakia. Use recipe for filling as in preceding recipe.

Lay filo pastry flat on a damp tea towel and cover with a second damp tea towel so pastry will not dry out. Cut each sheet of filo pastry in half lengthwise. Fold each piece in two lengthwise. Brush with melted butter. Place a teaspoonful of the filling in one corner of the pastry strip. Fold corner of pastry over filling until it meets the folded edge of pastry forming a triangle. Continue to fold pastry over in triangles until you come to the end of the pastry strip. Brush top with melted butter. Place on an ungreased baking tray and bake in a moderately hot oven (375°F.) for 45 minutes or until puffed and golden brown.

To make Cigarettes, spread tarragon flavoured cream cheese on thin slices of proscuitto. Roll up, chill and cut into halves. Dip one of each in a little softened butter, then into paprika.

To make Seafood Tricorns the circles of thinly rolled pastry are placed on aluminium foil and formed into triangular shapes by pinching foil together at 3 equal intervals. Filling is spooned into the baked and cooled pastry tricorns just before serving.

Tiropetes

Bourekakia

Strawberries Romanoff, Almond Lace Biscuits (Tuiles)

Small Cocktail Party 'At Home'

for twelve or less

If you are anti-cocktail parties, why not send invitations for an 'AT HOME'. The hours remain the same, 6.00 p.m. until 8.30 p.m. The food and drinks remain the same but the invitation has a different sound to it. Those who dread any kind of party, particularly a cocktail party, will accept gladly, knowing you are not expecting them to stay for hours.

Drinks: See chapter 'A Large Cocktail Buffet.'

Devilled Almonds
Cheese Caraway Crisps
Chicken Liver Pâté
Guacamole
Celery with Roquefort
Stuffed Eggs
Cocktail Pizza
Greek Meatballs

Devilled Almonds •

Blanch 8 oz. almonds, dry thoroughly. Heat 2-3 tablespoons olive oil in a frying pan, add almonds and cook, stirring constantly, until golden. Drain on absorbent paper and sprinkle with a little salt and chilli powder, about ⅛ teaspoon chilli to 1 teaspoon salt. Dust off excess salt and chilli powder and serve in small bowls.

Cheese Caraway Crisps •

1 cup (4 oz.) plain flour	2 teaspoons caraway
2 teaspoons dry mustard	seeds
1 teaspoon salt	3 oz. butter
½ cup shredded Cheddar	2 tablespoons cold water
cheese	

Sift flour, mustard and salt into a bowl. Add cheese and caraway seeds, mix well. Cut in butter with 2 knives until mixture resembles breadcrumbs. Make a well in the centre and add water. Stir with a knife until mixture forms a dry dough, adding more water if necessary. Form into two balls, wrap in greaseproof paper and chill for at least 30 minutes.

Roll out one portion of dough on a lightly floured board to an 8 x 9-inch rectangle. Cut into 3 x 1-inch strips. Place on ungreased baking trays and bake in a hot oven (400°F.) for 5-6 minutes or until a light golden brown. Repeat with remaining portion of dough. When cool store airtight. Makes 3½-4 dozen.

Note: The dough may be cut into rounds using a 2-inch fluted cutter. Toasted sesame seeds may replace the caraway seeds.

Chicken Liver Pâté ••

1 onion	few sprigs thyme or
1 clove garlic	oregano (or
3 oz. butter	pinch dried)
8 oz. chicken livers	2 teaspoons brandy
1 bay leaf	salt and pepper

Chop the onion finely and crush garlic. Heat 1 oz. butter and gently fry onion and garlic until onion is transparent. Add chicken livers and cook for 2-3 minutes. Add crumbled bay leaf and thyme and cook a further 1 minute. Cool. Chop chicken livers, then pound with a wooden spoon or blend in a blender. Stir in remaining butter, melted, and brandy. Season to taste with salt and freshly ground pepper. Pack into a mould and chill (or set mixture in a small crock and top with a little melted butter). Unmould the pâté before serving, place on tray and surround with hot toast or crisp crackers. Place a knife alongside the pâté for spreading.

Note: This pâté may be set in an earthenware crock or terrine or 2 small crocks or dishes. If these are to be kept for several days pour a little melted butter over top, this helps keep pâté fresh.

Guacamole •

2 ripe avocados
¼–½ teaspoon chilli powder
2-3 teaspoons lemon juice
2 teaspoons finely
** chopped onion**
salt
freshly ground pepper
2 tablespoons chopped
** canned pimiento**

Cut avocados in halves lengthwise, remove seeds and skin. Mash the avocados. Season with chilli powder, lemon juice, onion and salt and pepper to taste. Stir in the pimiento. Place in a bowl and serve chilled. Surround bowl with crisp fried prawn crisps or crackers. (Mixture may also be spread on crackers or fried bread).
Note: If preparing the Guacamole several hours before serving, place mixture in a bowl, return the seeds to prevent discolouration, then cover and chill. Remove seeds before serving.

Celery with Roquefort •

Choose tender, crisp sticks of celery. String and cut into 2-inch lengths. Cream 4 oz. Roquefort or a good blue cheese with a little brandy. Spoon into the curved part of celery and sprinkle with chopped chives. Serve chilled.

Stuffed Eggs •

If preparing Stuffed Eggs in advance, store the whites in a bowl of water to cover, in the refrigerator. The yolk mixture is kept in the piping bag or a bowl, ready to fill the whites as they are required.

Lower 6 eggs gently into a pan of cold water with a pinch of salt added. Bring to the boil and cook over a low heat for 15-20 minutes. Stir eggs for the first 10 minutes so the yolks will be centred. Place pan under running cold water until eggs are completely cooled. Shell eggs and cut into halves with a stainless steel or silver knife. Fill whites with one of the following mixtures:
Curry: Press egg yolks through a sieve, blend with 2-3 tablespoons mayonnaise, 1 teaspoon prepared mustard, ½ teaspoon curry powder and season to taste with salt and a few drops hot pepper sauce.
Devilled: Press yolks through a sieve, blend with 1 teaspoon each dry mustard and Worcestershire sauce, ½ teaspoon freshly ground pepper and 2-3 tablespoons mayonnaise. Season to taste with salt and beat in 2 teaspoons finely chopped parsley.
Pickled Walnut: Press yolks through a sieve and blend with 1½ tablespoons very finely chopped pickled walnuts. Season to taste with salt and pepper and blend in enough mayonnaise to give a smooth consistency. Decorate each with a small piece of pickled walnut.
Ham: Press yolks through a sieve and combine with 3 tablespoons finely chopped ham or ham paste, 1 teaspoon prepared mustard, 2 teaspoons finely chopped gherkins and enough paprika pepper to give a pink colour. Add enough mayonnaise to give a smooth consistency and season to taste with salt.
Cream Cheese: Press yolks through a sieve and mix in 2 oz. softened cream cheese, ½ teaspoon anchovy paste and mayonnaise to give a smooth consistency. Season

with salt and a squeeze of lemon juice. Garnish the filled eggs with snipped chives.
Smoked Oyster: Mash egg yolks and combine with half of a 3¾ oz. can smoked oysters which have been mashed finely. Add 1 teaspoon finely grated onion, 2-3 tablespoons mayonnaise and season to taste with salt, pepper and curry powder. Use remaining oysters for garnish.

Decorate eggs with chopped parsley, canned red pimiento cut into fancy shapes or a little of the selected flavouring if it looks decorative, a sprinkle of paprika pepper or anything savoury that will add to the appearance of the dish. Serve soon after filling for best results. Makes 12.

Greek Meatballs ••

1 onion
2 slices toast
12 oz. minced round steak
1 egg, slightly beaten
1 tablespoon olive oil
2 teaspoons lemon juice
1 tablespoon chopped
** parsley**
2 teaspoons chopped
** fresh mint**
¼ teaspoon ground
** cinnamon**
1 teaspoon salt
ground pepper to taste
plain flour
butter for frying

Finely chop onion. Soak toast in cold water and squeeze dry. Place meat in a bowl, add onion, toast and all the remaining ingredients except flour and butter. Blend well together, mixing lightly. Cover and chill for 30 minutes. Shape into small balls about 1-inch diameter. Dust evenly with a little flour and brown on all sides in the butter in a frying pan until cooked, cooking one layer at a time. Drain. Pierce meatballs with cocktail sticks and serve with a bowl of mustard or spicy tomato sauce for dipping. Makes about 25.

Cocktail Pizza ••

Crust:
1 cup (4 oz.) self-raising
** flour**
1 cup (4 oz.) plain flour
½ teaspoon paprika
** pepper**
½ teaspoon salt
Tomato Filling:
2 tablespoons olive oil
2 large onions, chopped
1 clove garlic, crushed
2 x 15 oz. cans whole
** tomatoes**
1 bay leaf
Topping:
4 oz. mozzarella cheese
1 x 1½ oz. can flat
** anchovy fillets**
4 oz. black olives
4 oz. pepperoni or Italian
** salami**

3 oz. butter
2 tablespoons lemon juice
3 tablespoons cold water
little olive oil
1 tablespoon grated
** parmesan cheese**

1 tablespoon brown sugar
1½ teaspoons salt
pinch ground oregano or
** basil**
freshly ground pepper to
** taste**

1 tablespoon olive oil
½ cup grated parmesan
** cheese**

For Crust: Sift both flours, paprika pepper and salt into a bowl. Rub in butter until mixture resembles breadcrumbs. Combine lemon juice and water, sprinkle over ingredients in bowl. Mix to a firm dough, adding a little more water if necessary. Chill 1 hour. Roll out thinly between sheets of plastic to fit a greased 12 x 10-inch shallow baking tray or use 2 smaller trays. Brush pastry with a little oil and sprinkle with grated parmesan.

For Filling: Heat oil in a saucepan and sauté onions until golden. Add garlic, drained and seeded tomatoes and all remaining ingredients. Bring to the boil, reduce heat and simmer, uncovered, for 30 minutes until thickened. Stir occasionally. Cool slightly, then spread on pastry.

For Topping: Slice cheese thinly, drain anchovies, halve olives and remove stones. Cut rind off salami, then slice the salami into fine strips. On one half of the filling, arrange overlapping slices of cheese, then garnish with anchovy fillets and olives. On other half of filling arrange the strips of pepperoni. Sprinkle olive oil evenly over surface, then sprinkle with the grated parmesan cheese.

Bake in a very hot oven (450°F.) for 10 minutes, reduce temperature to moderately slow (375°F.) and bake a further 15 minutes until crust is crisp and cheese golden. Cut into squares or finger lengths to serve. Serve hot.

The beef mixture for Greek Meatballs is formed into 1-inch balls dusted with flour and then fried.

The egg yolk filling for Stuffed Eggs is spooned or piped into whites just before serving.

Cheese Caraway Crisps.

Roast Chicken Provençal, Sauté Potatoes, Honey Glazed Carrots, Green Peas Bonne Femme, Strawberries Chantilly

Old Fashioned Family Get-together

for six or twelve people

This is just about the happiest kind of party in the world. Guests of all ages from grandma to grandchildren mix with friendly informality. Sisters help with the cooking. An aunt famous for her cheesecake waits to be told no family party would be the same without it. A special treat for the children is always in order.

Old fashioned roast chicken is loved by all. Give it new interest by serving at least one vegetable prepared in an unusual way. Plan to serve from both ends of the table— every family has at least two good carvers! Allow also for a choice of desserts and don't forget to provide drinks for the children. Strawberries Chantilly is made two ways —one without liqueur.

There will be lots of family news to catch up on, so don't interrupt the flow of conversation with the problem of different drinks. Prepare a bowl of punch and let everyone help themselves before the meal is served.

Serve dry sherry with the soup and a rich, highly flavoured Rhine riesling with the chicken. Champagne may be offered with dessert, tawny port would round off the meal.

Menu
Iced Tea Punch*
Cream of Mushroom Soup
Roast Chicken Provençal
Sauté Potatoes
Honey Glazed Carrots
Green Peas Bonne Femme
Strawberries Chantilly
and
Strawberries with Ice Cream
Fruit Cheesecake

*Consult index for recipe

Cream of Mushroom Soup •

1 onion	1 bay leaf
8 oz. mushrooms	1 teaspoon salt
2 oz. butter	1/4 teaspoon freshly ground
2 tablespoons (1 oz.)	black pepper
plain flour	1/4 pint cream
2 pints chicken stock	

Finely chop onion. Wash mushrooms and slice finely. Melt butter in a heavy pan, add onion and cook gently until transparent. Add mushrooms and cook, stirring for about 5 minutes.

Remove from heat and blend in the flour. Heat stock which may be home-made or prepared from stock cubes. Slowly add the stock to the mushroom mixture, stirring constantly. Add bay leaf, salt and pepper. Bring to the boil, stirring continually. Simmer for 5 minutes, then remove bay leaf. Before serving stir in the cream and heat through without boiling. Serves 6.

Make double quantity to serve 12 people.

Roast Chicken Provencal ••

1 x 4 lb. chicken	8 oz. button mushrooms
salt and pepper	6 canned anchovy fillets
3-4 oz. softened butter	parsley to garnish
6 small tomatoes	
Stuffing:	
2 rashers bacon	2 tablespoons chopped
liver of chicken	parsley
8 oz. pork sausage mince	pinch each sage, mace
1 onion, chopped	and thyme
1/4 cup chopped celery	salt and pepper
2 cups soft white	1 large egg
breadcrumbs	

Season chicken with salt and pepper and spoon the stuffing into cavity. Tie chicken legs together and place in a roasting pan which has been well buttered. Rub butter all over exposed surface of chicken and roast in a moderately hot oven (375°F.) for 20-25 minutes. Turn chicken over, spread with more butter and return to oven for another 20 minutes. Turn chicken breast side up for final roasting.

Wash and core tomatoes. Wash mushrooms. Place around chicken and cross each tomato with an anchovy fillet which has been halved lengthwise. Return to oven and roast a further 20 minutes until chicken is cooked and a beautiful brown all over. Serves 6.

Prepare two chickens for 12 people.

For Stuffing: Chop bacon and lightly fry in its own fat. Remove bacon and to pan add chicken liver, sausage mince, onion and celery. Fry until lightly browned. Add to breadcrumbs with bacon, herbs and seasoning to taste. Stir in beaten egg.

Note: If liked a pan gravy may be served with the chicken. Remove chicken from roasting pan, place pan on top of stove over direct heat and add ¾ cup chicken stock. Boil, stirring to lift off chicken drippings. Strain into a sauce-boat and serve separately. For a cream gravy boil the pan gravy until reduced to about ½ cup, then add ¼ pint cream. Cook until gravy thickens just a little.

Sauté Potatoes ••

2 lb. old potatoes	2 tablespoons oil
2 oz. butter	salt and pepper

Peel potatoes and slice into 1-inch lengths, ½-inch wide. Put into a pan with cold water to cover, bring to the boil and simmer for 3 minutes. Drain.

Heat butter and oil in a large frying pan or a shallow pan and fry potatoes, turning constantly until golden and cooked through. Season with salt and pepper to taste. Serves 6.

Three to four pounds of potatoes will be sufficient for 12 people.

Honey Glazed Carrots •

2 lb. young carrots	3 tablespoons honey
4 oz. butter	1 teaspoon salt
2 cups water	

Wash and scrape carrots, then cut into thin slices. Melt butter in a pan and add water, honey, salt and carrot slices. Cook gently, uncovered, for 15-20 minutes until tender, turning carrots occasionally and taking care not to break them. If liquid has not evaporated, place over a high heat and cook quickly until there is 2-3 tablespoons left.

Alternatively the carrots may be cut into quarters, then into 2-inch lengths, or if they are small carrots they may be cooked whole. Serves 6.

For 12 people allow 3 lb. carrots, but the other ingredients remain the same.

Strawberries Chantilly •

Wash and hull 3 punnets strawberries. Thirty minutes before serving sprinkle strawberries with castor sugar to taste (this will depend on ripeness and sweetness of the fruit, ½ cup is usually right for this quantity). Pour the juice of 1 orange over and flavour with a little cointreau or grand marnier. If serving to children remove enough strawberries for them before adding the liqueur. Serve with Cream Chantilly (½ pint cream whipped with 1 teaspoon vanilla essence). Serves 6.

Children may prefer the strawberries served over vanilla ice cream. For 12 people 4 or 5 punnets of strawberries may be used.

Green Peas Bonne Femme •

2 oz. butter	3 sprigs parsley
1 onion, sliced	2 lb. peas or 1 x 12 oz.
1 lettuce, shredded	packet frozen peas
½ teaspoon salt	½ cup water
2 teaspoons sugar	extra 2 teaspoons butter
1 sprig marjoram	1 teaspoon plain flour
1 sprig thyme	

Put 2 oz. butter into a saucepan. Add onion, lettuce, salt, sugar, herbs and peas. Mix all together well. Add water. Bring to the boil, cover and cook for about 20-25 minutes, or until peas are almost tender. Discard herbs. Blend 2 teaspoons butter with flour and stir into peas. Return to heat, shaking to roll peas around until butter and flour mixture has combined with the liquid. As soon as it boils again, remove from heat and serve. Serves 6.

Note: A good pinch dried herbs may replace the fresh sprigs of marjoram and thyme.

For 12 people double quantity of peas, the other ingredients remain the same.

Fruit Cheese cake ••

An extremely light textured cheesecake which rises to an impressive height on its base of fruit-topped pastry.

Pastry:

1 cup (4 oz.) plain flour	1 egg yolk
2 oz. butter	iced water

Filling:

1 x 15 oz. can sliced	½ teaspoon vanilla essence
pineapple	1 teaspoon grated lemon
1 x 14 oz. can sour	rind
pitted cherries	2 eggs
8 oz. cottage cheese	2 tablespoons melted
8 oz. cream cheese	unsalted butter
2 tablespoons (1 oz.)	½ cup hot milk
plain flour	3 egg whites
½ teaspoon salt	½ cup (4 oz.) castor sugar

Pastry: Sift flour into a bowl and rub in butter. Add beaten egg yolk and enough cold water to make a firm dough. Chill for 1 hour. Roll out pastry to a 10-inch circle. Press onto bottom of a greased 9-inch spring form tin, pressing pastry 1-inch up side of tin. Cover pastry with greaseproof paper, sprinkle a few dried beans over. Bake blind for 15 minutes in a moderate oven (350°F.), remove paper and beans and bake for a further 10 minutes or until a light golden brown. Pastry will shrink to form base with a small edge. Allow to cool.

For Filling: Drain pineapple and cherries while preparing cheese mixture. Sieve cottage cheese and beat with the cream cheese, flour, salt, vanilla, lemon rind and 2 whole eggs. When well mixed add melted butter and continue beating. Blend in hot milk, then fold in egg whites which have been whisked stiffly and mixed with the sugar. Arrange drained fruit over cooked pastry and carefully cover fruit with cheese mixture. Bake in a slow oven (300°F.) for 1 hour. Turn off temperature control and leave cake to cool in the oven. Chill before serving. Serves 10-12.

Young Fun Parties

Housewarming
for twenty people

Nearly everyone, at least once in their lifetime, knows the joy of this dream fulfilled—moving into a home of one's own. With or without furniture, a housewarming is soon on its way.

Plan on serving one large, rather than lots of small dishes. Lasagne Bolognese Bake is a great party dish, the filling can be made days ahead and the whole dish put together the day before the party. It even improves by the second day! Remove from the refrigerator and slip into the oven just as guests are arriving.

Sambal dip, garlic bread and salad greens are all do-ahead items, and so is the delicious ice cream dessert, important when catering for a crowd.

Instead of offering a variety of drinks make a large quantity of claret punch. It is so much easier, especially if there hasn't been time or money to stock the cellar.
Wines: Claret punch could be served throughout the evening. If toasts are being made for the new home, there is nothing more festive than Champagne.

Housewarming
Claret Punch*
Antipasto Tray
Sambal Dip*
Lasagne Bolognese Bake
Tossed Italian Salad*
Hot Garlic Bread
Cassata
Sherried Cheese
Potted Herb Cheese
*Consult index for recipe.

Antipasto Tray •

Arrange crisped fresh vegetables on a tray or in a Lazy Susan. Olives, cheese, anchovies, salami and any cold meats may be added. Serve a bowl of one of the good bottled dressings such as coleslaw or thousand island alongside for dipping.
Radish Roses: Wash small round radishes and remove all but the smallest leaf. Cut a small slice from root end of each radish, then cut 4 slices around radish from root end almost to stem. Use a thin bladed sharp vegetable knife. Chill in iced water until 'petals' open.

Celery Curls: Cut tender stalks of crisp white celery into 3-inch lengths. Make narrow, parallel slits from each end almost to centre. Soak in iced water until ends curl.
Carrot and Cucumber Sticks: Cut peeled, chilled vegetables lengthwise into $\frac{1}{4}$-inch slices and then each slice into thin strips.
Garlic Olives: Drain 8 oz. black olives, prick with a fork. Crush 3-4 cloves garlic and put into a jar with olives and a few sprigs parsley or dill. Top with olive oil and marinate for 2 days.
Stuffed Eggs: See recipe on page 29.

Chilli Con Carne, Corn Bread, Fiesta Salad.

Lasagne Bolognese Bake ••

2 carrots	4 teaspoons salt
2 stalks celery	1 teaspoon sugar
1 green pepper	4 teaspoons dried basil
1 large onion	pepper
6 tablespoons oil	2 lb. lasagne noodles
3 lb. minced steak	or spaghetti
2 x 30 oz. cans whole	4 oz. butter
tomatoes	8 tablespoons grated
1 x 8 oz. can tomato	parmesan cheese
paste	Cream Sauce (recipe
4 cups dry red wine	follows)

Peel and grate carrots. Finely chop celery, green pepper and onion. Heat oil in a large pan or casserole and sauté vegetables until soft, but not brown. Remove vegetables. Add meat to pan and stir until pinkness has disappeared. Add tomatoes, tomato paste, wine, salt, sugar, basil, pepper and sautéed vegetables. Bring to the boil, turn heat to low and simmer uncovered for 45 minutes or until thickened. Add more salt and pepper, if necessary, to taste.

Cook lasagne noodles in boiling salted water until tender, cooking only 1 lb. at a time (see page   for details of cooking spaghetti). Drain. Toss lightly in butter. Butter or oil two large casseroles about 13 x 8 x 2-inches. Place a layer of lasagne or spaghetti on the base of each, cover with meat mixture, sprinkle with parmesan cheese and finish with a layer of pasta (lasagne or spaghetti). Pour Cream Sauce over, top with remaining parmesan cheese and bake in a moderate oven (350°F.) for 30-40 minutes or until tops are nicely browned. Serves 20.

For Cream Sauce: Melt 3 oz. butter in a heavy saucepan, remove from heat, blend in 5 tablespoons plain flour, return to heat and cook for a minute. Add 1½ pints milk and 2 bay leaves, cook gently, stirring until sauce boils and thickens. Add ¼ pint cream, remove bay leaves and season to taste with salt and pepper.

Hot Garlic Bread •

4 large loaves French	2 teaspoons salt
bread	1 lb. butter or margarine
6 cloves garlic	

Cut French bread in two. Slash bread in 1-inch slices almost through to base. Crush garlic with salt. Soften butter and combine thoroughly with crushed garlic. Spread butter on both sides of each slice of bread. Remaining butter is spread on top of loaves. Wrap bread in aluminium foil until required. To heat, place foil-wrapped loaves in moderately hot oven (375°F.) for 15-20 minutes. Open foil for the last 5 minutes. Serve warm. Serves 20-24.

Variation:
For Herb Bread, substitute 3 tablespoons chopped, fresh herbs for garlic.

Sherried Cheese •

1 lb. Cheddar cheese	1 teaspoon prepared
8 oz. blue vein cheese	mustard
2 oz. softened unsalted	dash hot pepper sauce
butter	salt to taste
½ cup dry sherry	
1 teaspoon	
Worcestershire sauce	

Have cheeses at room temperature. Grate Cheddar cheese using finest grating edge. Crumble blue vein cheese and combine with Cheddar cheese and butter in a bowl. Blend well with a fork. Gradually beat in sherry. Add Worcestershire sauce, mustard, hot pepper sauce and salt. Continue beating either with an electric beater or wooden spoon until mixture is smooth and fluffy. Use at once or store in a covered crock in refrigerator. Bring to room temperature before serving. Use as a spread.

Potted Herb Cheese •

Add 2 tablespoons finely chopped fresh herbs to French Potted or Sherried Cheese. Parsley, sage, thyme, chives and basil are all good either alone or in combination.

Cassata ••

This is an easy-to-make adaptation of a classic Italian ice.

8 oz. coconut macaroons	2 x ½ gallon cans ice
½ cup sweet sherry	cream
8 oz. glacé cherries	½ pint cream
2 cups almonds	2 tablespoons castor sugar
8 oz. dark cooking	extra cherries to decorate
chocolate	

Crumble macaroons and sprinkle with sweet sherry. Chop cherries. Finely chop and toast almonds. Grate chocolate. Place each flavouring in four separate soup bowls. Scoop out large serves of ice cream, coat each scoop with one of the flavourings. Quickly spoon into one or two wetted moulds, or return to cans. Freeze 2-3 hours or longer. When nearly ready to serve, unmould and decorate with cream whipped with the sugar. Top with extra cherries. Return to freezer. Serves 20.

Parties for Teenagers

With one or more teenager in the family, it is fairly certain that at least once a year there will be a big, noisy but well-organised party. I have found the key to most successful young parties is to have a theme and a programme. Food is nearly always simple, but 'type-cast'; for example, a Pizza Party, a Hamburger Party, a Mexican Bean Feast or a Spaghetti Party.

Waxed paper plates in gay colours and plenty of paper napkins make for easy cleaning up and can be fun, but choose wild, way-out young colour combinations. Serve a punch. The punch bowl doesn't have to be heirloom silver—one I use for young parties is a large Fijian Kava bowl bought at an auction sale for $1.00, another, an old-fashioned Victorian wash basin. I've even used a large plastic salad bowl (the brand name is well known, world wide) garlanded with flowers from the garden.

The music should be in keeping with the times and the most important advice I can give is to supervise the early part of the evening, serve the food early, then leave the guests to enjoy the dancing and merry-making in their own way.

Wines? A matter of personal judgment here. In early teens it is wise to stick to a 'No Alcohol' rule. After that, select from punches in the Drinks chapter or buy flagons of red or white wine. Look for inexpensive French or Italian carafes for pouring the wines.

Pizza Party

for twenty people

Pizza fans come in all age groups. From teenagers to the decidedly mature, there are few who can resist Italy's gift to the rest of the world, the pizza pie. Of course, there are pizzas and pizzas, home-made ones can be among the best.

For parties where the accent is on having a good time, wedges of tasty pizza are easy to serve, you don't even need cutlery. Paper plates and napkins can be worked in with the colour scheme of the table setting.

Pizzas are both easy and fun to make. They take to freezing and the basic dough can be made and frozen weeks, even months, before the party. Some of the toppings should be limited to one or two weeks of frozen life.

Wines: In very hot weather, sangria goes well with pizza, so do bubbly wine punches. Flagons of dry red or chilled white wine are fine, but don't serve from the flagons. Inexpensive Italian or French type wine carafes are much more fun.

Antipasto Tray*
Neapolitan Pizza Marinara
Salami Pizza
Pizza con Cozze
Pizza Franciscana
Pizza Campofranco
Pepper Pizza
Tossed Italian Salad*
Cassata*

*Consult index for recipe.

Pizza Crust with Yeast ••

The traditional pizza dough is made with yeast, rolled thinly to form a crisp, golden base. This quantity makes two 12-inch pizzas or six individual pizzas.

1 cup lukewarm water	3¼ cups (13 oz.) plain
1 oz. compressed yeast	flour
3 tablespoons olive oil	1½ teaspoons salt
	¼ teaspoon pepper

Measure water into a large bowl. Crumble yeast into water and stir until smooth. Stir in olive oil. Sift flour, salt and pepper over yeast mixture. Blend thoroughly with a wooden spoon. Turn onto a lightly floured surface and knead gently until smooth and elastic.

Place in a large greased bowl, turn dough to grease all over. Cover with a clean tea towel and leave in a warm place for about 2 hours or until double in bulk.

Turn out on a lightly floured board and knead four or five times. Divide mixture into two. Roll out each portion about ¼-inch thick to a 12-inch circle. Press out to edge of greased pizza pans (do not cut) and continue in one of the following ways. (For individual pizzas divide dough into six, roll dough out to $\frac{1}{4}$-inch thickness and press into six rounds. Arrange on greased baking trays). Top with filling and bake for 15 minutes.

Note: Pizza dough can be prepared, rolled out to fit tin and stored in the refrigerator for 2-3 hours before cooking. Brush with olive oil to prevent a crust from forming.

Neapolitan Pizza Marinara ••

1 pizza base (see recipe page 37)	8 oz. cooked ham salt and pepper
3 tablespoons olive oil	6 oz. mozzarella cheese,
4 oz. mushrooms	sliced
Tomato Filling:	
1 small onion	1 teaspoon dried basil
1 clove garlic	2 teaspoons brown sugar
2 tablespoons olive oil	salt and pepper
1 x 7 oz. can tomato purée	2 tablespoons tomato paste

Brush dough in pizza pan with half the olive oil and sprinkle with half the parmesan cheese. Peel tomatoes, seed, drain and cut into slices. Arrange over dough. Sprinkle with garlic, oregano and pepper. Arrange strips of anchovies and thin slices of mozzarella over tomatoes. Sprinkle with remaining oil and parmesan. Bake in a hot oven (400°F.) for 20-25 minutes until crust is golden. Cuts into 8 wedges.

Variation:
Salami Pizza: Follow recipe for Neapolitan Pizza Marinara, omit anchovies and, instead, use 6 oz. sliced salami. Place on the mozzarella cheese slices and garnish the pizza with black olives. Sprinkle with the oil and parmesan cheese and bake as directed.

Pizza Con Cozze ••

Prepare as for Neapolitan Pizza Marinara but omit anchovies, use instead 1 cup of drained, cooked and shelled mussels. These may be freshly cooked or purchased in bottles from most fish shops. Drain off any liquor.

Pizza Franciscana ••

1 pizza base (see recipe above)	1 tablespoon fresh chopped oregano or 1 teaspoon dried
2 tablespoons olive oil	
$\frac{1}{2}$ cup grated parmesan cheese	pepper
1 lb. tomatoes	1 x 1$\frac{1}{2}$ oz. tin flat anchovy fillets
2 cloves garlic, chopped	6 oz. mozzarella cheese

Brush dough in pizza pan with 1 tablespoon olive oil. Spread with the prepared tomato filling. Wash and slice mushrooms, cook gently in remaining oil. Strew over tomato with thin strips of ham. Season with salt and pepper. Bake in a hot oven (400°F.) for 15 minutes, remove from oven, arrange sliced mozzarella over and return to oven for a further 5-8 minutes. Cuts into 8 wedges.

For Tomato Filling: Chop onion finely and crush garlic. Fry in hot oil until onion is transparent. Add tomato purée, basil, brown sugar and seasonings to taste. Cook, stirring for 10 minutes. Add tomato paste and mix well. Cool.

Pizza Campofranco ••

1 pizza base (see recipe page 37)	8 oz. bel paese cheese
3 tablespoons olive oil	4 oz. sliced ham
1 lb. tomatoes	$\frac{1}{2}$ cup grated parmesan cheese
1 teaspoon dried basil	

Brush dough with half the olive oil. Peel, seed and drain tomatoes. Cut into slices and cook gently in remaining olive oil. Season with basil. Spread over dough. Top with slices of bel paese and ham, then sprinkle with parmesan cheese. Bake in a hot oven (400°F.) for 20-25 minutes. Cuts into 8 wedges.

Variation:
Pepper Pizza: Prepare as for Pizza Campofranco and top the slices of cheese and ham with $\frac{1}{2}$-inch squares of banana pickles (available in jars). Sprinkle with a little olive oil and bake as directed. As the banana pickles are extremely hot, red and yellow or green peppers may be used. Cut the peppers into $\frac{1}{2}$-inch squares and blanch in boiling water for 3 minutes, drain and rinse with cold water.

Note: This pizza is often made as a closed pie, that is a second round of pizza dough is placed over the filling, glazed with a little beaten egg, and baked 25-30 minutes. However, the open pie is most suitable for a party.

To make Hot Garlic Bread the French Bread is cut into slices, almost through the base. If the loaves of bread are very long, cut each into half. Crushed garlic is beaten into butter which is then spread on both sides of each slice of bread.

Mexican Bean Feast

for ten or twenty people

This is not subtle, understated cooking and Chilli Con Carne is often as hot and fiery as the little red chillies that give this national dish its name. But to each his own, and even in Mexico the quieter temperament demands and gets a less pungent version of this dish—be assured, Chilli Con Carne need only be as hot as you like it, so experiment with the quantity of chilli powder, don't overdo it. For the venturesome guests, provide a small bowl of freshly chopped chilli and let them add to their own heat. If convenience foods are going to be a help, use canned kidney beans to make Chilli Con Carne. Be careful not to overcook as this dish should not become mushy.

Mexicans love chocolate, so serve Chocolate Ice Cream. Mexican Cheesecake is superbly rich, so serve small portions.

Fun and fiestas have always been one of the attractions of Mexico, so make this a very gay, bright fun party.

Wines: Sangria in very hot weather, flagon red wine, a good dry red or a fruity wine-based punch.

The character of Mexico shows up very clearly in its cuisine. Colourful, gay, unrepressed and decidedly fun.

Sangria*

Refried Bean Dip

Guacamole*

Acapulco Savoury Bites

Chilli Con Carne

Corn Bread

Fiesta Salad

Chocolate Ice Cream

or

Mexican Cheesecake

*Consult index for recipe.

Corn Bread ••

2 cups (8 oz.) self-raising
   flour
½ cup (4 oz.) sugar
6 teaspoons baking powder
1½ teaspoons salt

2 cups yellow cornmeal
4 eggs
2 cups milk
4 oz. softened butter

Grease a 13 x 9-inch shallow tin and set oven temperature at hot (400°F.).

Sift flour, sugar, baking powder and salt into a mixing bowl. Stir in cornmeal. Beat eggs slightly, add to dry ingredients with milk and softened butter. Beat with a rotary or electric beater until smooth, about 1 minute. Do not overbeat. Pour into prepared tin. Bake in a hot oven (400°F.) for 30-40 minutes. Serve cut into 2-inch squares. Serves 10.

Prepare this recipe twice for 20 serves.

Note: Although the amount of baking powder seems excessive when self-raising flour is used, it is necessary to give Corn Bread its light, even texture.

Mixture may also be baked in corn bread moulds. Grease the moulds and spoon in enough mixture to almost fill. Bake until golden and cooked when tested with a fine skewer. Baking time will depend on size of moulds.

Refried Bean Dip •

3 x 10 oz. cans kidney
   beans
4 tablespoons oil
1¼ cups grated Cheddar
   cheese

½-1 teaspoon salt
1 teaspoon chilli powder

Drain beans, reserving liquid. Heat oil in a frying pan, add beans and mash with a potato masher. Add ⅓ cup bean liquid and mix well, stir in cheese, salt and chilli powder. Cook, stirring, about 1 minute until cheese melts. Serve hot with crackers. If mixture gets too stiff for dipping, add a little more bean liquid or water.

Acapulco Savoury Bites •

Place cubes of salami, tasty cheese, prawns, radishes and cubes of avocado pear, which have been dipped in lemon juice, on toothpicks and serve the following sauce alongside for dipping.

Dipping Sauce:

1 onion	**4 tablespoons vinegar**
4 red tomatoes	**2 tablespoons olive oil**
3-4 red chillis	**salt to taste**

Chop onion finely, peel tomatoes and chop finely. Halve chillis, remove seeds and chop the chillis finely. Add vinegar, oil and salt to taste. Beat well until mixture is a smooth pulp, or blend in electric blender. Serve cold.

Fiesta Salad ••

All ingredients can be prepared ahead on day of party and chilled separately in covered containers.

3 lettuce (or mixture of salad greens)	**3-4 oranges**
2 green peppers	**¾ cup French dressing (see page 16)**
2 cucumbers	

Wash and dry lettuce and tear into bite-sized pieces. Chill well. Slice peppers into rings, discard seeds. Peel, score and finely slice cucumbers. Peel oranges, removing all white pith, and slice. Put all prepared ingredients into large salad bowls. Sprinkle French dressing over salads. Toss until every leaf is coated. Serve immediately. Serves 10-12.

For a larger party double all ingredients.

Chilli Con Carne ••

2 onions	**2-3 teaspoons salt**
2 cloves garlic	**1 teaspoon chilli powder or more to taste**
4 tablespoons olive oil	
2½ lb. minced steak	**2 teaspoons dried oregano leaves or ¼ teaspoon powdered oregano**
1 cup beef stock or water and beef stock cubes	
1 x 16 oz. can tomato purée	**1 teaspoon cumin**
	4 oz. pitted black olives
3 tablespoons tomato paste	

Mexican Beans:

1 lb. red kidney beans	**1 onion**
½ teaspoon ground cumin	**few whole cloves**
1 clove garlic	**2 bay leaves**
few parsley stalks	**2 teaspoons salt**

Chop onions and crush garlic. Gently cook onions in oil in a frying pan until transparent, add garlic, cook 1 minute and remove to a large pan. Add a little more oil if necessary to frying pan and brown meat, in two lots, over a high heat, stirring constantly. Add to onions. Stir in stock, tomato purée, tomato paste, salt, chilli powder, oregano and cumin. Cover and simmer 30 minutes. Add cooked drained beans (recipe follows) and simmer for a further 30 minutes until tender. If mixture cooks too quickly, it will be necessary to add a little water. Taste and add more seasoning if necessary. Just before serving, add olives and cook just long enough to heat through.
For Mexican Beans: Soak beans overnight. Next day, drain and put into a large saucepan. Add 6 cups water and all remaining ingredients. Cover and simmer gently 1½ hours until almost tender. Serves 10. For a larger party prepare two quantities.
Note: Two or three 10 oz. cans of kidney beans, rinsed in cold water and drained, may be used instead of the dried beans.

Chocolate Ice Cream •

1 x ½ gallon can chocolate ice cream	**¾ cup evaporated milk**
	2 oz. butter
¾ cup (6 oz.) sugar	**1 teaspoon vanilla essence**
3 tablespoons cocoa	
pinch salt	**1 teaspoon powdered cinnamon**
2 tablespoons hot water	

Combine sugar, cocoa and salt in a saucepan. Blend in water, gradually add milk and stir over low heat until cocoa and sugar dissolve. Bring to the boil and cook for 4-5 minutes until thickened, stirring constantly. Remove from heat and beat in butter. Flavour with vanilla and cinnamon. Cool and chill. Serve ice cream scoops topped with the cold chocolate cinnamon sauce. Serves 8-10.

For 20 guests prepare a double quantity.

Mexican Cheesecake ••

Combining Mexico's favourite flavours of chocolate and rum, this cheesecake has a light texture and crisp, crumbly topping.

4 oz. plain chocolate biscuits	**4 egg yolks**
	½ cup (4 oz.) castor sugar
1½ tablespoons melted butter	
	2 tablespoons rum
1 lb. packaged cream cheese	**2 egg whites**

Crush chocolate biscuits with a rolling pin. Mix half biscuits with butter and press crumb mixture in bottom of a greased 9 or 10-inch pie plate. Beat cream cheese until light and smooth. Beat egg yolks with sugar until thick and creamy and stir in rum. Add egg mixture gradually to cream cheese, stirring until it is smooth. Whisk egg whites until stiff, and fold into mixture. Pour into prepared pie plate and sprinkle top with remaining crushed chocolate biscuits. Bake in a slow oven (300°F.) 30 minutes. Remove from oven to cool. Serve chilled. Serves 8-10.

For 20 people, make 2 separate cheesecakes.

Spaghetti Party

for twenty people

Today's young party givers have one thing in common with their parents—they love giving and going to a spaghetti party. If the party is to be a group effort this party menù is just the thing. Four girls or less could manage this with ease, each making a sauce or a salad or the dessert. This is lots of fun and the cost is shared, important when a little money has to go a long way!

A great help at this kind of party is a pair of tongs to help serve the slippery spaghetti. Serve the spaghetti in large bowls and allow guests to help themselves, adding their choice of sauce. The salad and dessert may be prepared a day ahead and stored in the refrigerator and they do help to turn a simple spaghetti party into something special.

Wines: An Italian Chianti is right for this type of party. A light rosé wine or flagon red is also suitable.

Nuts and Bolts
Spaghetti
Bolognese Sauce
and
Milanese Sauce
Cauliflower Salad
Tossed Italian Salad
Italian Marsala Cream

Nuts and Bolts •

1 packet OK's	1½ teaspoons paprika pepper
2 packets long pretzels, broken into 1-inch pieces	2 teaspoons Worcestershire sauce
8 oz. salted peanuts	1 tablespoon chopped parsley
3 oz. butter	1 clove garlic, crushed, or ½ teaspoon garlic salt
4 tablespoons vegetable oil	
½ teaspoon salt	

Put cereal, pretzels and peanuts in a large baking dish. Melt butter, add oil, seasonings, Worcestershire sauce, parsley and garlic. Sprinkle evenly over the ingredients in baking dish and mix gently, taking care not to break cereal. Bake in a slow oven (300°F.) for 45 minutes, stirring occasionally. Cool and store in an airtight container. Serve in bowls for guests to nibble.

To cook spaghetti for a crowd

Use a large pan with plenty of room for spaghetti strands to cook separately and allow water to bubble briskly. Use lots of water for cooking—6 pints water for 8 oz. pasta. Add about 1 teaspoon salt to every 2 pints of water, and have water boiling vigorously before adding pasta. You may also like to add a teaspoon of olive oil to the water, this helps prevent sticking, a good tip especially if a large quantity of spaghetti is to be cooked at one time.

1 lb. of spaghetti will be sufficient for 6 guests, for 20 guests you cook 4 lb. spaghetti, but cook only 1 lb. at a time. If possible, use two really large saucepans or boilers. If you do not possess them, ask friends if they know where you can borrow them. It is fatal to attempt to cook spaghetti in too small a saucepan.

Using two large boilers, add enough water to two-thirds fill, add about 1 tablespoon salt and bring to the boil. Hold spaghetti at one end, and dip the other end into bubbling water. As spaghetti softens, curl it around in the pan until the length is submerged. Do not cover. Add a tablespoon of oil or butter and stir to prevent strands sticking. Cook until tender but firm, about 12-15 minutes. Remove from heat and drain immediately. Coat with 4 oz. melted butter and place in a hot serving bowl. Fill boilers with hot water, return to stove and proceed with cooking the next lot of spaghetti. As a spaghetti party is mostly very informal, commence serving the first lot of spaghetti while the next is cooking.

To keep spaghetti hot

For a short while, you may return drained spaghetti to the empty cooking pan, add some butter, then cover and keep warm.

For the best results serve pasta immediately, but if this is inconvenient, drain in a colander and set over a pan containing a small amount of simmering water. Coat pasta with a little butter to keep strands from sticking together. Cover the colander.

Remember, spaghetti is delicious served with butter, chopped fresh herbs and a grind of black pepper. Some guests may prefer this simple dish.

Bolognese Sauce ••

1 lb. chicken livers
8 oz. each lean beef and pork, finely minced
3 tablespoons olive oil
2 cloves garlic, peeled
2 small onions, finely chopped
1 tablespoon chopped parsley
2 bay leaves
2 x 15 oz. cans whole tomatoes or 2 lb. ripe tomatoes, peeled

½ pint beef stock or water and beef stock cube
4 tablespoons tomato paste
salt and pepper
1 teaspoon chopped basil or ½ teaspoon dried basil
2 oz. butter
parmesan cheese, grated

Soak chicken livers in salted water, dry on absorbent paper, halve and remove membrane. Put chicken livers, meat, oil, garlic, onions, parsley and bay leaves into a saucepan and brown slowly, stirring frequently to prevent meat from cooking in lumps. As soon as garlic turns golden, remove. Add tomatoes (with juice from can), stock, tomato paste, salt and pepper. Cover and simmer for 1 hour. Add basil, cook 1 minute longer. Remove from heat and add butter. Makes enough sauce for 2 lb. spaghetti.
Note: Bolognese sauce should be made with chicken livers but they may be omitted; if so, double the quantity of minced beef and pork. The stock may be made from bouillon cubes. This sauce is best spooned over, rather than mixed in with the spaghetti. Serve parmesan cheese separately.

Milanese Sauce •

1 lb. mushrooms
2 cloves garlic
2 oz. butter
1 lb. sliced ham or soft Italian salami

2 x 15 oz. cans whole tomatoes
1 teaspoon chopped oregano or ½ teaspoon dried oregano

Slice mushrooms, peel garlic and sauté in butter in a heavy saucepan for 4-5 minutes. As soon as garlic turns golden, remove. Cut ham into slivers, add to mushrooms with tomatoes from the can (include the juice but first cut tomatoes in two, remove seeds and chop roughly). Add oregano, cover and simmer gently for 20-25 minutes. Makes enough sauce for 2 lb. spaghetti. It may be spooned over individual servings, or mixed into spaghetti, then served.

Cauliflower Salad ••

1 large cauliflower
½ cup French dressing (see page 16)
Anchovy Dressing:
yolks of 2 hard-boiled eggs
1 teaspoon French mustard
2 tablespoons tomato purée or sauce
3 canned anchovy fillets

paprika pepper
watercress

½ pint mayonnaise (see page 14) or bottled salad dressing
salt and pepper
1-2 spring onions

Break cauliflower into flowerets. Plunge into boiling salted water and boil for 5-8 minutes until tender, but crisp. Pour into colander and place under cold running water. Drain thoroughly, put into bowl, sprinkle with French dressing. Cover and chill. Before serving, arrange cauliflower on a serving platter and top with the Anchovy Dressing. Sprinkle with paprika pepper. Garnish with watercress. Serves 20.
For Anchovy Dressing: Mash egg yolks, add mustard, tomato purée and pounded anchovies. Add to mayonnaise, season to taste with salt and pepper. Lastly fold in finely chopped onions.

Tossed Italian Salad •

3 lettuce
4 tomatoes, cut into wedges
8 oz. black olives

1 can flat anchovy fillets
1 cup French dressing (see page 16)

Tear the washed and chilled lettuce into bite-sized pieces. Keep in plastic bags in refrigerator until required. Put into two large bowls with tomato wedges, top with stoned olives and drained chopped anchovies. Sprinkle dressing over and toss well together. Serve immediately. Serves 20.

Italian Marsala Cream ••

1½ tablespoons (¾ oz.) gelatine
1 cup cold water
1 cup marsala
6 eggs, separated
¾ cup (6 oz.) sugar

1 scant tablespoon lemon juice
½ pint cream
extra ½ pint cream and hazelnuts for decorating

Soften gelatine in ½ cup cold water for 5 minutes. Stand over boiling water and stir until dissolved. Remove from heat and add remaining water and marsala. Cool. Chill until mixture begins to thicken. Meanwhile beat egg yolks until frothy, gradually add ¼ cup sugar and beat until thick and lemon coloured. Whisk egg whites until foamy. Gradually add ½ cup sugar, beating constantly Add lemon juice and beat until mixture is stiff but not dry. Add slightly thickened marsala and gelatine mixture to egg yolks and combine well. Whip cream and fold in. Gently, but thoroughly, fold in egg whites. Pour into one large or two small glass bowls. Chill until firm, overnight if possible. Serve decorated with additional whipped cream and hazelnuts or if liked, chocolate curls. Serves 10-12. Make two separate quantities for 20.

Wine and Pâté Party

One of the many pleasant things about pâtés and terrines is that they go so well with wine. As a quick lunch, a bite to eat with friends before the theatre, something to take to a picnic, a starter course for a dinner party or even a barbecue, this formidable twosome is hard to beat. A wine and pâté party seems one of the most logical kinds of parties. Ideal for a Sunday luncheon or a buffet party or if you want to show off a new cellar or just have a few friends in for a casual buffet meal.

Pâtés and terrines improve by being made a few days in advance. They will mature in the refrigerator, but they should be covered. Serve an interesting assortment of breads and crisp-breads and an assortment of salads. Butter can be unsalted or salted, and there should be plenty of it. Provide a pile of plates, plenty of knives, napkins, glasses for wine and bowls of fresh fruit which perform the dual roles of decoration and dessert.

Wines: The choice of wines to serve is as wide as the variety of pâtés you prepare. Milder pâtés call for a crisp full bodied wine or a fruity and fragrant traminer. Many people will prefer red wine. If it is a very informal party flagon wines are ideal, although better wines will still be shown to advantage with these pâtés and terrines.

Pork and Veal Terrine*
Veal Saumone*

or

Crusted Veal Pie*
Country-Style Pâté
Vegetable Platter
Hot French Bread
Assortment of Crispbreads
Fresh Fruit

*Consult index for recipe.

Country-style Pâté ••

1 lamb's fry
3 eggs
1 lb. minced pork and
　veal
4 shallots, chopped
4 oz. streaky bacon,
　chopped
6 slices white bread

½ cup brandy or port wine
½ teaspoon ground allspice
2 teaspoons salt
1 teaspoon dried
　marjoram
extra 6-8 rashers bacon,
　rind removed

Roughly chop lamb's fry and put into blender container with beaten eggs. Mix minced meat with chopped shallots and bacon. Add to blender. Remove crusts from bread, cut into cubes and sprinkle with brandy. Allow to soak for 10 minutes. Add to blender with seasonings. Blend at high speed until all ingredients are thoroughly combined. (It may be necessary to blend ingredients in two or three lots, depending on the size of your blender container). Spoon mixture into a 9 x 5 x 2½-inch loaf tin lined with extra bacon rashers. Smooth over the top, cover with aluminium foil or a double sheet of greaseproof paper.

Bake in a moderate oven (350°F.) for 1¼-1½ hours. The pâté is cooked when firm to the touch. Leave pâté in the tin and press down with a light weight. Cool and then chill in the refrigerator. Before serving, turn out and cut into slices.

Note: Pig's liver may be used instead of lamb's fry. Ingredients may be minced finely together twice if no blender is available.

Vegetable Platter ••

1 small cauliflower
1 lb. carrots
1 lb. green beans
1 lb. button mushrooms
2 lb. tomatoes, peeled

1 bunch radishes
watercress and parsley
1 cup French dressing
　(see page 16)

Cut cauliflower into small sprigs. Wash and scrape carrots, cut diagonally into ¼-inch slices. String beans. Cook each of these vegetables separately in boiling salted water until barely tender. Drain and marinate in separate bowls in French dressing.

Carefully clean mushrooms and cut into slices and marinate in a little French dressing. Prepare radish roses, wash and crisp watercress and parsley.

Arrange vegetables on one large or two small platters

or place in separate bowls on a platter. Garnish with watercress or parsley. Serves 10-12.

Hot French Bread •

Cut one French loaf in two. Slash bread almost through to bottom at 1-inch intervals. Brush with a little softened butter, wrap in aluminium foil. Heat in moderately hot oven (375°F.) for 15-20 minutes. Open foil for last 5 minutes to crisp the bread.

(a) For Italian Marsala Cream the stiffly beaten egg whites are piled on top of mixture and folded in gently but thoroughly.

(b) Pour into a serving bowl and chill. Serve topped with whipped cream and decorate with chopped hazelnuts and chocolate curls.

(a) When preparing Cauliflower Salad, separate the cauliflower into sprigs, par-boil, drain thoroughly and sprinkle with French dressing.

(b) After the cauliflower has marinated in the dressing, it is turned into a serving bowl and topped with anchovy dressing. Serve the salad garnished with a sprinkling of paprika.

Beer and Sausage Party

for ten or twenty people

No one knows for sure how, when, where and why the first meat was chopped, seasoned or smoked. It is certain, however, that medieval European towns produced their own specialities, bologna, frankfurts, hamburgers, berliners. Now sausages are international and have travelled wherever people have roamed.

For an evening of nostalgia a Beer and Sausage Party is just the thing. Some like it hot! In Germany, Holland, Italy and even England (Toad-in-the-hole), there are wonderful ways of serving sausages hot. There is no reason in the world why many of the great national dishes should not find their way to the party table. When you shop for sausages, a good Continental delicatessen man should be able to advise you on how to use any that may take your fancy. For the party photograph I used sauerkraut as a base for one sausage and creamy mashed potato for the other.

Some like it cold! Arrange sausages and salami that don't need further cooking on a large board with crusty bread and sharp knives and allow guests to cut themselves a slice or chunk of sausage and bread and eat heartily to their hearts content. Serve salad greens or make a large salad, and have plenty of well chilled beer. If you can find some German beer hall gramophone records, the party will be made.

Wines: No wines, but serve plenty of ice cold beer.

*Nuts and Bolts**

Salted Pretzels

Olives

Knackwurst with Sauerkraut

Polish Sausage in Red Wine

*Creamy Mashed Potatoes**

or

*Buttered New Potatoes**

Crusty Bread

*Green Salad**

*Picnic Apple Pie**

*Consult index for receipe.

Knackwurst with Sauerkraut •

2 x 16 oz. cans sauerkraut
2 onions, finely chopped
1 oz. butter
1 tablespoon oil
2 cooking apples
1 tablespoon brown sugar

1 teaspoon dry mustard
½ cup dry white wine
salt and pepper
2 x 8 oz. knackwurst
  sausage or Polish
  colbassy

Toss sauerkraut with a fork to separate. If packed in brine, wash and drain thoroughly. Sauté onion gently in hot butter and oil until transparent. Mix in the sauerkraut, then add peeled and sliced apples, brown sugar, mustard and wine. Season to taste with salt and pepper. Place into one or two greased shallow ovenproof dishes.

Put knackwurst into a large pan of cold water. Bring to the boil and drain. Cut knackwurst into thick diagonal slices and place on sauerkraut. Cover with aluminium foil and bake in a moderate oven (350°F.) for 20-30 minutes until thoroughly heated. Serve accompanied by German mustard and dill pickles. Serves 6-10 when accompanied by another sausage dish.

For 20 people double the recipe.

Polish Sausage in Red Wine •

1 cup finely chopped
  shallots
3½ cups red wine

2½ lb. smoked colbassy
  or kransky sausage

Combine shallots with red wine in a heavy frying pan or electric frypan. Place sausage in the wine and bring to the boil. Lower heat and simmer, turning several times, for 20-25 minutes or until sausages are glazed with the wine. Slice and serve on a bed of creamy mashed potatoes. Serves 6-10 when accompanied by another sausage dish.

For 20 people use 2 cups chopped shallots, 5 cups red wine and 5 lb. sausages.

Parties for the Very Young

Two simple rules for successful children's parties are keep them amused and feed them well. Games and amusements vary with age groups but have everything very simple for the young ones.

Food should be plentiful but very simple. Young children dislike anything rich or highly seasoned. Serve food that has novel touches to attract them but is basically good wholesome food.

There are lots of ways to take the headache out of playing hostess to a houseful of children, and one is to save breakages by using only paper plates and cups. No broken crockery to worry about and no washing up. Anyway, paper items come in matching sets—invitations, table decoration, napkins and plates, and they look so gay that their convenience becomes almost incidental.

Parties for the 3-5 age group

These parties should be held quite early in the afternoon —say 2.30 p.m. or 3 o'clock—and should not go on for longer than three hours, as young children tire from all the excitement. The food should be simple and easy to eat. Plain iced sponges, sandwiches, fairy bread, biscuits —the kind of food they know and like.

Games should be simple and not too rough. Musical games such as 'Here We Go Round the Mulberry Bush' or 'Farmer in the Dell' are a good choice. Other suitable indoor games are musical chairs or musical cushions, pinning the tail on the donkey, and ring o'roses. Outdoor games can include lemon-and-spoon race or a simple treasure hunt.

See that every child gets a prize, even if it is only a few sweets. An idea that proves very popular (and not only among this age group) is a lucky dip. A clothes basket or wastepaper tidy covered with coloured crepe paper will do. In it place little toys. Those suitable for boys wrap in blue paper and those for girls in pink. Let each child pick out a parcel.

Parties for the 5-9 age group

The young members of this group will like musical games such as 'Oranges and Lemons' and 'Nuts in May'. The latter can end up in a tug of war, two teams standing in line behind their leaders, facing each other. Between the leaders place a broom or other stick on the ground. The team that succeeds in pulling the opposing side over the stick is the winner.

'Hunt the Thimble' or a scavenger hunt are also popular, but *do* define the boundaries of the hunt. For the scavenger hunt, give each player or team of players a list and place the objects they are required to find in a certain room or in the garden. A potato race is fun and a good way of working off excess energy. A lemon and spoon race is still a good idea, but make it more difficult by requiring the spoon to be held in the mouth, instead of in the hand as with the younger children. If there are many children it can be played as a relay race (in this case the spoon would be held in the hand).

Children of this age are very fond of savoury food so concentrate on such items as cocktail frankfurts, savoury dips, cheese biscuits, sausage rolls. Ice cream, of course, is always popular. Use cones to save breakages and washing up and dip each filled cone into crushed peanut brittle, chopped nuts or grated chocolate.

Parties for the 9-12 age group

You will probably find that where previously your children have invited friends of both sexes, they are now having all girl or all boy parties. Tastes in food are also becoming more sophisticated, which gives you more freedom with the menu. A popular idea is to let the meal take the form of a barbecue. Hamburger parties or pizza parties are good for this age group. For dessert, long-handled forks enable the children to toast their own marshmallows at barbecues. An adult should preside as

To make Traffic Light Sandwiches cut 6 circles from half the bread slices and place on remaining buttered bread slices which have been buttered and topped with tomato, cheese (in centre) and lettuce. Cut into halves so each sandwich has a green, an orange and a red light.

The baked pastry cases for Mushroom Tarts are filled with raspberry jam and butter cream. The top is marked with a fork and dusted with drinking chocolate to resemble mushrooms. Stalks add the finishing touch.

chief cook and keeper of the peace.

Games they like are treasure hunts, blind man's bluff, twos and threes. Indoor games can include pencil/paper games such as Truth or Consequences, Crazy Animals, or memory games such as trying to memorise about 15 items displayed on a tray. The tray is shown to them for a minute or two, then removed and each player writes down all the items he or she can remember. The one with the most correct items is the winner. Word games are also popular.

Party food

Here is a suggested party menu with young children in mind. You can add other favourites such as Fairy Bread (thin slices of buttered white bread thickly sprinkled with hundreds and thousands) and Jelly Oranges (orange half-shells with the flesh scooped out and filled with chopped orange jelly). On the following pages are recipes for these party treats as well as others that have proved popular for a long time.

Sausage Rolls
Traffic Light Sandwiches
Cocktail Frankfurts
*Coffee Meringue Kisses**
Chocolate Butterflies
Ice Cream Cones
*50/50 Punch**
The Birthday Cake

* * *

Other Favourites
Fairy Cakes
Mushroom Tarts
Toffee Cups
Ice Cream Sodas

*Consult index for recipe.

Sausage Rolls •

| 8 oz. puff pastry | 1 small egg, |
| 8 oz. sausage meat | beaten |

Cut pastry into two pieces and roll each into a strip 4-inches wide and 12-inches long. Divide sausage meat into two and form each portion into a neat roll 12-inches long. Place a roll of sausage meat in the centre of each strip of pastry, dampen edges with beaten egg, fold pastry over the sausage meat and seal. Mark pastry with the back of a knife and cut each roll into 1½-inch lengths (8 pieces).

Rinse a large baking tray with cold water and place the sausage rolls on it. Brush pastry with beaten egg. Bake in a very hot oven (450°F.) for 10 minutes, reduce heat to moderate (350°F.) and bake a further 10 minutes until golden brown. Cool on a wire cooling rack. Keep airtight and heat rolls in a moderate oven (350°F.) for 5-8 minutes before serving. Makes 16.

Traffic Light Sandwiches •

Add a novel touch to the party table with these gaily coloured 'traffic light' sandwiches.

24 slices brown bread	4 small tomatoes
butter	6 lettuce leaves
½ packet processed cheese slices	salt and pepper

Spread slices lightly with butter. Trim crusts from bread. Using a round ¾-inch biscuit cutter, press 6 holes into each of 12 of the bread slices.

Cut each slice of processed cheese evenly into 3. Slice tomatoes thinly and finely shred lettuce. On 12 plain slices of bread arrange alternately the tomato, cheese (in centre) and lettuce. Season with salt and pepper. Top with cut-out slices of bread and cut each sandwich in half. Cover with clear plastic food wrap and chill until ready to serve. Makes 2 dozen.

Cocktail Frankfurts •

Separate each frankfurt and place in a large saucepan of cold water. Bring slowly to the boil. When water rises in pan, cover and allow to stand off the heat for 2-3 minutes. Drain and serve piping hot with a bowl of tomato sauce and toothpicks.

Chocolate Butterflies • •

1¾ cups (7 oz.) self-raising flour	¾ cup (6 oz.) castor sugar
¼ cup cocoa	1 teaspoon vanilla essence
½ teaspoon baking powder	2 eggs, beaten
pinch salt	¾ cup milk
4 oz. butter or margarine	raspberry jam
	whipped cream

Place paper cases in patty tins. Set oven temperature at hot (400°F.).

Sift flour, cocoa, baking powder and salt together. Beat butter until light and creamy. Add sugar and vanilla. Continue beating until mixture is light and fluffy. Gradually add eggs, beating until blended. Fold in sifted dry ingredients alternately with milk. Using two teaspoons drop enough mixture into patty cases to two-thirds fill.

Bake in a hot oven (400°F.) for 10-15 minutes until well risen and cooked. Cool on a wire cooling rack. Using a sharp knife, cut circular slice off top of each cooled cake. Cut slice in half to form 'wings'. Spread a little raspberry jam on top of each cake, top with whipped cream. Place halves of cake slice butterfly-wing fashion on top.

The Birthday Cake • •

Keep the birthday cake simple, as young children like light cakes such as sponges and light butter cakes. Slightly richer cakes like rainbow and marble cakes are enjoyed by older children. To decorate choose a pale coloured Warm Icing, arrange birthday candles on top and cover sides with ribbons or cake papers.

To make Silhouette Pattern: Trace shape (animal, flower or any simple shape) on heavy paper or thin cardboard. Cut out shape with razor blade to make the pattern. Sift icing sugar over top of the cake and place paper pattern on this. Sift cocoa through a fine sieve over the pattern. Carefully lift paper off cake. Place cake paper around sides and candles on top.

Fairy Cakes • •

2 cups (8 oz.) self-raising flour	1 teaspoon vanilla essence
pinch salt	2 eggs
4 oz. butter	¾ cup milk
¾ cup (6 oz.) castor sugar	Warm Icing
	hundreds and thousands

Place paper cases in patty tins. Set oven temperature at hot (400°F.).

Sift flour and salt together. Beat butter until light and creamy. Add sugar and vanilla. Continue beating until mixture is light and fluffy. Beat in eggs, one at a time, beating until well blended. Fold in sifted flour alternately with the milk. Using two teaspoons, drop enough mixture into patty cases to two-thirds fill. Bake in a hot oven (400°F.) for 10-15 minutes until well risen and golden. Cool on a wire cooling rack. When cold, top with Warm Icing and sprinkle with hundreds and thousands.

Warm Icing •

Sift 1 cup (5 oz.) icing sugar and mix in 1 tablespoon water or fruit juice. Warm slightly over low heat until icing will cover back of spoon smoothly. Use immediately.

Mushroom Tarts • •

Pastry:

3 oz. butter or margarine	1 egg
¼ cup (2 oz.) castor sugar	1½ cups (6 oz.) plain flour
	½ teaspoon baking powder

Filling:

4 oz. butter	raspberry jam
½ cup (4 oz.) sugar	drinking chocolate
vanilla essence	

Pastry: Cream butter and sugar until light and fluffy. Beat in egg. Sift flour and baking powder and stir into butter mixture. Knead into a smooth ball, wrap and chill for at least 1 hour. Keep aside a little of the pastry to make stalks. Roll remaining pastry out thinly on a floured board. Cut into rounds to fit greased patty tins with rounded bases. Prick with a fork. Chill while preparing stalks. Roll the reserved pastry between palms of hands to make a long narrow roll. Cut at ¾-inch intervals. Bake, with the shells, in a hot oven (400°F.) for 5-7 minutes. Cool.

For Filling: Cream butter and sugar well. (Use crystal granulated sugar—not castor). Cover with cold water and pour it straight off. Beat mixture again and repeat the process until sugar has dissolved. Flavour with vanilla essence.

Spoon a little raspberry jam into each pastry case. Top with the butter filling and smooth over with a spatula. Mark cream with a fork to resemble mushrooms and dust lightly with drinking chocolate. Place stalks in centre of tarts. Makes about 30.

Ice Cream Cones • •

Half gallon cans of ice cream are easy for children's parties. Scoop into cones just before serving or try one of the following flavour suggestions.

Choose your flavour combination, get the additional ingredients ready, using a large serving spoon remove large scoops of ice cream, return each scoop to container generously coated with selected flavouring and pop back in the freezer quickly. The quantities given are for a ½ gallon can of ice cream.

Coconut Crunch: Toast 8-10 tablespoons desiccated coconut.

Strawberry Swirl: Crush 3 punnets of strawberries with a fork (or purée in electric blender) and sweeten to taste with icing sugar.

Peanut Brittle: Crush 1 lb. peanut brittle with a rolling pin (or use an electric blender).

Coffee Coquette: Chop 2 cups blanched almonds and brown in 4 oz. melted butter. Cool. Dissolve 2 tablespoons instant coffee powder and 2 tablespoons icing sugar in 2 tablespoons water. Dip ice cream scoops into this, return to cans and freeze. Serve sprinkled with the almonds.

Whisky: A treat for the adults. Mix 1 cup finely chopped raisins and 4 tablespoons whisky.

Toffee Cups •

This quantity makes about 3 dozen toffee cups. Before starting place paper patty cups in patty tins (to keep good shape) and have ready the nuts, hundreds and thousands and coconut for decoration. It is a good idea to make the toffee in a saucepan that has a lip for easy pouring.

2 lb. sugar	coconut
3 tablespoons liquid glucose	hundreds and thousands
1½ cups water	paper patty cases
chopped nuts	

Stir sugar, glucose and water in a saucepan over low heat until sugar dissolves. Brush sides of pan with hot water to wash off sugar grains. Increase heat and boil quickly until mixture cracks when a little is dropped into cold water, or to 310°F. Allow bubbles to settle, pour into patty cases. Sprinkle with nuts, coconut or hundreds thousands.

Note: Toffee cups need only to be half filled. A deep toffee is difficult to eat.

Ice Cream Sodas •

For each person, place a scoop of vanilla or other flavoured ice cream in a tall glass. Fill glasses with chilled soft drinks. Serve with long straws.

Popular party fare for the very young includes cocktail frankfurts, sausage rolls, Meringue Kisses, Chocolate Butterflies, Fairy Bread and of course the birthday cake.

Sausage Rolls are easy to prepare using bought puff pastry and sausage mince. Roll pastry into 4-inch wide strips, place a roll of sausage meat down centre and fold edges over. Cut into 1 and a half inch lengths and bake.

Sausage Rolls, Traffic Light Sandwiches and Mushroom Tarts.

Festive Parties and Dinners

Christmas Dinner
for eight to twelve people

Christmas Dinner is one of the big family meals of the year, intimately connected with the ceremony of breaking bread together, feasting and rejoicing. A Christmas Dinner can be an overwhelming job, especially if you are having all the trimmings. Thanks to the general feeling of goodwill, it is a time when the family is eager to join in and help with the preparations. They have stirred the pudding and on the great day will string the beans, baste the noble bird and set the festive table with dazzling household treasures.

This Christmas menu, although up-dated, is still rich in the flavours that for centuries have filled many a house with steaming spicy fragrances, stimulating the appetite for that biggest, most joyous meal of the year.
Wines: Prepare a bowl of punch and let everyone help themselves as the final preparations are made. Champagne may be served throughout the meal, a full flavoured white burgundy could be served with the turkey.

Florida Cocktail
or
Jellied Wine Consommé
Roast Turkey
Orange Rice
Lingonberry Sauce
Giblet Gravy
Vegetables
Christmas Pudding
or
Eggnog Fruit Cream

Choosing your turkey

It is advisable to order your turkey at least two weeks before Christmas to get the size of bird you want. These suggestions for the size of bird to choose will allow enough meat to be served hot then cold and there should be a little left over for a third meal:

Roast Turkey with its garland of chipolata sausages, Orange Rice served in the orange shells and Lingonberry Sauce

For two people:	4-5 lb. dressed turkey
For four people:	6-7 lb. dressed turkey
For eight people:	10-12 lb. dressed turkey
For twelve people:	14-16 lb. dressed turkey

When catering for twelve people, check that the size of the bird is not going to be too big for the oven. If the oven is too small, wings and legs may burn before the rest of the bird is completely cooked.

Christmas eve preparations

Preparing turkey for the oven is quite an undertaking, not difficult but time consuming. If the turkey has been frozen, allow ample time for complete thawing. At average room temperature, a bird weighing up to 10 lb. takes about 24-36 hours to thaw, up to 16 lb. takes at least 36 hours. Remove the bag of giblets from inside and pat the bird dry.

Make the stuffing and have the turkey ready for the oven, even to the wrapping of brown paper or aluminium foil. Refrigerate until it is time to cook it.

Vegetables may also be prepared on Christmas Eve. Modern plastic airtight containers will keep them fresh overnight.

You will, of course, have made the pudding weeks ago. Cover it with a freshly scalded and floured pudding cloth or greased aluminium foil, tied with sturdy string.

If serving Florida Cocktail, chill fruit, or prepare Jellied Wine Consommé and chill. Cover each with aluminium foil or plastic wrap.

You may be tired after doing all this. If you don't get around to it all, at least have the turkey ready for the oven, the family will pull their weight on Christmas Day!

Jellied Wine Consommé •

1 tablespoon gelatine
3 cups chicken stock,
  skimmed of fat

1 cup dry white wine
sliced lemon and
  watercress to garnish

Sprinkle gelatine over ½ cup cold chicken stock, then dissolve over hot water. Add to remaining stock and stir in wine. Chill in refrigerator until firm. Spoon into soup cups, breaking up jelly with a fork before serving. Garnish with lemon slices and sprigs of watercress. Serves 6. Add 1 extra cup chicken stock and 1 extra teaspoon gelatine to serve 8. Double recipe to serve 12.
Note: Canned consommé may be used in this recipe, dilute if using concentrated consommé.

Florida Cocktail •

2½ x 20 oz. cans
  grapefruit segments
2 x 11 oz. cans mandarin
  segments
1 x 7 oz. jar maraschino
  cherries in syrup

½ teaspoon angostura
  bitters
mint sprigs

Empty all fruit with syrup into a large bowl or jar, add bitters. Mix gently. Chill thoroughly. Prepare mint sprigs and keep in a plastic bowl with lid or covered jar in refrigerator. To serve, spoon fruit cocktail into small glass coupes just before required. This dish should be well chilled for best flavour. Decorate with mint sprigs. Serves 8-12.

Roast Turkey • • •

A favourite trick for turkey is to use two kinds of stuffing—a meat stuffing for the breast which gives delicious flavour and keeps the flesh moist and a bread stuffing for the cavity. Walnuts added to the bread

stuffing give good texture contrast but do make sure you use fresh walnuts otherwise they can be rancid and bitter. Alternatively, the Orange Rice may be doubled and used instead of the bread stuffing. You will not require as many oranges, just enough to give 2 cups juice.

1 x 10-12 lb. turkey
1 quantity Pork and Veal
  Stuffing or Chestnut
  and Sausage Stuffing

1 quantity Bread Stuffing
6-8 oz. butter, melted
2 lb. chipolata sausages

Remove giblets from turkey and keep for gravy. Wash turkey inside and out and dry well. Spoon pork and veal stuffing into neck cavity, bring skin of neck over back and secure with a skewer. Spoon bread stuffing into body.

Secure wings close to body with small skewers. With string, lace cavity closed, and tie legs together. Brush turkey with plenty of melted butter. Wrap in three thicknesses of well-buttered brown paper or heavy aluminium foil. Put turkey in a roasting pan and roast in a moderate oven (350°F.) for approximately 3½ hours. Unwrap, baste with melted butter and pan juices, and cook uncovered for a further 1-1½ hours or until done, basting regularly.

Transfer turkey to heated platter and allow to stand 20 minutes before carving. Keep hot. Garnish with a garland of chipolata sausages.

To Cook Sausages: Buy the bulk chipolatas from your delicatessen, do not separate the links. Put into a pan with enough cold water to cover, bring to the boil, drain immediately and allow to cool. Before serving, grill the sausages until brown and cooked.

Pork and Veal Stuffing • •

1 tablespoon oil
1 small onion, chopped
1 lb. pork and veal mince
4 oz. bacon, chopped
2 sticks celery, chopped
salt and pepper

2 cups (4 oz.) soft white
  breadcrumbs, lightly
  packed
1 egg, beaten
2 teaspoons chopped
  parsley

Heat oil in frying pan and cook onion gently until transparent. Add meat, bacon and celery. Cook, stirring until meat browns. Season with salt and pepper to taste, then transfer to a bowl and allow to cool. Add breadcrumbs, egg and parsley. Mix well and, if necessary, add more salt and pepper to taste. Enough stuffing for the breast of a 10-12 lb. turkey. If using this mixture for cavity and breast of a 10-12 lb. turkey, treble quantities.

Bread Stuffing •

4-6 oz. butter
½ cup finely chopped
  onion or shallots
4 cups (8 oz.) soft white
  breadcrumbs, lightly
  packed
1 teaspoon dried
  tarragon

½ cup finely chopped
  parsley
1 egg
1 teaspoon salt or more
  to taste
1½ teaspoons freshly
  ground black pepper
¾ cup walnut halves

Melt butter, add onion and cook gently until transparent. Combine with breadcrumbs, add remaining ingredients and toss lightly. Add more melted butter if mixture is too dry.

Chestnut and Sausage Stuffing ••

1 lb. chestnuts	2 oz. butter
1 pint chicken stock	8 oz. pork sausage meat
1 stick celery	4 oz. chopped walnuts
salt and pepper	1 cup fresh breadcrumbs
1 large onion	

Remove the shell from the chestnuts with a sharp knife, then blanch and peel off the inner skin. Place the chestnuts in a saucepan, with the stock to cover, the chopped celery, and seasoning. Cook until the chestnuts are quite tender and all the stock has been absorbed, put into a bowl to cool. In the meantime chop the onion finely, cook in the butter until soft and when cool add to the sausage meat. Mix with the chestnuts, walnuts and enough breadcrumbs to bind.

Note: When fresh chestnuts are not available, use 8 oz. dried chestnuts (available at most continental delicatessen shops), soak overnight, then cook in stock until tender as above.

Orange Rice ••

5-6 oranges	2 cups long grain rice
1 onion, chopped	2½ cups water
3 oz. butter	2½ teaspoons salt

Finely grate the rind of 1 orange. Squeeze juice and put into a measuring cup. Halve remaining oranges and gently squeeze enough juice into cup to measure 1 cup. Carefully remove pulp with a teaspoon. Gently cook onion in butter until soft and golden, add washed and drained rice and fry for 3-4 minutes. Add orange juice, grated rind, water and salt. Bring to the boil, cover, then lower heat and cook without stirring for 20-25 minutes until tender. Turn off heat, fluff up with fork. Serve hot in the orange cups.

A less elaborate way to serve the rice is to pile it into a heated serving bowl, the orange cups are more festive for Christmas.

Lingonberry Sauce •

A tart-sweet sauce that goes well with hot or cold turkey, chicken and ham. Preserved lingonberries or cranberries in syrup can be purchased in cans and jars from delicatessens and good supermarkets which specialise in imported foods. Simply empty contents of can or jar into a sauceboat or bowl and serve.

Giblet Gravy •

Use the turkey or chicken giblets to make delicious stock for gravy. Keep the liver refrigerated until needed and put the giblets and neck into a pan with 5 cups water, pinch of herbs, few peppercorns and a bay leaf. Simmer for 1½-2 hours. Add liver and simmer a further 15 minutes.

Remove liver from stock and chop coarsely. Set aside. Strain the stock. Pour off all but 3 tablespoons of drippings from pan in which turkey was cooked. Add 2 tablespoons plain flour and stir over a low heat until flour browns, about 5 minutes. Remove from heat and gradually add 3 cups stock, stirring until smooth. Bring to the boil, stirring continuously. Season with salt and pepper to taste and simmer the gravy until slightly thickened. Add the chopped liver. Serve in a sauceboat.

Note: Prepare stock day before and keep in refrigerator with the chopped liver.

Vegetables

Select three or four vegetables from the following, including at least one green vegetable. You may like to serve a bowl of creamy mashed potatoes as well as crisp roast potatoes, simple yet delicious buttered asparagus, baked tomatoes or whichever of these recipes are your family's favourites.

Other vegetable dishes that can be served are zucchini, honey glazed carrots and green peas bonne femme. Consult the index for these recipes.

Caramelised Butter Onions ••

1½ lb. spring onions	1½ teaspoons sugar
or small white onions	¼ teaspoon salt
2 oz. butter	2 tablespoons water

Peel onions and cut off the roots. Parboil for 2-3 minutes, drain. Melt butter in a frying pan over a low heat, stir in sugar, salt and water. Add onions and shake pan so onions are well coated.

Cover pan and simmer for 10-15 minutes, depending on size of onions, until just cooked and lightly browned. Shake pan constantly to brown onions evenly. Serves 6-8.

Note: Onions may also be cooked in oven. After parboiling, drain and put into a shallow greased ovenproof dish. Dot with butter, then sprinkle with sugar. Add salt to water, pour around onions. Cover with aluminium foil and bake in a moderate oven (350°F.) until tender, about 30 minutes, adding a little more water if necessary. Remove foil for last 10 minutes.

Roast Potatoes •

Choose even sized, small potatoes for an attractive appearance, otherwise halve or quarter large ones.

Peel potatoes and boil for 5 minutes. Drain and mark surface with fork. Put into a roasting pan containing ½-inch hot fat, sprinkle lightly with salt and bake in a moderate oven (350°F.) for 1¼ hours or until golden and crusty, turning and basting occasionally. Drain before serving.

Buttered Asparagus •

Prepare recipe on page 62 using 2 x 16 oz. cans giant asparagus and half quantity of the remaining ingredients Serves 8.

Candied Sweet Potatoes ••

2-3 lb. sweet potatoes
3 oz. butter
½ cup (2½ oz.) brown sugar, lightly packed
½ cup water

Wash potatoes and boil in salted water until tender but still firm. Peel and cut into halves. (If potatoes are large, cut into quarters). Melt butter and sugar in a heavy frying pan, add potatoes and turn until brown on all sides. Add water, cover and reduce heat. Cook until potatoes are tender and delicately brown. Serves 6-8.

Note: Potatoes may also be finished in a baking dish and baked in a moderate oven (350°F.) until tender.

Creamy Mashed Potatoes •

8 medium sized potatoes
salt to taste
½-1 cup milk
2 oz. butter
freshly ground pepper

Peel potatoes (cut into halves if large) and put into saucepan with cold, lightly salted water to cover. Bring to boil, cover and cook gently for 20-30 minutes until potatoes are easily pierced with a fork. Drain thoroughly then shake pan over heat a few minutes until all surplus moisture has evaporated and potatoes are quite dry. Mash with potato masher. Beat potatoes with wooden spoon until very smooth. Heat milk and butter, add to potatoes, beat well until potatoes are light and fluffy. Season to taste. Serves 8-10.

To keep mashed potatoes hot without spoiling: Boil potatoes as described above, then mash and press down well in saucepan with potato masher. Pack tightly, levelling top. Add butter, spoon ½ cup hot milk over, cover with a well fitting lid. Keep warm, beat well before serving, adding more hot milk if needed.

Herbed Baked Tomatoes ••

8-12 small tomatoes
salt and pepper
1 cup (2 oz.) soft white breadcrumbs
½ teaspoon dried rosemary or basil
2 oz. butter, melted

Cut tops off tomatoes, scoop out some of the seeds. Arrange cut sides up in a greased baking dish. Season with salt and pepper. Combine breadcrumbs, rosemary and butter. Season to taste with salt and pepper. Spoon on tops of tomatoes and bake, uncovered, in a moderate oven (350°F.) for about 15 minutes. Serves 8-12.

Note: If tomatoes are large, use 4 or 6 and cut each into halves crosswise.

Traditional Christmas cooking

Christmas Cake and Fruit Mince Tarts are all part of the traditional Christmas season fare. Make the cake and fruit mince well ahead to allow flavours to blend and mellow. The Fruit Mince Pie may be served instead of the pudding in our menu.

Christmas Pudding •••

A plum pudding always improves with keeping. Make it ahead and simply reheat for Christmas dinner.

1⅓ cups (8 oz.) raisins
⅓ cup (2 oz.) mixed peel
1⅓ cups (8 oz.) sultanas
⅔ cup (4 oz.) currants
⅓ cup (2 oz.) glacé apricots or pineapple
3 tablespoons rum
8 oz. butter
1⅓ cups (8 oz.) firmly packed brown sugar
1 orange
4 eggs, beaten
⅓ cup (2 oz.) almonds
1 cup (4 oz.) plain flour
1 teaspoon mixed spice
½ teaspoon ground ginger
½ teaspoon cinnamon
¾ cup (2 oz.) grated carrot
2 cups (4 oz.) soft white breadcrumbs

Chop raisins and mixed peel. Put into a large bowl, add sultanas, currants and roughly chopped glacé apricots. Sprinkle with rum and leave overnight.

Next day, cream butter and brown sugar with the finely grated rind of the orange. Add eggs gradually, beating well between additions. Fold in fruit alternately with blanched chopped almonds, sifted flour and spices, carrot and breadcrumbs. Put in a large well greased pudding basin lined with a circle of greased greaseproof paper cut to fit base. Top with a circle of greased grease-proof paper cut to fit over top of pudding basin. Cover pudding with a cloth which has been scalded, wrung out and floured. Or use a double thickness of greased aluminium foil. Tie firmly with string.

Steam in a large saucepan of boiling water, covered, for 6 hours. Water should not come more than half way up side of basin. Add more boiling water as necessary. When cooked, remove cloth and allow pudding to cool. Cover with fresh greaseproof paper or aluminium foil and store in a cool place or in the refrigerator. Before reheating cover pudding with cloth prepared as before or greased aluminium foil. Boil for a further 2½ hours, turn out and decorate with glacé fruits. Serve with Hard Sauce or Custard and ice cream or pouring cream. Serve hot. Serves 8.

If you wish to flame the pudding, turn the hot pudding out carefully on to a serving plate, and surround pudding with the glacé fruits. Heat about ¼ cup brandy in a small saucepan, ignite and pour over the pudding at the table.

Custard •

3 egg yolks
pinch salt
½ cup (4 oz.) sugar
½ pint milk, scalded
¼ pint cream
1-inch vanilla bean or 1 teaspoon vanilla essence

Combine beaten egg yolks, salt and sugar. Gradually stir in scalded milk and cream. Add vanilla bean if used. Cook in top part of double boiler or in a bowl over hot water until mixture coats spoon, stirring constantly. Remove from heat, cool. Take out vanilla bean.

Hard Sauce •

3 oz. butter
1 cup (5 oz.) icing sugar
2 teaspoons rum or more to taste

Cream butter until soft. Sift icing sugar, add to butter

Ice Cream Cones, Strawberry Swirl, Coffee Coquette and Coconut Crunch

and beat until white and light. Work rum into mixture and chill.

Note: If liked, use ¾ cup icing sugar and ¼ cup ground almonds instead of 1 cup icing sugar. This will give a less sweet result, with a slightly grainy texture.

Fruit Mince •

2 cups (12 oz.) seedless raisins	2 cups (12 oz.) firmly packed brown sugar
1⅓ cups (8 oz.) mixed peel	1 lemon
1⅓ cups (8 oz.) sultanas	1 small orange
8 oz. apples	2 teaspoons mixed spice
⅓ cup (2 oz.) glacé cherries	½ teaspoon grated nutmeg
⅔ cup (4 oz.) blanched almonds	4-6 oz. butter, melted
1⅓ cups (8 oz.) currants	½ cup brandy or rum
1 cup canned crushed pineapple, drained	3 bananas

Finely chop raisins, mixed peel, half the sultanas, apples, cherries and almonds (or put through a mincer). Add remaining sultanas, the currants and crushed pineapple. Stir in brown sugar, grated lemon and orange rind and lemon juice, spices, melted butter and brandy. Mix well and put into jars. Cover and chill, stirring every day for a week. Fruit mince can be kept for a few weeks in refrigerator. Add peeled and finely diced bananas 1-2 days before using.

Eggnog Fruit Cream ••

3 eggs, separated	½ pint cream, whipped
⅓ cup (2½ oz.) sugar	2 tablespoons rum
1 tablespoon (½ oz.) gelatine	½ cup Fruit Mince (see above)
¼ cup cold water	extra whipped cream to decorate
1 cup hot milk	

Beat egg yolks and sugar in a bowl or the top part of a double boiler until the mixture is thick and pale in colour. Stir in gelatine which has been softened in the water, and add milk. Cook over boiling water, stirring constantly, until mixture thinly coats the back of a silver spoon. Chill until just beginning to set. Fold in the whipped cream, stiffly beaten egg whites, rum and fruit mince. Turn into a glass serving bowl. Chill until set, decorate with whipped cream. Serves 8.

Lattice Fruit Mince Pie ••

1¼ cups (5 oz.) plain flour	½ cup (4 oz.) castor sugar
scant ½ cup (2 oz.) cornflour	1 egg yolk
½ teaspoon baking powder	about 1 tablespoon iced water
¼ teaspoon salt	Fruit Mince (see above)
5 oz. butter	

Sift flour, cornflour, baking powder and salt into a bowl. Rub in butter until mixture resembles coarse crumbs. Blend in sugar. Make a well in the centre and add egg yolk beaten with water, stirring with a knife to form a

dough. Knead lightly. Divide into two portions, one slightly larger than the other and chill for 1 hour.

Roll out the larger portion of pastry on a lightly floured board to fit a greased 9-inch pie plate. Chill. Spoon in enough Fruit Mince to almost fill. Roll out remaining pastry to ¼-inch thickness, cut into ½-inch strips and arrange in lattice pattern on top of pie. Trim and flute edge. Brush pastry with egg glaze and bake in a moderate oven (350°F.) for 30-35 minutes until pastry is golden. Serve warm with cream or ice cream. Serves 10-12.

Little Mince Pies ••

Make pastry as for Lattice Fruit Mince Pie. Chill. Roll out thinly on lightly floured board or sheet of plastic. Cut into rounds and fit into small greased tartlet tins. Cut small rounds for tops. Put 2 heaped teaspoons Fruit Mince into each tart. Place smaller rounds on top and press around edges with a fork to seal. Cut small slit in top of each to allow steam to escape. Brush with egg glaze and bake in a moderate oven (350°F.) for 20-25 minutes. Remove from tins while hot. Makes about 16 pies.

Christmas Cake •••

2 cups (12 oz.) each raisins and sultanas	3 tablespoons golden syrup
	5 eggs
1⅓ cups (8 oz.) currants	2½ cups (10 oz.) plain flour
⅔ cup 4 oz. each mixed peel and glacé cherries	1 teaspoon garam masala or mixed spice
⅓ cup (2 oz.) each glacé apricots and glacé pineapple	½ teaspoon each cinnamon and nutmeg
3 tablespoons each brandy and rum	½ teaspoon salt
8 oz. butter	⅔ cup (4 oz.) blanched almonds
1⅓ cups (8 oz.) firmly packed brown sugar	about 1 tablespoon extra brandy
finely grated rind of 1 lemon and 1 orange	extra blanched almonds to decorate

Wash raisins, sultanas and currants, dry thoroughly. Chop raisins and finely chop the peel. Put into a bowl, add sultanas, currants and the coarsely chopped glacé fruits. Sprinkle with brandy and rum and leave overnight.

Next day grease a deep 8-inch cake tin and line with two thicknesses of brown and two thicknesses of greased greaseproof paper. Set oven temperature at slow (300°F.).

Cream butter and brown sugar with lemon and orange rind. Add golden syrup and beat well. Add eggs one at a time, beating well after each. If mixture shows signs of curdling beat in 1 tablespoon of the measured flour with the next egg. Sift flour, spices and salt. Stir into creamed mixture alternately with fruit which has been dusted with a little of the sifted flour and chopped almonds. Spoon mixture into prepared tin, arrange extra blanched almonds in a pattern on top. Bake in a slow oven (300°F.) for 4-4½ hours. When cooked remove from oven, quickly turn cake upside down on to a clean tea towel, lift tin, peel away paper and sprinkle with rum and brandy. Replace paper, place tin on cake and gently ease over cake. Turn over, wrap in a cloth and cool.

If cake is not to be cut for several weeks, peel away paper, wrap cake in aluminium foil, then a cloth and store in an airtight container.

Note: If you prefer to ice your Christmas cake, omit the almond decoration.

(a) When cake is cooked, after 4-4½ hours, remove from oven. Have rum and brandy ready for sprinkling over cake.

(b) Immediately turn the cake upside-down on to a cloth, lift off the tin, peel away paper and sprinkle base of cake with the brandy and rum. Replace paper and tin, turn cake over and leave wrapped in a cloth until cool.

21st Birthday or Engagement Party

for twenty five people

Naturally, for a party as important as this, you don't just pick at random among your party dishes and allow three or four to share the honours. Let one superb dish star, in this case Chicken Tetrazzini. Chicken Tetrazzini is creamy chicken baked on a bed of buttery noodles. Apart from the good flavour, the added charm of this dish is that it can be made days ahead and stored in the refrigerator until required. If you own a freezer it can be made and frozen weeks in advance. Thaw completely before cooking.

Choose 25 small bread rolls or use 3 long French loaves of bread. If necessary, heat the bread in a moderately hot oven (375°F.) for 3-5 minutes to crisp.

Wines: Iced Tea Punch or Wedding Punch (but this time why not call it Temptation Punch) could see the party through from beginning to end. Champagne for toasts (see the wedding plan for quantities). If you prefer to serve wine with the chicken, select a crisp light riesling type wine, if the weather is hot chilled rosé wine.

Iced Tea Punch*
Sambal Dip*
Celery with Roquefort*
Saffron Rice Salad with
Stuffed Eggs*
Chicken Tetrazzini
Crusty Bread Rolls
Nut Crunch Slaw*
Sherry Soufflé

*Consult index for recipe.

Chicken Tetrazzini ••

This entire dish can be done the day before the party and layered in casseroles with the noodles, then chilled ready to bake.

1 quantity Wedding	salt and pepper
Chicken (see page 62)	1 cup grated parmesan
2 lb. ribbon noodles	cheese
8 oz. butter, melted	little extra butter

Prepare the recipe for Wedding Chicken using the same quantities.

Cook noodles in two separate lots. To a large pan of boiling salted water, add 1 lb. noodles and cook for 10-15 minutes until tender, drain. Melt 4 oz. butter in pan, add noodles and season with salt and pepper. Repeat with remaining noodles. Toss together off the heat.

Place noodles in two large buttered shallow casseroles, place the Wedding Chicken mixture on top, sprinkle with cheese and dot with butter. Cover with aluminium foil or clear plastic food wrap and refrigerate. Remove from refrigerator at least 1 hour before heating. Bake, uncovered, in a moderately hot oven (375°F.) for about 1 hour, until completely heated through. Serve in casseroles. Serves 25.

Crusty Bread Rolls •

Crusty bread rolls and coleslaw, highly seasoned, crisp and colourful, offset the main dish to perfection. The dessert, Sherry Soufflé, is elegant and needs no last minute preparation.

Nut Crunch Slaw •

½ medium size cabbage	1 cup French dressing
8 shallots	(see page 16)
1 red and 1 green	salt and pepper to taste
pepper	dash hot pepper sauce
2 stalks celery	4 oz. walnuts or toasted
3 cups grated carrot	almonds, chopped

Wash cabbage, dry and chill. Shred finely with a sharp knife. Chop shallots, peppers and celery. Place cabbage into one large or two smaller bowls, add shallots, peppers, celery and carrot. Cover and chill. Before serving, beat French dressing, salt, pepper, hot pepper sauce together and pour over salad. Toss to coat and add walnuts. Serves 6-8.

For a larger party double quantities.

Sherry Soufflé

Sherry Soufflé •••

**1 tablespoon (½ oz.)
  gelatine
½ cup cold water
1½ cups sweet sherry
6 eggs, separated
¾ cup (6 oz.) castor
  sugar**

**1 scant tablespoon
  lemon juice
½ pint cream
savoy fingers
extra sweet sherry
extra cream for
  decorating**

Cut a strip of aluminium foil or greaseproof paper 6-inches wide and long enough to fit around a 1 pint soufflé dish. Fold to make a double strip 3-inches wide. Tie strip around dish, so that it stands like a collar above the edge.

Sprinkle gelatine on water and allow to soften for 5 minutes. Stand over boiling water until dissolved. Remove from heat and add sherry. Chill for 30 minutes or until mixture begins to thicken. Meanwhile beat egg yolks until frothy, gradually add ¼ cup sugar, beating until mixture is thick and lemon coloured. Whisk egg whites until foamy and gradually whisk in remaining sugar. Add lemon juice and beat until mixture is stiff, but not dry.

Add slightly thickened sherry mixture to egg yolks and combine well. Whip cream and fold in. Lastly fold in egg whites gently but thoroughly. Pour half mixture into the soufflé dish which has been lined with savoy fingers. Cut 4-6 savoy fingers into halves crosswise to fit across dish, sprinkle with extra sherry and place on top of mixture. Pour remaining mixture on top. Chill until firm, overnight if possible. Before serving, remove paper collar from dish and spoon extra whipped cream on top.
Serves 10-12.
Note: Make two separate quantities of this recipe for a large party.

Chilled cabbage is shredded finely with a sharp knife for making Nut Crunch Slaw.

Wedding Reception

for twenty five guests

Nothing is more heart warming or adds more to the charm of that very special day in a girl's life than a wedding reception held at home. However, the mother of the bride should not have to worry about food on the day of the wedding, so it needs careful organising and planning.

The menu has been chosen so that everything may be prepared days before, leaving the principal members of the wedding free of this responsibility. There is usually someone in the locality whose help can be enlisted for serving the food, and she should be made familiar with the arrangements well in advance of the day so that there is no need even for last minute instructions to be given. There will be excitement enough without that!

Buffet service is best when space is limited and this allows for friendly mixing of the guests, but do allow for adequate seating. Trestle tables, chairs and large tablecloths can usually be hired from a catering firm together with crockery, cutlery and glassware. It is a good idea to plan seating well ahead, so place cards are in order. Informality is the keynote, but it must be accomplished without confusion. Arrange the food on sideboards or a large table as attractively as possible. Floral arrangements, the wedding cake and tempting food all contribute to atmosphere.

The first course and dessert may be prepared well ahead of the day. The hot dish may be made a day or two beforehand, refrigerated, then reheated on the day of the wedding. For fifty guests it is better to make each recipe twice. Doubling the quantity of ingredients is not recommended.

Wedding Punch*
Florida Cocktail*
or
Florida Cocktail Sorbet
Wedding Chicken
Fluffy White Rice
Buttered Asparagus
Minted Green Peas
Wedding Trifle
Wedding Cake
Champagne
Coffee

*Consult index for recipe.

Florida Cocktail •

Follow recipe on page 52 using double quantity given for all ingredients.

Florida Cocktail Sorbet •

Sorbet is most refreshing during the hot summer months.

Double the ingredients given for Florida Cocktail on page 52. Blend grapefruit and mandarins with juice in cans in an electric blender until the fruit is mushy, do not over-blend or fruit will become too liquid. Pour into refrigerator trays and place in freezer. The fruits do not freeze hard and there may be tiny splinters of ice which add to the refreshing qualities of the dish. Add bitters to maraschino cherries. Serve in individual glasses and top each sorbet with a cherry, a little juice and mint sprig. Serves 25.

Fluffy White Rice •

Allow 2 oz. raw rice per person. For 25 guests allow 3 lb.

Cook rice in boiling salted water, allowing 12 cups of

water to each pound of rice. Unless equipped with a very large boiler it is better to cook only 1 lb. rice at a time. Bring water to a rolling boil, add rice gradually so that water continues to boil all the time. Boil rice for 12-15 minutes. Drain in colander, cool and chill.

The rice may be cooked a day before required and stored overnight in the refrigerator. About 1 hour before serving melt 2 oz. butter and pour into a large ovenproof dish or roasting pan. Spread rice in pan. Heat 1 cup milk and 1 oz. butter until almost boiling and pour over rice. Put dots of extra butter on top and cover completely with aluminium foil. Bake in a moderately hot oven (375°F.) until heated through, about 1 hour. Occasionally fluff up with fork. Serve sprinkled with 1 cup finely chopped parsley.

Buttered Asparagus •

7 x 10 oz. cans asparagus tips	8 oz. butter
freshly ground white pepper	1 tablespoon lemon juice

Open asparagus and drain. Lightly butter a large baking dish. Season asparagus with freshly ground pepper. Melt half the butter and drizzle over asparagus. Cover asparagus with plastic wrap or aluminium foil and stand aside or refrigerate if keeping overnight.

To heat, place in moderately hot oven (375°F.) for 45 minutes until heated. Serve on two or three silver entrée dishes.

Melt remaining butter until it froths and turns a pale golden colour. Add lemon juice and pour over asparagus.

Wedding Chicken ••

4 x 5-6 lb. chickens or boiling fowls	4 teaspoons salt
16 cups cold water	2 teaspoons mixed poultry herbs (thyme, sage, rosemary)
4 carrots, scraped and halved	
4 onions, peeled and halved	
Cream Sauce:	
4 oz. butter	pepper
1 cup (4 oz.) plain flour	½ teaspoon grated nutmeg
4 cups chicken stock	
1 tablespoon salt	2 cups cream
Additions to sauce:	
2 lb. button mushrooms	½ cup lemon juice
3 oz. butter	

Put each chicken or boiling fowl into a large saucepan and add 4 cups cold water, 1 carrot, 1 onion, 1 teaspoon salt and ½ teaspoon herbs to each pan. Cover and simmer gently for about 1 hour or until tender. Boiling fowls will take 2-2½ hours and should be completely covered with water. Cool in broth, then lift out and strip meat from bones. Remove skin. Cut meat into bite-sized pieces, about 1½-inches square. Return bones to broth and simmer about 1 hour longer. Strain and chill broth and remove fat from surface.

For Cream Sauce: Melt butter in a saucepan and add

flour. Cook, stirring for a few minutes and add chicken stock. Season with salt, pepper and nutmeg to taste. Cook gently and stir until sauce boils and thickens. Stir in cream and cook a further 5 minutes.

Wipe mushrooms with a damp cloth and slice. Gently sauté mushrooms in butter until lightly cooked. Drain on absorbent paper. Combine chicken and mushrooms with sauce.

Prepare the recipe up to this point the day before the wedding. Store in the refrigerator overnight. Reheat over gently simmering water about 1 hour and just before serving add lemon juice and mix well. Serve with fluffy white rice. Serves 25.

Minted Green Peas •

5 lb. frozen peas	2 tablespoons freshly chopped mint
8 oz. butter	1 tablespoon lemon juice
salt and pepper	

Cook frozen peas as instructed on packages. If cooking has to be done ahead of time, plunge drained cooked peas into iced water. Stand in a minimum of water until required. Melt the butter in a large saucepan, add 2 heaped teaspoons salt and ½ teaspoon pepper, chopped mint and lemon juice. Toss drained cooked peas in hot butter and heat through gently. Serve in heated vegetable dishes.

Rich Wedding Cake •••

5⅓ cups (2 lb.) raisins	4 eggs
2⅔ cups (1 lb.) sultanas	3 cups (12 oz.) plain flour
1⅔ cups (10 oz.) currants	
⅔ cup (4 oz.) mixed peel	1 scant teaspoon baking powder
1 slice glacé pineapple	
2 glacé apricots	1 teaspoon mixed spice
2 tablespoons each brandy and rum	1 teaspoon salt
	⅔ cup (4 oz.) blanched almonds
8 oz. butter	
1⅓ cups (8 oz.) firmly packed brown sugar	extra brandy and rum
finely grated rind of 1 lemon	

Wash raisins, sultanas and currants. Drain and dry thoroughly. Put into a large bowl and add finely chopped peel, chopped pineapple and apricots. Sprinkle with brandy and rum and leave overnight. Line a deep 9-inch cake tin with two thicknesses brown paper and two thicknesses greased greaseproof paper.

Next day, beat butter and sugar to a cream with lemon rind. Beat in each egg separately. If mixture shows signs of curdling, sprinkle in a little of the measured flour before adding next egg. Mix in sifted dry ingredients alternately with chopped almonds and fruit which has been lightly dusted with part of the measured flour.

Chicken in Wine

Put mixture into prepared tin. Level top and bake in a slow oven (300°F.) for about 3½-4 hours until cooked. Remove from oven and immediately sprinkle with extra brandy and rum (about 1 tablespoon each). Wrap in a cloth and leave until cold. Remove from tin, peel away paper and wrap in aluminium foil. Store in an airtight container until ready to ice.

Two-Tiered Wedding Cake •••

Follow recipe for Rich Wedding Cake using the following quantities.

16 cups (6 lb.) raisins	**grated rind of 3 lemons**
8 cups (3 lb.) sultanas	**12 eggs**
5⅓ cups (2 lb.) currants	**9 cups (2¼ lb.) plain flour**
2 cups (12 oz.) mixed peel	**2½ teaspoons baking**
3 slices glacé pineapple	**powder**
6 glacé apricots	**3 teaspoons mixed spice**
6 tablespoons each brandy	**2 teaspoons salt**
and rum	**2 cups (12 oz.) blanched**
1½ lb. butter	**almonds**
4 cups (1½ lb.) firmly	**extra rum and brandy**
packed brown sugar	

Place mixture in deep 11-inch and 6-inch cake tins both lined with two thicknesses of brown and greased grease-proof paper. The 11-inch cake will take about 8 hours to cook, the 6-inch cake about 3½ hours.
Note: The smaller cake can be kept in the refrigerator several hours or overnight while the larger cake bakes.

Most people order the wedding cake from caterers. We have included this recipe for those who prefer to make the cake at home.

Champagne

Wine for toasting the bridal couple: One bottle of champagne or sparkling white wine (26 fl. oz.) serves 6-8 persons. For more than one toast and sufficient for the main course, a modest amount of wine would be 8 bottles (in champagne this would allow approximately 60 glasses to be poured).

One dozen bottles of champagne would yield about 90 glasses. For 25 guests this allows 3½ glasses per person.

If serving champagne for the toasts one or two quantities of punch will be sufficient. If toasts are to be made with the punch allow three quantities of the basic Wedding Punch recipe.

Wedding Trifle •

2 packets port wine jelly	**½ cup slivered toasted**
3 pints custard	**almonds**
3 oblong sponge cakes	**2 x 1 lb. 13 oz. cans**
(11 x 7-inches)	**apricot halves**
1 cup sherry	**½ cup passionfruit pulp**
1 lb. strawberry	**1 pint cream, whipped**
conserve	**2 punnets strawberries**

Make port wine jelly according to instructions on packet. If liked, substitute port wine for half the quantity of water in the jelly. Cool until almost set.

Make 3 pints pouring custard using custard powder and follow instructions on packet, but replace ½ pint of the milk with ½ pint cream for a richer custard. Cut sponge cakes into 2-inch squares.

In two large or four smaller bowls arrange trifle in the following order, making layers of each ingredient: 1 layer sponge cake squares sprinkled with a little sherry, topped with strawberry conserve and toasted almonds, port wine jelly, custard, cake, sherry, almonds, apricot halves, passionfruit pulp, custard. Cover with clear plastic food wrap or aluminium foil.

Just before serving, top with whipped cream and decorate with strawberries which have been carefully washed. If strawberries are very large slice just before serving. Serves 25.

Coffee for 25 •

6 oz. finely ground coffee	**1-1½ lb. coffee crystals**
8 pints water	**1 pint cream**

Prepare urns or large pots by scalding with boiling water, then rinsing out with cold water. Pour in water and bring to boil. Add coffee tied loosely in a fine cheesecloth or muslin bag. Cover and stand for 10 minutes over a very gentle heat, stirring the bag around occasionally. Do not allow to boil. Remove bag of coffee grounds. Transfer coffee to pots. Serve coffee crystals and cream separately.

(a) To prepare radish roses for the antipasto tray, wash radishes well and remove all but the smallest leaf. Besides being decorative it serves acting as a "handle" to pick up the radish. Trim off the root.

(b) Use a small sharp knife and make four cuts from root end towards the leaf. Put into iced water to crisp and allow petals to open.

Chicken and Champagne Wedding Breakfast

for twenty five guests

'Let's have the wedding at home even if it's just sandwiches and champagne. It will mean so much more to everyone and especially to us.' When a bride and her mother agree about this, it is the start of much planning and preparation. The choice of the day, the time of day, the reception, the menu—it is all up to the bride and many of today's brides want to keep it simple but perfect.

A word of warning—simple does not necessarily mean easy. 'Perfect' is the key word which means the sandwiches must be dainty and absolutely fresh with no dry edges, the champagne well chilled, the glasses sparkling, the coffee good and strong and piping hot. Follow instructions for keeping everything in tip-top condition and the wedding will be one to remember with pleasure and pride.

Chicken and Ham Sandwiches

Asparagus Rolls

Almond Crescents

Wedding Cake*

Champagne

Coffee

*Consult index for recipe.

Chicken Sandwiches •

The bread should be sliced very thinly for these dainty sandwiches. Ask your grocer or delicatessen dealer to slice the bread on his machine. This quantity makes 66 small sandwiches, allowing $2\frac{1}{2}$ per guest.

10 lb. chicken breasts	salt and pepper
$1\frac{1}{2}$ x 2 lb. sandwich loaves, thinly sliced	good mayonnaise
12 oz. softened butter, beaten with $\frac{1}{4}$ cup milk	

Simmer chicken breasts in well flavoured poaching liquor (add salt, peppercorns, onion, bay leaf and tarragon to water) over very low heat for 15-20 minutes or until just tender. Allow to cool in the liquid.

Using a 2-inch cutter, cut two rounds of bread from each slice. This will give 132 rounds of bread, making 66 sandwiches.

Remove chicken meat from bone in one piece. Cut into thin slices. Using a 2-inch cutter, cut rounds of chicken from each slice. Remaining chicken meat is used for a chicken and mayonnaise spread for the asparagus rolls or other chicken sandwiches.

Butter bread rounds and assemble sandwiches. Season chicken slices with salt and pepper and spread a little mayonnaise on chicken. Store in covered containers or cover with clear plastic wrap. Keep in the refrigerator.

To serve, arrange sandwiches on plates and garnish with sprigs of watercress or parsley.

Note: Save the stock in which chicken was cooked and use as a base for soups.

Chicken Spread •

There should be approximately $2\frac{1}{2}$ lb. of chicken trimmings after cutting circles for the sandwiches. Chop finely and mix with $1\frac{1}{2}$ cups mayonnaise. Add 4 tablespoons very finely chopped olives and 3 tablespoons finely chopped celery. Season to taste with salt and pepper and add a few drops of hot pepper sauce. Use as a spread for the asparagus rolls or as a filling for extra chicken sandwiches.

Ham Sandwiches •

Makes 66 sandwiches. Bread should be sliced as for chicken sandwiches.

$1\frac{1}{2}$ x 2 lb. sandwich loaves thinly sliced	French mustard
	salt and pepper
4 lb. sliced leg ham	
12 oz. softened butter beaten with $\frac{1}{4}$ cup milk	

With a 2-inch cutter cut two rounds of bread from each slice. Cut ham into circles with 2-inch cutter. Spread bread on one side with softened butter, top with ham, a smear of French mustard, salt and pepper to taste, and top with other round of buttered bread.

These sandwiches, like the chicken sandwiches, may be prepared ahead and stored as for chicken sandwiches in the refrigerator.

Asparagus Rolls ••

1½ x 2 lb. sandwich loaves,
  thinly sliced
12 oz. softened butter,
  beaten with ¼ cup milk

chicken spread
salt and pepper to taste
5 x 10 oz. cans asparagus
  spears, drained

Remove crusts from bread and cut the slices into 3-inch squares. Spread with butter, then top with the chicken spread. Season with salt and pepper and place one asparagus spear on each square. Roll up and secure with a toothpick. Store in covered, shallow containers in refrigerator. Remove from refrigerator 30 minutes before serving.

Note: Bread may be cut into squares the night before and stored in suitable containers. The number of cans of asparagus required may vary according to the size of asparagus spears.

Almond Crescents ••

1½-inches vanilla bean
1 cup (5 oz.) sifted icing
  sugar
2 cups (12 oz.) blanched
  almonds

1 lb. butter
1½ cups (12 oz.) castor
  sugar
5 cups (1¼ lb.) plain
  flour

Chop vanilla bean and pound in a mortar, or mix in an electric blender with 1 tablespoon of the icing sugar. Mix with remaining icing sugar, put into an airtight container and allow to stand overnight.

Grind almonds or chop finely. Beat butter and sugar until light, blend in almonds and sifted flour. Form into a dough and chill at least 1 hour. Shape teaspoonfuls of dough into small crescent shapes about 1½-inches long.

Place on ungreased baking trays and bake in a moderate oven (350°F.) for 15-18 minutes until pale golden brown. Cool 1 minute and while still warm roll in vanilla flavoured icing sugar. Cool completely before storing in airtight containers.

Note: The vanilla flavoured icing sugar gives these biscuits a delicious coating. If you do not have access to a blender or mortar, store a whole vanilla bean, which has been split lengthwise, in the icing sugar for at least two days before using. Failing this, 2 teaspoons vanilla essence may be beaten with the butter and sugar. Roll the cooked biscuits in plain icing sugar.

Champagne •

A 26 fl. oz. bottle of champagne pours 6-8 glasses. On this basis 8-12 bottles of dry champagne will see you through the meal for 25 guests.

8 x 26 fl. oz. bottles of champagne will pour 60 glasses, allowing 2 per person, extra for the bridal table.

1 dozen 26 fl. oz. bottles of champagne will pour 90 glasses, allowing 3½ glasses per person.

If champagne proves too costly, one of the sparkling white wines may be served.

Serve champagne well chilled. Lay flat in refrigerator for 2-3 hours (not overnight) or preferably in tubs of ice for 1 hour.

Coffee

Consult Wedding Reception menu on page 64 for instructions on making coffee.

Christmas Pudding.

Lattice Fruit Mince Pie.

Chicken and Ham Sandwiches, Asparagus Rolls and Almond Crescents—part of the Chicken and Champagne Wedding Breakfast menu.

Picnics, Barbecues and Luaus

The Family Picnic
for eight people

Anywhere you unpack a hamper, be it in the fields, by a stream or just at the side of a road, the change of scene brings back childhood appetites and a feeling of gay abandon. Does a family picnic mean to you, as it does to me, sitting on the grass, or a rug, leisurely eating food that wouldn't seem half as good anywhere else?

Childhood memories have someone slicing home-cooked meat, a terrine or cold pie with a really sharp knife, someone else is arranging a crisp, colourful salad, the crusty French bread is sliced and buttered and someone else is handing around icy cool drinks.

A funny thing, too, most people develop a 'sweet-tooth' on a picnic! Picnic Apple Pie and Sticky Gingerbread, which improves on keeping (about 1 week is ideal) will ensure no one is disappointed.

Wines: A chilled rosé would be ideal. Or, if you have no way of keeping the wine cold, a light red wine. Include a flask of tea or coffee, and fruit juices or bubbly drinks for the children.

Veal Saumone
Picnic Salad
Crusty Bread
Picnic Apple Pie
Cream
Sticky Gingerbread
with Gouda Cheese
Fresh Iced Fruit

Veal Saumone ● ● ●

1 x 5 lb. leg or shoulder of veal	pinch each thyme and tarragon
salt and pepper	2 cups white wine vinegar
4 onions, sliced	5 pints water
$\frac{1}{2}$ lemon, sliced	3 cups dry white wine
8 juniper berries	8 peppercorns
4 sprigs parsley	salt to taste
4 whole cloves	$\frac{3}{4}$ cup chopped chives
2 bay leaves	

Ask your butcher to bone the veal. Season veal, form into a roll and tie with string. Place the sliced onions and lemon in a glass dish. Add juniper berries, parsley, cloves, bay leaves, thyme, tarragon and vinegar. Marinate veal, covered, in the refrigerator for 1-2 days, turning twice each day. Place veal in a large pan, add the marinade, water, wine, peppercorns and salt to taste. Simmer the veal over very low heat for about $2\frac{1}{2}$ hours or until a skewer inserted into the thickest part of the meat comes out easily. Allow the meat to cool in the stock and then chill thoroughly.

Remove string and place the veal in an airtight container. Spread chopped chives over the top of veal. Cover and chill. Serve cold in thin slices with Shallot Mayonnaise. Serves 8-10.

Good food suitable for outdoor eating, packed and presented attractively, contributes in no small measures to successful picnics.

Shallot Mayonnaise •

4 tablespoons soft white breadcrumbs	6-8 shallots, chopped
warm water	¼ teaspoon salt
	1 cup mayonnaise

Soak breadcrumbs in a little warm water. Press them to drain. Put shallots, salt and breadcrumbs into a blender container. Add mayonnaise and blend at high speed for a few seconds until combined, or chop shallots very finely and add to mayonnaise with the breadcrumbs and salt. Carry to picnic site in a covered container.

Picnic Salad •

Wash and trim shallots or spring onions, radishes, celery sticks, small tomatoes, cucumbers and lettuce. Cut cucumber and lettuce into wedges and pack all ingredients in separate containers or polythene bags. Seal, then chill. Carry them all in an insulated container with ice. Take along Shallot Mayonnaise or Horseradish Cream (see page 126) in a separate covered container for dipping. Other ingredients that may be included are wedges of pineapple and watermelon, olives and carrot sticks.

Picnic Apple Pie ••

Canned pie apples may be used instead of fresh for this simple picnic apple pie but remember to sweeten apples with sugar. The pulp of 2 passionfruit stirred into the apples is a delicious variation.

4 oz. butter	1 cup (4 oz.) plain flour
½ cup (4 oz.) castor sugar	pinch salt
1 egg	4 cooking apples
1 cup (4 oz.) self-raising flour	1 teaspoon cinnamon
	1 tablespoon sherry

Cream butter and sugar, beat in egg. Sift flours with salt and stir into mixture, adding a little more flour if required to make a firm dough. Chill for 30 minutes. Roll out two thirds of pastry on a lightly floured surface and line a lightly greased 8-inch pie plate. Chill.

Meanwhile, peel and slice apples. Put into saucepan with cinnamon, sherry and about 1 tablespoon water.

Cook gently until tender. Cool. Pile into pastry case.

Roll out remaining pastry to cover top, crimp edges and bake in a moderately hot oven (375°F.) for about 35 minutes until golden brown. Cool and put into an airtight container. Whip cream, flavour and sweeten to taste, if liked. Chill pie and cream until ready to pack for the picnic. Serves 8.

Sticky Gingerbread ••

Gingerbread and cheese—a wonderful flavour combination and so good for picnics. Make the gingerbread several days, even weeks ahead and store airtight for best flavour.

4 oz. butter	⅔ cup (4 oz.) sultanas
⅔ cup (4 oz.) brown sugar, firmly packed	½ teaspoon bicarbonate of soda
2 eggs	2 tablespoons warm milk
1¼ cups golden syrup	unsalted butter
2 cups (8 oz.) plain flour	gouda cheese
pinch salt	
1 teaspoon ground ginger	

Grease and lightly flour a deep 8-inch square tin. Set oven temperature at moderately slow (325°F.).

Beat butter and sugar until creamy, then add eggs, one at a time. When well beaten add golden syrup. Sift flour, salt and ginger, fold into creamed mixture with sultanas. Dissolve bicarbonate of soda in milk and carefully stir into cake mixture. Put into prepared cake tin and bake in moderately slow oven (325°F.) for 1½-2 hours. After 1 hour reduce temperature to slow (300°F.).

When gingerbread is cold cut into slices and spread each slice with unsalted butter. Put a slice of cheese on each piece, join together again and wrap. If you are uncertain that everyone will enjoy the combination, take gingerbread to picnic unsliced and let people add cheese themselves.

Fresh Iced Fruits •

Before leaving for picnic, pack firm fruits in season (melons, cherries, apples, oranges, etc.) in a large covered container. Cover with ice cubes, then place lid on top.

Crusted Veal Pie.

Cherry Almond Cake.

A Hamper Picnic

for eight people

Getting away from it all can often be no more than driving into the country to some scenic spot, leaving daily routine behind. It is wonderful just to have a change of scene or activity. If the outing is planned around being on the move or watching a favourite sport—cricket, football or racing—the kind of food you take with you is important. Don't make an elaborate meal that needs a lot of setting out.

Scotch Eggs, Hero Rolls and if the occasion is to be even slightly festive, an old fashioned Crusted Veal Pie accompanied by finger salads such as tiny whole tomatoes, crispy celery sticks and crunchy radishes. The Coconut Tart and Cherry Almond Cake may even be left for afternoon tea. It is all special food, but food that can be eaten with the fingers, food that doesn't need knives and forks—just provide plenty of large paper napkins.

Wine: This depends on the event. A claret style wine would be ideal. Of course, there should be a flask of tea or coffee. For children, fruit juice.

Scotch Eggs

or

Hero Rolls

Crusted Veal Pie

Tomatoes

Radishes, Celery Sticks

Coconut Tart

Cherry Almond Cake

Scotch Eggs ••

6 hard-boiled eggs	½ cup (2 oz.) plain
few drops hot pepper	flour
sauce	salt and pepper
few drops Worcestershire	beaten egg
sauce	breadcrumbs
1 lb. sausage mince	oil for deep frying

Shell eggs. Add hot pepper sauce and Worcestershire sauce to sausage mince and mix well. Divide meat mixture into 6 equal portions. Dust eggs lightly with flour mixed with salt and pepper, cover each egg with sausage mince, pressing and moulding on well. Brush with beaten egg and roll in breadcrumbs. Chill for at least 1 hour.

Heat oil for deep frying and cook eggs until golden brown. Remove and drain on absorbent paper. Cool and chill, before packing.

Hero Rolls •

These hearty rolls travel well, tie with string to keep fillings intact. Cut each into three or four pieces to serve.

Cut 3 long rolls of crusty bread in halves. Scoop out some of the bread from bottom half and spread rolls with butter. Fill liberally with slices of ham, cheese, tomato and lettuce leaves. Season well. Replace top and tie both ends and the middle of each roll with string. Wrap in clear plastic food wrap or aluminium foil.

Alternative Fillings: Any of these fillings may be used for the hero rolls or for sandwiches.

Sliced ham and chutney.
Cooked crumbled bacon and dill pickle.
Sliced salami, teawurst or devon.
Cooked sliced chicken and mayonnaise.
Sliced cheese and cheese spreads.
Salmon, tuna, sardines.
Cooked sliced beef and horseradish.

Crusted Veal Pie •••

2 veal knuckles	1 lemon
1 teaspoon salt	3 hard-boiled eggs
1 onion	3 rashers bacon
1 small carrot	beaten egg to glaze
1 bay leaf	
Pastry:	
4 oz. butter	3 oz. boiled, sieved
1½ cups (6 oz.) plain	potatoes
flour	1 tablespoon water

Ask butcher for 'meaty' knuckles and cut each into 3

pieces. Put into a large pan with salt, peeled and halved onion, scraped carrot, bay leaf and add enough cold water to cover. Bring to the boil, lower heat and simmer for 2-3 hours. Strain stock into a basin and to stock add the grated rind of $\frac{1}{2}$ lemon and juice of the whole lemon. Measure stock and, if necessary, simmer gently until there is $2\frac{1}{2}$ cups (1 pint) remaining. Discard vegetables and bay leaf. Remove meat from bones and cut into pieces. Slice eggs. Fry bacon lightly and drain.

Prepare pastry and cut into two pieces, one larger than the other. Line a deep 7-inch round tin or a raised pie mould with the larger piece of pastry, rolled thinly. Fill lined tin with layers of meat, bacon and sliced hard-boiled eggs. Cover with remaining pastry. Make a hole in centre. Glaze with beaten egg. Bake in a hot oven (400°F.) for 10 minutes, reduce to moderate (350°F.) and continue baking a further 30-35 minutes or until cooked. When cold remove pie from tin. Fill pie with stock through centre hole. Allow stock to set. Serve cold. Serves 8-10.
For Pastry: Rub butter into flour. Add sieved potato. Mix to a firm dough with water. Knead until smooth. Chill for 1 hour.

Coconut Tart ••

Pastry:

3 oz. butter	1 egg
$\frac{1}{4}$ cup (2 oz.) castor sugar	$1\frac{1}{2}$ cups (6 oz.) plain flour
1 teaspoon vanilla essence	$\frac{1}{2}$ teaspoon baking powder

Filling:

$\frac{3}{4}$ cup milk	1 cup (8 oz.) sugar
1 teaspoon butter	$1\frac{1}{3}$ cups (4 oz.) desiccated coconut
4 eggs	

Pastry: Cream butter, sugar and vanilla essence. Add egg and beat well. Stir in sifted flour and baking powder. Turn on to a floured board and knead lightly. Chill 1 hour. Roll out on a floured board and line a greased 8 or 9-inch pie plate. Chill while preparing filling.
For Filling: Warm milk, add butter and allow to melt. Beat eggs and sugar until combined, add coconut and milk mixture and mix well together. Pour into pastry shell and bake in a moderate oven (350°F.) for 30 minutes. Reduce heat to moderately slow (325°F.) and bake for a further 40 minutes or until filling is set. Cover pastry edges with aluminium foil if pastry browns too quickly. Cool and chill. Serves 8-10.

Cherry Almond Cake ••

10 oz. butter	3 cups (12 oz.) plain flour
1 cup (8 oz.) castor sugar	1 teaspoon baking powder
$\frac{1}{2}$ teaspoon almond essence	$\frac{3}{4}$ cup milk
5 eggs	extra cherries and
$1\frac{1}{3}$ cups (4 oz.) glacé cherries, chopped	almonds to decorate
$\frac{1}{3}$ cup (2 oz.) blanched almonds, chopped	

Line a deep 8-inch round cake tin with greased grease-proof paper. Set oven temperature at moderate (350°F.).

Cream butter and sugar with almond essence, until light and fluffy. Add eggs one at a time, beating well after each. Dust cherries and almonds with a little of the flour. Sift remaining flour and baking powder together. Add to creamed mixture alternately with the milk. Lastly fold in cherries and almonds. Put mixture into prepared tin and arrange cherries and almonds in a pattern on top. Bake in a moderate oven (350°F.) for $1\frac{1}{2}$-2 hours, until a skewer inserted comes out clean. Cool.

Scotch Eggs

Bean Salad

Barbecues

Everybody loves a barbecue, meat, fish, fruit—everything seems to taste so much better. The aroma of food cooking over hot coals—nothing equals the smokey, charcoal flavour of barbecued steak and chops. Today's barbecue meals have come a long way from early attempts at cooking picnic fashion over an open fire. They have progressed to patio and terrace and with new portable barbecue equipment even countryside barbecue cooks can produce food of gourmet quality.

Marinades

Explore the use of marinades. These aromatic mixtures of oil, wine or vinegar, herbs and vegetables do wonders for barbecued foods. They tenderise the meat as they penetrate. After soaking the meat, the marinade liquid is often used to brush over the grilling food.

Red Wine Marinade: Combine ½ pint red wine, 1 sliced onion, 1 teaspoon peppercorns, 1 bay leaf, 4 sprigs parsley, ½ teaspoon dried thyme and 4 tablespoons oil.

Marinate steak or lamb in this mixture for several hours or overnight. Sufficient for 2½-3 lb. steak.

White Wine Marinade: Use the same recipe replacing white wine for red wine. Marinate chicken or lamb several hours.

Minted Wine Marinade: A particularly good marinade for lamb. Follow the recipe for White Wine Marinade, add 1 tablespoon honey and 1 teaspoon chopped mint.

Cooking know-how

All meats for grilling should be at room temperature. Sausages are better if first blanched (put into cold water and brought slowly to boiling point, simmered a few minutes, then drained) before cooking on the barbecue.

They will not split or spit and do not require pricking. All grill racks or rods should be greased with fat or oil before placing food on to keep it from sticking. Use a sturdy brush to grease frequently.

Grease aluminium foil well before wrapping food to cook over the fire.

Do not rush the cooking. Keep meats well above fire. They cook better and taste more delicious if cooked slowly and are not charred by intense heat of a direct fire.

Building a fire

When using charcoal, make sure there is enough to last for the entire cooking process. More added during cooking causes smoke and flames. Judging the amount of fuel comes with experience, but a 12 oz. pack of charcoal briquettes is usually sufficient for a meal for four.

The charcoal should be reduced to glowing coals with just a brush of white ash on top before any cooking is started. This will take up to one hour or more for a deep bed of coals, so get the fire going well before the meal starts. Wood takes longer to reduce to live coals.

Barbecue equipment

Folding grid-irons are a necessity when barbecuing foods that are difficult to turn without breaking, and are ideal when using an open fire without a grid.

Tongs, spatulas and long handled forks are basic implements for the barbecue chef and a collection of skewers is necessary for kebabs and other skewered foods. Salt and pepper shakers on long handles are also available for seasoning foods while cooking.

Thick, charcoal grilled steak is cut into slices and served with Mushrooms with Herbed Butter and Shallot Grilled Tomatoes.

Barbecue at Home
Marinades

There are still a few men left who can be justly proud of their skill at carving the great Sunday roast. With the advent of backyard barbecues, men have something new to boast about—their skill as a barbecue chef and that not only means steak, chops and sausages, but spareribs and other specialities.

It is a good idea to make use of the kitchen oven as well as the barbecue. Plan spareribs or a shoulder of lamb along with the usual steaks, chops and chicken which never seem to go out of date. Salads should be varied. Fresh fruit makes a welcome added touch. Appetites have an uncanny knack of returning, even after generous servings of barbecue food. Prepare a pie or cake, it is sure to be a welcome finale. Marbled Cheesecake Squares, an American recipe, is a perfect choice.

Wines: Flagons of chilled dry white wine and red wine. Sangria (see index) is an excellent barbecue drink.

Antipasto Tray*
Barbecued Spareribs
or
Herbed Shoulder of Lamb
Steaks, Chicken, Lamb Chops or
Hamburgers
Shallot Grilled Tomatoes
Mushrooms with Herbed Butter
Foil-Roasted Potatoes
Corn Grilled in Husks
Parsley Butter Loaf
or
Hot Garlic Bread
Deluxe Tossed Salad
Bean Salad
Nut Crunch Coleslaw
Beetroot Relish
Marbled Cheesecake Squares

*Consult index for recipe.

Barbecued Spareribs ••

It is wise to order pork spareribs well in advance from your butcher to be sure of a supply.

6 lb. spareribs	5 tablespoons tomato sauce
1½ teaspoons salt	3 tablespoons honey
3 tablespoons soy sauce	1½ cups chicken stock
1½ tablespoons (1 oz.)	or water and chicken
sugar	stock cubes

Mix salt, soy sauce, sugar, tomato sauce, honey and stock well together. Pour over the spareribs in a large dish, cover and marinate for 12 hours or overnight if possible.

Lift spareribs out of the marinade and place on a rack in a roasting pan. Pour a little water into pan to prevent smoking. Roast in a moderately hot oven (375°F.) for about 1¼ hours, turning the spareribs occasionally. Put cooked spareribs on serving dish, bring marinade to the boil with a little extra stock if necessary, and pour over

the meat. Serve hot.
Note: Spareribs may also be cooked over low coals for 1-1½ hours, until brown and tender. Brush with the marinade while cooking.

Herbed Shoulder of Lamb ••

The lamb may be cooked over glowing coals or in a moderate oven (350°F.) for 1½ hours. If your barbecue has a rotisserie attached, a leg of lamb may be marinated in the same mixture and cooked for about 2 hours, basting frequently as the rotisserie turns.

1 shoulder of lamb	1 tablespoon grated onion
1 cup dry red or white wine	2 teaspoons dried
¾ cup chicken stock or	rosemary
water and chicken	2 teaspoons dried
stock cube	marjoram
2 tablespoons orange	1 bay leaf, crumbled
marmalade	1 teaspoon salt
1 tablespoon white vinegar	½ teaspoon ground ginger

Ask the butcher to cut shank almost off but without separating it from shoulder so it can sit flat. Combine all remaining ingredients in a pan and simmer for 20 minutes, stirring occasionally. Cool, pour over lamb, and allow to stand for several hours or overnight.

Start barbecue about 1 hour before cooking so that the fire is reduced to glowing coals. Lift meat from the marinade and wrap securely in a large sheet of heavy duty aluminium foil. Place on barbecue grid and cook for 1 hour, turning once. Remove foil and cook a further 30 minutes, turning and basting frequently with the marinade. Slice and serve while hot. Serves 6.

Barbecued Meat •

Lamb Chops on the Grill: Rub 1-inch thick loin or chump chops with salt and pepper and, if liked, a little powdered rosemary. Or marinade in one of the mixtures on page 73. Cook over hot coals for 12-15 minutes, turning occasionally.

Glazed Chicken on the Grill: Brush chicken pieces (legs and thighs or whole chicken cut into portions) with Barbecue Baste (see page 77) or marinate chicken in white wine marinade (see page 73) for several hours. Cook over hot coals for 25-30 minutes, turning and brushing occasionally with the barbecue baste or marinade.

Barbecued Hamburgers on the Grill: Lightly but thoroughly combine 2 lb. minced steak with ¾ cup evaporated milk, 2 beaten eggs, 1 cup soft white bread-crumbs, 2 teaspoons salt, good pinch pepper, 1 teaspoon dry mustard, ½ cup grated onion and ½ cup finely chopped green pepper. Shape into 8 patties and cook over hot coals or on a greased barbecue griddle for 12-15 minutes, until cooked. Serve on toasted, buttered hamburger buns.

Steaks on the Grill: Prepare and grill steaks according to the recipe on page

Fruits on the Grill: An ideal accompaniment to barbecues is fruit cooked on the grill. Slices of fresh or canned pineapple, sprinkled with brown sugar, may be cooked over the coals until the sugar caramelises. Bananas in their skins are delicious when cooked over the coals (place them around edge of grill) for 10 minutes or until the skins become black in colour. Peel and sprinkle lightly with salt and pepper.

Shallot Grilled Tomatoes •

Halve tomatoes if large or cut tops off small tomatoes and season with salt and pepper. Place on hot greased barbecue plate or in a greased frying pan over hot coals and cook, cut side down for a few minutes. Turn and continue cooking until tomatoes are soft and tender. Add chopped shallots with a little butter to barbecue plate or pan, cook 2-3 minutes, then spoon on tomatoes to serve.

Mushrooms with Herbed Butter •

12 button mushrooms	1 tablespoon snipped
8 oz. butter	chives
salt and pepper	1 clove garlic, crushed
2 teaspoons chopped parsley	

Wash mushrooms, remove stems. Heat 2 oz. butter and gently cook mushrooms until tender. Season with salt and pepper. Cool and chill mushrooms. Beat remaining butter with parsley, chives and garlic. Season if necessary with salt and pepper. Spoon or pipe this mixture into the mushroom caps and serve chilled as an accompaniment for grilled chops or steak. Serves 4-6.

Foil-Roasted Potatoes •

Scrub 6-8 medium sized potatoes. Cook in salted water until almost tender, about 20 minutes. Drain. Wipe well, brush with oil and wrap each potato in a piece of aluminium foil. Cook on the coals or in a moderately hot oven (375°F.), turning occasionally, for 15-20 minutes. To test if done, pierce with a skewer. To serve, cut a cross on top of each potato, squeeze to open and add a pat of butter. Serves 6.

Parsley Butter Loaf •

1 round cottage or French	1 tablespoon lemon juice
loaf	2 tablespoons grated
½ cup chopped parsley	tasty cheese, optional
4 oz. softened butter	

Cut bread into ¾-inch thick slices, almost through to the bottom crust. Combine parsley, butter and lemon juice and spread between the slices. Wrap loaf in heavy duty aluminium foil and place over hot coals for 10-15 minutes. Or put into a moderately hot oven (375°F.) for 15-20 minutes. Open foil for last 5 minutes, sprinkle bread with cheese and leave foil open to crisp the crust.

Corn Grilled in Husks •

Strip outer husks of 6 corn cobs, leaving 3-4 husks on corn. Place in iced water for 30 minutes or longer. Drain well and grill over glowing coals 15-20 minutes, turning occasionally. Strip away husks and serve the cooked corn topped with a dab of butter. Serves 6.

Hot Garlic Bread •

Prepare bread as described on page 36, using half the ingredients. Bake according to directions in recipe. Or place the foil-wrapped bread on the barbecue for 10-15 minutes. Serves 6.

Deluxe Tossed Salad •

2 lettuce	4 stalks celery
1 large white onion (or 4-5 spring onions)	¾ cup French dressing (see page 16)
3 ripe tomatoes	2 hard-boiled eggs, quartered
1 cucumber	
1 green pepper, cut into fine strips	

Wash lettuce, dry and chill until crisp. Tear into bite-sized pieces, place in a salad bowl. Slice onion finely, place on lettuce, with quartered tomatoes, peeled and thinly sliced cucumber, pepper strips and sliced celery. Cover with aluminium foil or plastic food wrap.

When ready to serve, pour dressing over salad, toss the salad well and garnish with eggs. Serves 6.

Bean Salad •

1 small onion, finely chopped	1 tablespoon chopped parsley
1 teaspoon prepared mustard	1 clove garlic, optional
salt and pepper	½ cup oil
1 tablespoon lemon juice	1 x 10 oz. can lima beans
1 tablespoon vinegar	1 x 10 oz. can kidney beans

Combine onion, mustard, salt and freshly ground pepper, lemon juice, vinegar, parsley and crushed garlic in a bowl. Gradually mix in oil. Drain beans, add to dressing and toss well to coat evenly with the dressing. Cover and chill. Before serving, toss again and add more salt and pepper to taste if necessary. Serve in lettuce lined bowl. Serves 4-6.

Beetroot Relish •

Grated onion and horseradish add piquant flavour to this crisp beetroot relish.

1 bunch young beetroot	¾ cup French dressing (see page 16)
2 white onions	
1 tablespoon bottled horseradish relish	salt and freshly ground pepper
1 teaspoon sugar	

Peel uncooked beetroot and grate coarsely. Peel onions

and grate. Combine in a bowl together with horseradish and sugar. Toss well with French dressing, season with salt and pepper. Cover and chill. This relish develops a better flavour if it is prepared a few hours before required.

Marbled Cheesecake Squares ••

A variation of the usual cheesecake, this one is deliciously marbled with chocolate and has walnuts for texture and flavour contrast.

Cheese Mixture:

2 oz. butter	1 egg
4 oz. cream cheese	1 tablespoon (½ oz.) plain flour
¼ cup (2 oz.) castor sugar	½ teaspoon vanilla essence

Chocolate Mixture:

4 oz. dark cooking chocolate	¼ teaspoon baking powder
3 oz. butter	¼ teaspoon salt
2 eggs	½ cup coarsely chopped walnuts
¾ cup (6 oz.) castor sugar	¼ teaspoon almond essence
½ cup (2 oz.) plain flour	

Grease a shallow 9-inch square cake tin and set oven temperature at moderate (350°F.).

For Cheese Mixture: Cream butter with cream cheese. Gradually add sugar, beating until light and fluffy. Add egg and beat in well. Stir in flour and vanilla. Set aside.

For Chocolate Mixture: Melt chopped chocolate and butter in a bowl over hot water, stirring constantly. Cool. Beat eggs until thick and light, gradually beating in sugar. Fold in the sifted flour, baking powder and salt, then blend in the cooled chocolate mixture, walnuts and almond essence.

Measure 1 cup chocolate mixture and set aside. Spread remaining chocolate mixture into prepared tin. Top with cheese mixture, then drop spoonfuls of reserved chocolate batter on top. Swirl a knife through batter to make a marbled pattern. Bake in a moderate oven (350°F.) for 40-45 minutes. Cool in tin, cut into squares, cover and allow to set in refrigerator.

Parsley Butter Loaf goes well with any barbecue. A round cottage loaf is sliced, not quite through to bottom crust, in four different directions. The slices are spread with flavoured butter and the whole loaf wrapped in aluminium foil and cooked over the coals.

A Barbecue in the Country

With the wide range of equipment available, outdoor cooking is a breeze! There is a portable barbecue to suit every need. The accessories, designed with imagination, make everyone want to be a barbecue chef and, with good equipment, you are left to choose your site with complete freedom.

Small barbecues like Japanese hibachis are inexpensive and ideal when cooking for small numbers. They are so compact and well designed that they can be used indoors or out. (For an Eastern meal, skewered appetisers grilled before the guests on one of these hibachis are delicious and most impressive). There are other portable barbecues which pack neatly for easy carrying. Some have convenient attachments like the clip-on side trays useful for holding sauces or marinades, stacking plates, and so on.

For picnickers and campers, a primus stove with liquid fuel is a great asset. They are clean, compact, light to carry and take no time at all to set up and use.

Containers that Travel

Thanks to modern spill-proof and insulated containers, there is no limit to what you can take on a picnic or barbecue. Look for plastic bowls with airtight seals, plastic meat and bread keepers, carriers for meat, salads and accompaniments! Remember aluminium foil, plastic food wraps and polythene bags. Light foam insulted carriers can be packed with a little ice, providing a travelling ice box for your precious food.

Wines: A flagon of red wine or cans of chilled beer, cola or any popular bubbly drink.

Steaks on the Grill
Bean Salad*
Beetroot Relish*
Nut Crunch Slaw*
Buttered Rolls
Sticky Gingerbread with
Gouda Cheese*

*Consult index for recipe.

Steaks on the Grill •

Allow 8-12 oz. of rump, T-bone or sirloin steak per person, cut 1-inch thick for individual steaks, 1½-2 inches thick if barbecuing a big piece of meat. Trim off excess fat and score edges so that steak will not curl during cooking.

Grease the rack and put rack with meat 3-inches from the heat over a deep bed of glowing coals. For rare steaks, allow 4-5 minutes on each side for meat 1½-inches thick. If too rare, cook a few minutes more on each side as required.

Steaks may be seasoned before cooking in one of the following ways. Or, if liked, marinate meat in Red Wine Marinade (page 73) for several hours or overnight.

Steak Seasonings: Flavour steak, chicken or lamb chops in one of the following ways to give good flavour and appetising appearance.

Mustard Steaks: For each steak beat 1 oz. butter with ½ teaspoon dry mustard and spread on meat before cooking.

Pepper Steak: Press coarsely ground pepper into steak on both sides and allow to stand 30 minutes or more before cooking.

Herbed Steak: Press dried rosemary, thyme or oregano into steaks, season with salt and pepper and cook.

Oriental Baste: Combine 1 teaspoon grated fresh ginger (or use chopped canned green ginger), 1 small clove crushed garlic, ¼ cup soy sauce, 1 tablespoon mirin (sweet sake) or sherry, 2 teaspoons sugar and 2 teaspoons oil. Brush on meat before cooking.

Barbecue Baste: Finely chop 1 small onion and put into a small pan with 3 tablespoons oil, 1 tablespoon tarragon vinegar, 2 tablespoons Worcestershire sauce and ¾ cup tomato sauce. Bring to the boil, cover and simmer for 10 minutes, stirring occasionally. Cool and use to brush on meat while cooking.

Barbecues from the Sea

The mating of fried fish with chips has been called 'one of the happiest marriages in history'. If you have lived by the sea and know and love the smell of the sea, you know, as I do, that fresh fish should smell of the sea. I prefer fish cooked in a simple way and what could be simpler, more natural than barbecued fish.

If you are lucky enough to have a fisherman in the family or have access to fresh fish, then you will want to include something from the sea in your barbecues. The secret of good fish eating is to guard against overcooking, for that is what makes all fish tough and dry.

Marinated Prawn Kebabs
Barbecued Fish
Grilled Fish with Fennel
Barbecued Rock Lobster
(Crayfish)
Barbecued Scallops

Marinated Prawn Kebabs ••

2 lb. large raw shelled prawns.	salt and pepper to taste
½ cup coconut milk	2 teaspoons ground cumin
2 teaspoons soy sauce	1 tablespoon lemon juice
1 clove garlic, crushed	lemon wedges
Coconut Milk:	
½ cup desiccated coconut	1 cup hot water

Marinate prawns in a mixture of ¼ cup coconut milk, soy sauce, garlic, salt and pepper to taste for 1 hour. Thread on to 6 long skewers. Wrap aluminium foil around wooden handles to prevent burning. Combine remaining ¼ cup coconut milk with cumin and lemon juice. Brush over prawns and grill over hot coals on barbecue, turning and brushing prawns frequently. Do not overcook. Serve with lemon wedges.
For Coconut Milk: Infuse desiccated coconut in hot water for 10 minutes. Squeeze the coconut well for a few minutes to extract the milk, then strain through a fine strainer.

Barbecued Fish ••

1 x 2-4 lb. whole fish	1 teaspoon ground cumin
4 oz. butter	
1 teaspoon salt	fresh banana leaves
2 teaspoons ground coriander	

Clean and scale fish. Slash flesh in 2-inch wide strips down to bone. Blend together butter, salt, coriander and cumin. Spread in slashes on both sides of fish. Pour boiling water over banana leaves to soften, and cut leaves from centre rib. If fish is large put a long skewer lengthwise through fish. This holds it firm for turning. Wrap in banana leaves, then in a large sheet of heavy aluminium foil. Put fish on grid over hot coals. Allow 20 minutes for a 2 lb. fish or 30 minutes for a 4 lb. fish. Turn fish every 5 minutes.

This method is ideal for big fish and as the flesh is slashed every 2-inches right to the bone the cooking time increases only 5-10 minutes per pound. Allow 45 minutes for a 6-8 lb. fish. The spiced butter may also be varied in the following ways:
Garlic Butter: To 4 oz. butter add 2 cloves crushed garlic, juice of ½ lemon, 1 teaspoon salt, good pinch cayenne.
Mustard Butter: Add 2 teaspoons dry mustard, 1 teaspoon salt, dash Worcestershire sauce to 4 oz. butter.
Herb Butter: Add 2 teaspoons chopped parsley, 1 teaspoon each marjoram, thyme and salt, good squeeze of lemon juice to 4 oz. butter.

Grilled Fish with Fennel ••

Fish may be cooked this way at home under a grill and finished over the flaming fennel branches or cooked at the seaside in a barbecue grid over charcoal and the fennel added to the charcoal at the end of cooking time (the brandy would not be necessary). Fennel is a perennial herb found growing wild along many river banks.

1 x 2½-3 lb. fish	1 large bunch of dried fennel branches
6 short pieces of dried fennel	½ cup brandy
olive oil	

Make three crosswise deep incisions on each side of fish. Put a piece of fennel in each incision. Brush fish with oil. Place fish in barbecue grid and grill fish for 7-10 minutes on each side, turning over only once.

Place dried fennel branches on a large ovenproof dish

and place fish in grid on top. Warm the brandy, set alight and pour flaming over the dried fennel which catch alight and give out a strong scent which flavours the fish. When the flames die down remove fish from grid to a heated serving dish.

Note: Any white fleshed fish may be used for this dish. Both salt water or fresh water small fish may be prepared in the same way.

Barbecued Rock Lobster ••
(Crayfish)

1 medium sized live	lemon juice
rock lobster or crayfish	salt and pepper
2-3 oz. butter	
Beurre Noisette:	
2 oz. butter	salt and freshly ground
good squeeze of lemon	pepper to taste
juice	

To kill the lobster plunge the point of a knife into the head, between the tail and body shell, aiming between the eyes. A firm grip on the lobster is necessary. Use kitchen towels to safeguard against spines, which can be very sharp.

Split the lobster in two lengthwise. Remove the dark vein that runs through the tail. Brush lobster meat with melted butter and place lobster, cut side down on grill about 4-inches from coals and cook for 6-8 minutes, turn over, spread thickly with butter. Sprinkle with a squeeze of lemon and season with salt and pepper. Continue to cook for 8-10 minutes, until lobster is cooked through at the thickest part. Brush constantly with more butter while cooking. Serve accompanied by Beurre Noisette or dabs of butter. Lobster may also be cooked under a hot grill. The times are the same.

For Beurre Noisette: Melt butter and continue to cook until a light nut brown, shaking pan occasionally. Add remaining ingredients, swirl around in pan and serve immediately.

Note: When lobster is large, over 3 lb., it is better to plunge it into boiling salted water and simmer gently for 10-15 minutes before barbecuing.

Barbecued Scallops ••

1½ lb. scallops	½ teaspoon salt
¼ cup dry vermouth	1 tablespoon chopped
¼ cup olive oil	parsley
¼ teaspoon finely chopped	
garlic	

Wash scallops, cut away the dark vein, but leave the coral on. Mix vermouth with the remaining ingredients, add scallops and marinate for several hours in the refrigerator. When ready to serve, place the scallops and the marinade in scallop shells or a shallow pan. Place the shells on barbecue griddle plate (if coals are very hot, move the shells to outer edge) and cook for 8-10 minutes.

Note: Scallops may also be cooked in a frying pan, on the barbecue or over the stove.

The brandy for Grilled Fish with Fennel is warmed and poured, while flaming over dried fennel which ignites and flavours the dish.

An Island Luau

for twenty people

The luau (rhymes with moo-cow), traditional feast of Hawaii, is as completely informal as a feast could be. The food is set out all at once on a 'tablecloth' of ferns and other leaves on the ground or table. In a 'genuine' luau no plates or forks are used, everything is eaten with the fingers, the plates are ti (pronounced tea) leaves. Canna leaves or banana leaves can be used. Banana leaves can also be used for cooking food in much the same way as we use aluminium foil.

The feature of a real island luau is the whole roast pig. Sometimes the local baker can be talked into cooking it in his big oven, otherwise cook loins of pork. A Chinese food chopper will help chop the pork into chunky pieces for easy finger eating.

If the party is to be out-of-doors, set Hawaiian flares in the garden, available at all 5 and 10 cent stores. Provide plenty of cushions if the feast is set on the ground. Remember, the emphasis is on informality, friendliness and fun. Create a fabulous atmosphere with Hawaiian background music playing softly and welcome guests with a lei of flowers (plastic? So what!) or a single flower —yes, the men wear them too, behind the left or right ear depending on whether they are available or not!

Learn a few Hawaiian words to greet your guests:—

Aloha—	Literally, means love and affection, used as a welcome or goodbye.
Hoolaulea—	A gathering for fun.
Kaukau—	Food, meals.
Lomi—	To rub or massage.
Luau—	Leaf of taro—name of festive Hawaiian dinner.
Mahola—	Thank you.
Mai Kai—	Good, wholesome.
Mele Kali Kimaka—	Merry Christmas.
Ono Ono—	Delicious.
Okole Maluma—	'Bottoms up!'—a toast.
Wahine—	Female.
Wikiwiki—	Very quick, hurry up.

The mind boggles at just how you are going to weave these words into conversation. Anyway, '*Ono ono kaukau* to you, and all your *hoolauleas*!''
Wines: Trader Vic's punch bowl may be replenished throughout the feast.

Trader Vic's Punch*
Curried Macadamia Nuts
Fried Prawn Crisps
Butterfly Prawns
Sweet and Sour Sauce*
Barbecued Fish*
Skewered Beef Satay
Island Roast Pork
Glazed Sweet Potatoes
Kona Coast Rice Salad
Baked Bananas
Tropical Fruit Platter

*Consult index for recipe.

Curried Macadamia Nuts •

Follow recipe for Curried Walnuts (see page 24) using macadamia nuts or cashew nuts instead of walnuts. Cook the nuts well ahead of time and store in airtight containers when cool. Serve in bowls for guests to nibble with drinks.

Fried Prawn Crisps •

These can be purchased from large supermarkets, some delicatessens and Chinese grocery stores. Fry crisps a few at a time, in deep hot oil for a few seconds. Do not allow to brown. Drain and store in airtight containers until ready to serve.

Butterfly Prawns ••

4 lb. raw shelled king prawns	6 tablespoons oil
1½ cups (6 oz.) plain flour	2 egg whites
1 teaspoon salt	deep oil for frying
1½ cups lukewarm water	

Purchase the shelled raw prawns which have the tails intact. Devein prawns and dry well. Press open to flatten slightly. Sift flour and salt into a bowl, make a well in the centre and add water and oil. Stir to combine but do not beat. Allow to stand, covered, for 3 hours or until required. Before using, fold in the stiffly beaten egg whites. Add prawns, stir lightly to coat and deep fry until golden and cooked, about 3 minutes. Take care not to fry too many prawns at a time. Drain. Serves 20.

Serve on a platter lined with wild ginger or banana leaves. A bowl of Sweet and Sour Sauce (see page 116) may be placed alongside for dipping.

Island Roast Pork ••

2 x 5-6 lb. loins of pork	2 cloves garlic, crushed
2 tablespoons light soy sauce	4 teaspoons salt
3 teaspoons grated fresh ginger	1 tablespoon oil

Order the pork loins in advance and ask the butcher to score the skin. Mix soy sauce, ginger, garlic, salt and oil. Rub over pork. Cover and chill overnight.

Place the pork in a shallow roasting pan and roast in a very hot oven (500°F.) for 30-40 minutes, until skin is starting to bubble and crisp. Lower heat to moderate (350°F.) and roast for 2 hours. Do not cover the pork while roasting.

Serve on two large platters accompanied by Glazed Sweet Potatoes and Baked Bananas. Serves 20.

Glazed Sweet Potatoes •

8 lb. sweet potatoes	4 tablespoons honey
8 oz. butter	½ teaspoon ground ginger

Peel potatoes, cut into about twenty five even pieces. Put into a pan of boiling water, cover and simmer 5 minutes.

Drain. Melt 4 oz. butter in baking dishes. Stir in honey and ginger. Add potatoes, dot with remaining butter. Bake in a moderate oven (350°F.) for 1 hour or until tender. Brush with glaze every 15 minutes. Serves 20.
Note: If oven space is unavailable continue to cook the potatoes in boiling water until almost tender. Drain. Heat butter, honey, ginger in frying pans and brown a layer of potatoes at a time, turning constantly.

Skewered Beef Satay ••

Marinate the beef the evening before party, then thread onto bamboo skewers and arrange on tray. Have a barbecue with glowing coals ready and the guests can join in and cook their own satays.

4 lb. rump steak, cut into 1-inch cubes	3 teaspoons ground cumin
⅔ cup light soy sauce	1 tablespoon lemon juice
⅔ cup peanut oil	salt and pepper to taste
2 onions, thinly sliced	
3 cloves garlic, crushed	
4 tablespoons toasted sesame seeds	

Cut the steak into 1-inch cubes. Put the meat in an earthenware or glass bowl and add soy sauce, peanut oil, onions, garlic and toasted sesame seeds. Marinate the meat for at least 3 hours, then drain, reserving the marinade. Thread the steak cubes onto bamboo skewers and brush with a mixture of the ground cumin and lemon juice. Grill the meat over hot coals or under the grill, basting it with marinade and turning the skewers from time to time, until meat is tender. Season with salt and pepper to taste.

Kona Coast Rice Salad ••

2 lb. rice	1 cup sliced water chestnuts
salt	salt and pepper
2 red peppers	toasted halved almonds to garnish
2 green peppers	
4 sticks celery	
12 shallots	
Dressing:	
2 cloves garlic, crushed	1 teaspoon ground cumin
1-inch fresh ginger, grated	¼ cup vinegar
1 cup oil	salt and pepper

Cook rice in two large saucepans in plenty of boiling salted water for 15-20 minutes until tender. Drain.

Dice peppers and celery, chop shallots. Add all the vegetables to the rice and mix well. Pour dressing over and toss well to coat. Season to taste with salt and pepper. Cover and chill until ready to serve. Toss again before serving and garnish with almonds. Makes 20 small portions.
For Dressing: Beat all ingredients well together.
Note: For a more elaborate salad, add a choice of sliced cooked chicken, strips of ham, prawns, crab and/or pineapple pieces.

Tropical Fruit Platter •

Serve peeled, quartered or sliced fresh fruit on leaves on a bed of ice. Choose fruit such as pineapples, mangoes, melons, mandarins, oranges, bananas, pawpaws, Chinese gooseberries, strawberries, custard apples, and passion-fruit. Fruits that discolour should be dipped in lemon juice. If liked, sprinkle fruits with a little light rum before serving.

Iced Tea and Iced Coffee.

Baked Bananas •

Choose 20-25 firm, green tipped bananas and bake in a moderate oven (350°F.) for 20 minutes until a fork pierces the skin easily. Guests peel the bananas and sprinkle lightly with salt. Bananas may be cooked in their skins over the barbecue.

82

Plan an outing soon and enjoy a super picnic spread with food which packs well and can be served easily. Scotch Eggs, Hero Rolls, Crusted Veal Pie and Cherry Almond Cake

Daytime and Small Parties

Afternoon Tea

So you were the lucky one to inherit Grandma's silver tea tray or Aunt Jean's fine bone china tea service, or perhaps you have taken to collecting Victoriana at auction sales or antique shops. However you came by such treasures, you have the perfect setting for that most evocative of parties—a turn-of-the-century afternoon tea party. The dainty collation of fresh bite-sized sandwiches, fresh fruit tarts, simple but perfectly baked biscuits and always a featherlight sponge cake is, even with today's fast moving moderns, a feast to be wondered at.

My friend Mary, a most beautiful and trendy girl, knows how I adore her afternoon teas. Pure Victoriana using auntie's old tea cups, sugar tongs and a choice of two teas. My friend June, also beautiful and trendy, does it quite differently. Madly modern with Scandinavian tea pot, cups aesthetically pure and simple. How I enjoy afternoon tea with June. Both girls know the pleasures of an afternoon tea, the wonderful ritual that gives them a chance to play 'ladies' and show off their baking skills at the one time. Both girls know that, apart from the lovely cakes, biscuits and sandwiches they make, the cup of tea must be just right.

The Choice of Tea
It is fun to be able to offer a choice: Ceylon, Earl Grey, Orange Pekoe, Darjeeling, Prince of Wales; the best grocery departments keep an infinite variety. The green China teas are most refreshing when served not too strong, with or without a thin slice of lemon. Milk will spoil the delicate flavour of China tea. With other teas it is very much a matter of personal choice whether milk is served and there are two schools of thought whether the milk should be put into the cup first or last. I think that tea has a more blended flavour when milk is poured first, but others claim it is more correct to pass the sugar and the milk separately. (A good hostess asks her guest's preference, then pours accordingly). A jug of hot water is a practical refinement, the cups rinsed in hot water before the tea is poured assures that the tea will be served piping hot.

How To Make A Pot of Good Tea
1. Run fresh cold water from the tap, bring to a full rolling boil. Water from a hot water service has a flat taste.

2. As water comes to the boil, rinse the tea pot with boiling water so that the tea pot is thoroughly heated. Pour off water, none should remain in the bottom of the tea pot.

3. Use one teaspoon of tea per cup. Don't guess. Measure. Pour briskly, boiling water over tea. Replace lid, keep hot under tea cosy while tea infuses.

4. Infuse or brew the tea by the clock, 3-5 minutes depending on the strength you like. It takes time for the leaves to unfold and release their flavour. Don't guess the time.

5. Use a tea strainer if necessary, and should you be serving tea to a group, ask preferences. Milk? With lemon? Strong? Weak? It is so easy to serve this simple beverage to every liking.

The Food
As afternoon tea may vary from a simple cup of tea with a biscuit to a conventional, elegant affair, we have included a few additional recipes that would be just right for any afternoon tea.

Orange Rock Cakes and Syrup Pikelets served with a choice of butter or jam and whipped cream.

Serve Crêpes Louise hot garnished with slivered, toasted almonds.

Avocado Sandwiches
Cheese Sables
Coffee Meringue Kisses
Fruit Tarts
Swedish Brandy Knots
Chocolate Log
Lemon Sponge Roll
Chocolate Ripple Roll
Sultana Cake
Coffee Melting Moments

Avocado Sandwiches •

Chill avocado for 30 minutes. Slice thinly and sprinkle with lemon juice. Remove crusts from thinly sliced bread. Spread bread with butter, place avocado slices on half of the bread slices, season with salt and freshly ground black pepper and cover with remaining bread slices. Cut each sandwich into four triangular pieces to serve.

Cheese Sables ••

4 oz. butter	pinch cayenne pepper
1 cup (4 oz.) plain flour	2 oz. grated Cheddar cheese
½ teaspoon salt	

Beat butter until creamy and light coloured. Sift flour with salt and cayenne pepper and add to butter together with cheese, mixing to a dough. Form into a ball and chill for 1 hour. Roll out on a lightly floured board to ¼-inch thickness. Cut into rounds with a 2-inch cutter. Place on greased baking trays, mark with a fork, and bake in a hot oven (400°F.) for 15-20 minutes, until light golden brown. Cool on wire cooling racks. Serve plain or joined in pairs with a cream cheese filling.

To make the cheese filling, beat cream cheese with salt and pepper to taste. Flavour with paprika pepper, chutney or bottled horseradish relish.

Coffee Meringue Kisses ••

3 egg whites	½ teaspoon instant coffee powder
⅛ teaspoon cream of tartar	whipped cream
1 cup (7 oz.) castor sugar	vanilla essence to flavour

Brush baking trays with oil. Sift a little plain flour over, shaking trays to spread flour evenly. Invert and tap to remove excess flour.

Beat egg whites on very low speed of electric mixer (or use a rotary whisk) until frothy. Add cream of tartar and beat on highest speed until peaks hold their shape. Sift sugar and gradually beat 2 tablespoons of the measured sugar into the egg whites and continue beating for 2-3 minutes. Add coffee powder and remaining sugar and fold in quickly and carefully with a metal spoon. Use a piping bag and a plain tube. Pipe small mounds on to the prepared trays. Alternatively, use a teaspoon to make well shaped mounds of meringue on trays.

Bake in a very slow oven (250°F.) for 1½ hours. Turn meringues with a spatula and leave in oven for a further 30 minutes to dry out completely. Cool. Join in pairs with whipped cream flavoured with vanilla and serve in small paper cases. Makes 2 dozen.

Note: Meringues may be prepared well in advance and stored in airtight containers. Join with cream just before serving.

Fruit Tarts ••

Use fresh fruits in season such as strawberries, cherries, black or green grapes for these tarts. Canned fruits like cherries and pineapple may be used when fresh fruits are not available but drain well before using.

Pastry:

1 cup (4 oz.) plain flour	⅓ cup (2½ oz.) castor sugar
pinch salt	
2 oz. butter (at room temperature)	2 egg yolks

Filling:

fresh fruits in season	2 tablespoons water
1 cup apricot jam	

Pastry: Sift flour and salt into a bowl. Make a well in the

Miniature Fruit Tarts, Cheese Sables, Avocado Sandwiches, Lemon Sponge Roll

bake in a moderately hot oven (375°F.) for about 10 minutes until golden and cooked.

For Filling: Wash fruits and dry thoroughly. Put apricot jam and water into a saucepan and stir over low heat until combined. Press through a fine sieve and return to saucepan. Bring to the boil and boil gently until glaze thickens.

Brush insides of tart cases with the glaze and leave to cool. Arrange fruits in one layer in the tart cases and brush again with warmed glaze. Leave to cool.

Swedish Brandy Knots ••

½ cup (4 oz.) castor sugar	1¾ cups (7 oz.) plain
½ cup finely chopped	flour
unblanched almonds	2 tablespoons brandy
6 oz. butter	egg white to glaze

Mix 2 tablespoons of the measured sugar with the almonds in a bowl. Cream butter with remaining sugar, then stir in sifted flour until mixture resembles coarse breadcrumbs. Add brandy and mix to a smooth dough. Break off a small portion of dough and roll between palms of hands, which have been lightly floured, into pencil-thin rolls. Shape into a bow, brush with beaten egg white and dip into almond mixture. Arrange almond side up on greased baking trays. Bake in a moderate oven (350°F.) for 8-10 minutes. Cool on wire cooling racks. Makes 2-2½ dozen.

Chocolate Log •••

½ cup (2 oz.) plain flour	1 teaspoon vanilla essence
½ teaspoon baking powder	¼ teaspoon bicarbonate
¼ teaspoon salt	of soda
2 oz. dark cooking	2 tablespoons cold water
chocolate	icing sugar
4 eggs	1 quantity Chocolate
¾ cup (6 oz.) castor sugar,	Cream Filling
sifted	chopped nuts to decorate

Chocolate Cream Filling:

½ pint cream	2 tablespoons brandy
2 oz. chocolate	

Grease a 15 x 10 x 1-inch Swiss roll tin and line with greased greaseproof paper. Set oven at hot (400°F.).

Sift together flour, baking powder and salt. Melt chocolate in a bowl over hot water. Break eggs into a large bowl, sift in sugar and beat at high speed until very light and thick. Fold flour mixture and vanilla all at once into egg mixture. Add bicarbonate of soda and cold water to chocolate. Stir until smooth and light and fold quickly and evenly into egg and flour mixture. Pour into prepared tin and bake in a hot oven (400°F.) for 15 minutes or until cake top springs back when centre is gently touched. When cake is cooked, loosen edges and turn onto a clean tea towel thickly sprinkled with icing sugar.

Peel off paper and trim edges of cake with a sharp knife. Roll immediately in towel, first folding hem of towel over edge of cake and rolling towel in the cake to prevent sticking. After cake is rolled, leave to cool on a wire cooling rack for at least 1 hour.

Carefully unroll cake and spread with the Chocolate

centre, add butter, sugar and egg yolks. Mix with fingertips to form a dough. Chill for 1 hour. Roll out thinly on a lightly floured board, cut into circles and line greased patty tins or tartlet cases. Prick with a fork and Cream Filling. Re-roll cake and chill until serving time.

For Chocolate Cream Filling: Whip cream until thick. Chop chocolate and melt over hot water, allow to cool a little. Fold cooled chocolate into cream then carefully fold in brandy. Chill.

Lemon Sponge Roll ••

3 eggs, separated	3 tablespoons hot water
⅔ cup (5 oz.) castor sugar	¼ pint cream
finely grated rind of	1-2 tablespoons lemon
1 lemon	cheese, optional
1 cup (4 oz.) self-raising	sugar to taste
flour	

Grease and line a 13 x 10-inch Swiss roll tin with greased greaseproof paper. Set oven temperature at moderately hot (375°F.).

Whisk egg whites with electric or rotary beater until peaks form. Gradually add sugar, beating all the time until mixture is thick and glossy. Beat in lemon rind and egg yolks, all at once. Sift flour three times and fold through egg mixture. Quickly and lightly fold in hot water. Immediately pour mixture evenly into prepared tin. Bake in a moderately hot oven (375°F.) for 15-20 minutes, until centre will spring back when lightly touched with finger.

Have ready a clean tea towel sprinkled with castor sugar. Remove cake from oven and turn over onto towel. Quickly peel off paper and trim edges. Roll up in the towel. Whip cream until stiff, blend in lemon cheese and sugar to taste. Unroll the cooled sponge, spread cream over the cake and roll up. Sprinkle top with icing sugar.

Chocolate Ripple Roll •

Simply and quickly made, this delicious dessert type roll has a pretty, striped appearance when cut. Dipping the biscuits in sherry adds flavour, gives them a cake-like texture.

1 x 8 oz. packet chocolate	½ pint cream, whipped
biscuits	chocolate curls to
sweet sherry	decorate

This quantity is sufficient for 2 rolls. Divide ingredients and prepare the one roll completely, then start on the other.

Dip chocolate biscuits, one at a time into sweet sherry. As each one is dipped, sandwich with cream, placing one on top of the other until all biscuits are used. Lay the roll on its side and cover with remaining whipped cream. Spread with a spatula or knife to smooth. Repeat with remaining biscuits. Chill at least 3-4 hours. Decorate with chocolate curls which can be simply made using milk chocolate and a potato peeler. To serve, slice the roll diagonally. Makes 2.

Sultana Cake ••

12 oz. butter	3½ cups (14 oz.) plain flour
1½ cups (12 oz.) castor sugar	1¾ cups (7 oz.) self-raising flour
grated rind 2 lemons	1¼ cups sour milk
4 eggs	2 cups (12 oz.) sultanas

Grease and line a 10-inch cake tin. Set oven temperature to moderately slow (325°F.).

Cream butter and sugar until light and fluffy. Add grated lemon rind, then eggs, one at a time, beating well after each. Fold in sifted dry ingredients alternately with sour milk. Lastly mix in sultanas and place into prepared tin. Bake in moderately slow oven (325°F.) for 1½-1¾ hours or until a skewer inserted in the middle comes out clean. Allow to cool in tin before turning out. Serve sliced, either plain or buttered.
Note: To sour fresh milk, add a good squeeze of lemon juice or ½ teaspoon vinegar and allow to stand, if possible, for at least 1 hour.

Coffee Melting Moments ••

4 oz. butter	½ cup (2 oz.) self-raising flour
2 tablespoons icing sugar	½ cup (2 oz.) cornflour
1 teaspoon instant coffee	
1 teaspoon boiling water	

Lightly grease baking trays and set oven temperature at moderate (350°F.).

Cream butter and icing sugar together and stir in the coffee which has been dissolved in the boiling water. Sift flour and cornflour together and add to mixture, stirring to form a dough. Pipe biscuits onto trays and bake in a moderate oven (350°F.) for about 10 minutes. Remove from trays, cool and store in an airtight container.
Note: The biscuits may also be rolled into small balls, placed on a baking tray and flattened with a damp fork.

(a) For the Basic Crêpes, sufficient batter is poured on a hot greased pan to cover the base with a thin layer.

(b) When golden brown on one side, turn over and cook other side. As each crêpe is cooked, stack between squares of greaseproof paper to prevent sticking.

(c) The filling for Crepes Louise is spread thickly in centre of each crêpe.

(d) Roll up the crêpes and arrange in a greased ovenproof dish, ready to bake.

Morning Coffee

Morning coffee is one of the most friendly events in a day. A nice way of saying 'Welcome' to a new neighbour or having a chat with an old friend. The food should be simple, one freshly baked item and something home-made from the biscuit barrel adds a personal touch. Good hot coffee will never taste so good as it does at this time of the day.

What Coffee to Buy
When you are buying coffee, buy only a small quantity at a time and, if possible, have it freshly ground. The ideal way is to buy the coffee beans and to grind them as they are needed. But to do this you must have a coffee grinder. On the other hand, you may find ground coffee in a vacuum pack that suits your taste. When choosing coffee, buy the best you can afford. Mocha coffee, which comes from Aden and Mocha, is generally considered the best but you will find by experience which blends you prefer. If you like your coffee with a strong flavour, choose one to which a little chicory has been added. This will also make the coffee go further.

To store coffee, take care that it is not near any strong smelling foodstuff, as it quickly absorbs other odours and is spoiled. When you open a tin, if you have bought the vacuum packed kind, or a packet, transfer the coffee immediately to a screw-top jar. This will help to keep it fresh.

When making coffee, remember the following points:

Use sufficient coffee. About 4-6 tablespoons to each pint of water is correct for breakfast use, and for after dinner coffee use 6-8 tablespoons to a pint of water.

Use fresh water as you would for tea making. Never allow coffee to boil. Bring it just to boiling point. Add hot, not boiling, milk to breakfast coffee.

Breakfast coffee is usually a lighter roast than after dinner coffee. For after dinner, or black coffee, choose the darker kind. This is sometimes called Continental Roast and is much stronger and richer in flavour.

How to Make Perfect Coffee
There are many ways of making coffee and dozens of pieces of coffee making equipment to choose from.

The simplest way of all is to use a tall earthenware jug that has been well warmed. Put in the correct amount of coffee and pour over freshly boiled water. Put a lid on the jug or cover with a folded cloth. Leave for about 1 minute, then stir. Stand for another 5 minutes. The grains will drop to the bottom of the jug, leaving clear coffee on top. Strain to serve. The same can be done if coffee is made in a heavy saucepan.

If a percolator is used there is no need to worry about straining. Fill percolator just over half full with water. Put filter in position and measure in the coffee. Put lid of filter in position and then percolator lid. Put over heat and percolate for as long as required, usually about 5 minutes after boiling point is reached.

Syrup Pikelets
Orange Rock Cakes
Caraway Cake
Mrs. Seymour's Currant Cookies

Mrs. Seymour's Currant Cookies ••

4 oz. butter
½ cup (4 oz.) castor sugar
1 egg
1½ cups (6 oz.) plain flour
¼ cup (2 oz.) self-raising flour
3 tablespoons custard powder
pinch nutmeg
2 tablespoons currants
little beaten egg
sugar for sprinkling

Cream butter with sugar and then add beaten egg. Stir in sifted dry ingredients and fold in currants. Form into a ball and chill for 30 minutes. Roll out dough thinly on a floured board and cut into shapes with a biscuit cutter. Put on greased baking trays, brush with a little beaten egg and sprinkle with sugar. Bake in a moderate oven (350°F.) 12-15 minutes. Makes about 3½-4 dozen.

Orange Rock Cakes •

2 cups (8 oz.) self-raising flour
½ teaspoon cinnamon
3 oz. butter or margarine
finely grated rind of 1 orange
½ cup (4 oz.) sugar
2 tablespoons each currants, raisins and chopped mixed peel
1 egg
4 tablespoons milk
extra tablespoon sugar

Grease baking trays and set oven temperature at hot (400°F.).

Pepper Pizza, Salami Pizza, Pizza Campofranco and Neapolitan Pizza Marina, Tossed Italian Salad (garnished with shallot curls) and bread sticks. Start the party with Antipasto Tray

Sift flour and cinnamon into a mixing bowl. Rub in butter, then stir in orange rind, ½ cup sugar, fruits and peel. Beat egg and milk together and add to mixture. Stir with knife until stiff dough is formed. Put small table-spoonfuls of mixture in little heaps about 1½-inches apart on prepared trays. Sprinkle a little extra sugar on top of each rock cake. Bake in a hot oven (400°F.) for 10-15 minutes. Serve warm, plain or with butter.

Syrup Pikelets •

1 cup (4 oz.) self-raising flour
pinch salt
¼ teaspoon bicarbonate of soda
1 tablespoon (½ oz.) castor sugar
1 egg
½ cup sour milk (or fresh milk with 1 teaspoon vinegar added)
1 tablespoon golden syrup
2 teaspoons butter
extra butter for frying

Sift flour, salt and bicarbonate of soda into a mixing bowl. Make a well in the centre and add sugar, egg, sour milk and golden syrup which has been melted with 2 teaspoons butter. Stir mixture, gradually incorporating flour, to make a smooth batter. Grease a hot griddle or shallow frying pan and drop tablespoonfuls of the batter onto griddle. Cook until bubbly on top and brown underneath, turn and brown other side. Serve warm with butter or cold with raspberry jam and whipped cream.
Note: If batter thickens, add a little more milk.

Caraway Cake ••

4 oz. butter
½ cup (4 oz.) castor sugar
3 eggs, beaten
1½ cups (6 oz.) self-raising flour
Icing:
1 cup (5 oz.) sifted icing sugar
1 tablespoon boiling water
pinch salt
2-3 tablespoons milk
2 teaspoons caraway seeds
cinnamon
½ teaspoon butter
few drops vanilla essence

Grease a 4½ x 8½ x 2½-inch loaf tin and set oven temperature at moderate (350°F.).

Cream butter, add sugar and beat until light and fluffy. Add the beaten eggs a little at a time, mixing well. Sift flour with salt and fold one third into creamed mixture. Add remaining flour, milk and caraway seeds and mix gently but thoroughly. Put into prepared tin and bake in a moderate oven (350°F.) for 1-1¼ hours. When cold top with icing and sprinkle with cinnamon.
For Icing: Mix icing sugar, boiling water, butter and vanilla in a bowl. Stir until smooth and use immediately.

Semolina Cheesecake.

Mother's Day Breakfast

for one

There is something wonderful about the earnest efforts of a young family preparing breakfast for Mother on 'her day'. The main thing about this breakfast is that it should be as near to perfection as possible. This means heat the plate for the egg dish and set the breakfast tray before you start to cook. Serve the tea or coffee piping hot. It needs careful timing, but with family co-operation it should be the start of a wonderful day for a wonderful person.

Honey Grilled Grapefruit
Egg Scramble with Ham
Toasted English Muffins
Crescent Rolls with
Black Cherry Jam
Tea or Coffee

Honey Grilled Grapefruit ••

½ grapefruit	1 teaspoon butter
2 teaspoons honey	
pinch ground cinnamon	
· or mace	

Remove seeds from the grapefruit and separate the sections, spread with honey, sprinkle with cinnamon and place dots of butter on the top. Grill 4-inches from heat for 5 minutes until top is bubbling and grapefruit is hot.

Egg Scramble with Ham ••

1 oz. butter	salt and pepper
2 oz. ham or bacon, diced	1 teaspoon chopped
2 eggs	parsley
1 tablespoon cream or	toasted English muffins
milk	or toast triangles

Heat butter in a frying pan and fry ham for 2 minutes. Beat eggs, cream and seasoning until thoroughly combined. Add to pan and stir gently over a low heat until eggs are lightly set. Stir in parsley and serve immediately on a hot plate with toasted buttered muffins or toast triangles. Sprinkle with extra parsley if desired.
Note: English muffins are available from good bakeries and supermarkets.

Crescent Rolls with Black Cherry Jam •

Bake a packet of refrigerator crescent rolls according to the directions on the package and serve warm with pats of butter and a good black cherry jam or apricot conserve.

Note: If able to purchase croissants from a good bakery, wrap in foil, freeze overnight and warm in a moderately hot oven (375°F.) before serving.

How to make tea

1. Heat your teapot by filling it with boiling water.
2. Use freshly drawn, briskly boiling water for making tea. (Always use water from the cold tap and bring to a rolling boil).
3. Measure tea correctly. One teaspoon for each person.
4. Pour the briskly boiling water onto the measure of tea.
5. Stir once or twice, cover and brew for 3-5 minutes.
6. Pour tea through a strainer into cups with milk added, or serve plain with lemon slice.

How to make coffee

Measure 1 heaped tablespoons freshly ground coffee into a jug. Pour in ½-pint boiling water, stir well, cover and allow to stand in a warm place for 5 minutes. Strain into warm cup. Makes 2-3 cups.
For Milk Coffee: Heat milk gently in saucepan while brewing coffee. Pour milk and coffee simultaneously into cup so they blend smoothly as they are poured.

Ladies Luncheon
for six people

One of the most delightful books in my library is 'Oh! For a French Wife'.** In case you don't know, it's a cookbook. Louise Coleman, wife of the co-author, a brilliant hostess whether entertaining in Sydney, Cannes or Paris, taught me a lot about entertaining. (Any transgressions in this book cannot be blamed on Louise). I discovered that a French crêpe differs from the average pancake in more ways than one. Louise taught me that they should be as fine as lace doyleys, as light as a tu-tu, and with a flavour that could stand on its own. The main dish for this luncheon is named after Louise. It combines two great basics of French cookery, crêpes and Sauce Béchamel. Use good quality canned King Crab meat unless fresh crab is available. It is a superb dish. Serve it as a first course at a dinner party, too.

Wines: A light, chilled white wine or chilled rosé wine.

**Written by Ted Moloney and Deke Coleman and illustrated by George Molnar, published in Australia by The Sheppard Press.

Tomatoes Farçi

Crêpes Louise

or

Asparagus Quiche

Green Salad*

Chocolate Strawberry Cream

*Consult index for recipe.

Crêpes Louise •••

8 basic crêpes	2 hard-boiled eggs,
6 shallots	chopped
2 oz. butter	2 teaspoons snipped
1 x 6½ oz. can king crab	chives
1 pint béchamel sauce	2 tablespoons whipped
1 egg yolk	cream
2 teaspoons Madeira	toasted slivered almonds
or port	to garnish

Finely chop shallots and sauté in butter until softened. Flake crab and remove any bony tissue. Add to shallots. Prepare béchamel sauce (recipe follows), set 4 tablespoons aside for topping. To remaining sauce add the egg yolk, Madeira, hard-boiled eggs, chives and crab

Tomatoes Farci

6-8 small tomatoes	1 x 14 oz. can artichoke
1 tablespoon capers,	hearts, cut into
chopped	quarters
1 tablespoon chopped	freshly ground pepper
parsley	sliced black olives to
1 cup sour cream	garnish

Cut tops off tomatoes and scoop out centres. Mix remaining ingredients together except olives. Pile into tomatoes and garnish with olive slices.

Knackwurst with Sauerkraut, Polish sausage in Red Wine served on a bed of Creamy Mashed Potatoes and Green Salad

94

mixture. Spread on the crepês, roll up and arrange in one layer in a buttered baking dish. Cover dish with aluminium foil and bake in a moderate oven (350°F.) for 15 minutes. Fold cream into the reserved 4 tablespoons sauce, spoon along centre of crêpes and return to oven, uncovered, for 5 minutes until sauce browns. Garnish with toasted, slivered almonds. Serves 6.

Basic Crêpes ••

1⅛ cups (4½ oz.) plain flour	1½ cups milk
pinch grated nutmeg	2 teaspoons melted butter
pinch salt	2 teaspoons brandy
pinch pepper	butter for frying
3 eggs, beaten	

Sift flour, nutmeg, salt and pepper into a mixing bowl. Combine eggs and milk, stir into dry ingredients and continue stirring until batter is smooth. Add melted butter and brandy.

Heat a little butter in a frying pan or pancake pan and when sizzling, pour in sufficient batter to cover bottom of pan with a thin layer. Rotate quickly to spread batter as thinly and evenly as possible. Cook each pancake about 1 minute on each side. Stack pancakes flat between layers of greaseproof paper and keep on a hot dish until all are made. Each should be about 5-inches across. Makes about 20 thin crêpes.

Note: Since crêpes freeze well they may be cooked ahead and stored for future use. Place squares of greaseproof paper between, wrap in groups of six and freeze.

Béchamel Sauce •

1 pint milk	2 oz. butter
1 bay leaf	4 tablespoons (2 oz.)
½ onion, chopped	plain flour
5 peppercorns	salt and pepper

Heat milk slowly in a saucepan over low heat to scalding point with bay leaf, onion and peppercorns. Remove from heat, cover and infuse for 7-8 minutes. Melt butter in a small heavy saucepan, draw away from heat, stir in flour, cook for about 1 minute, then add the strained and slightly cooled milk. Stir continuously over medium heat until boiling. Simmer 2-3 minutes. Add salt and pepper to taste.

Asparagus Quiche ••

1 quantity short crust pastry (see page 25)	salt and freshly ground black pepper
1 x 16 oz. can asparagus cuts	pinch grated nutmeg
4 egg yolks	4 oz. gruyère cheese
½ pint cream	1 oz. butter

Prepare pastry and roll out on a floured board to fit a greased 8 or 9-inch greased flan ring. Trim edge with a knife. Chill while preparing filling.

Drain asparagus. Lightly beat egg yolks and cream with salt, pepper and nutmeg. Slice cheese and cut into ½-inch squares. Place in pastry case and top with the asparagus. Strain the cream and egg mixture over ingredients in flan ring, dot with butter and bake in a hot oven (400°F.) for 10 minutes. Reduce temperature to moderate (350°F.) and bake for a further 20 minutes until golden and set. Serve warm. Serves 6.

Chocolate Strawberry Cream •

½ pint cream	1 punnet strawberries
few drops vanilla essence	sugar
4 oz. dark cooking chocolate	

Whip cream with vanilla until thick, but not stiff. Grate chocolate and stir lightly into cream. Hull strawberries and reserve a few for decoration. Slice remaining strawberries and sweeten with a little sugar if needed. Fold into cream mixture and spoon into 6 individual serving dishes. Chill until ready to serve. Decorate with reserved strawberries. Serves 6.

Jellied Avocado Soup.

Luncheon

for four or eight people

In some countries turtle is so common it is sold like fish. In England it has always been highly esteemed and considered a luxury. Avocado comes into the same class, a luxury for some, for others a bountiful fruit growing on huge backyard trees. It is inevitable that the two should get together. The two soups suggested for this menu combine these two luxurious foods.

Fish, especially fish fresh from the sea, is a luxury too. All too often it is yesterday's fish. In France, fish is always treated with great respect. It is said that the finest whiting is caught in the Mediterranean, the flesh is flaky,

tender and light, and it lends itself to convalescent cookery as well as to meals for the more robust. If your guests enjoy fish, this is a superb way to make the most of whiting or other fresh fish.

A simple fruit and cheese tray is suggested for dessert. Show that you care by selecting only the most perfect fruit at its peak and offer it with the right cheese.

Wines: Serve a dry white wine, chablis style, with the fish and accompany the cheese and fruit tray with a full bodied white wine.

Jellied Avocado Soup

or

Jellied Consommé with Avocado
Baked Whiting with Olives and
Capers
Cheese and Fruit Tray

Jellied Avocado Soup •

1 ripe avocado pear	dash hot pepper sauce
1 x 10 oz. can consommé	sour cream
or clear turtle soup	diced avocado for
lemon juice	garnish (optional)
salt	

Peel avocado pear and remove seed. Rub avocado through a sieve and combine at once with well chilled consommé diluted with 1 can water, or put avocado into blender container and blend with consommé until smooth. Add a few drops of lemon juice, and season to taste with salt and hot pepper sauce. Serve chilled, topped with sour cream and garnish with diced avocado, if liked. Serves 4.

Note: Double this recipe if preparing for 8 people.

Jellied Consommé with Avocado •

2 x 10 oz. cans consommé	2 tablespoons dry
or clear turtle soup	sherry
1 ripe avocado pear	dash hot pepper sauce

Chill consommé for several hours. Halve avocado pear, remove seed and cut into thin slices, sprinkle with sherry and hot pepper sauce. Serve soup in jellied chunks in bowls, top with sherried avocado slices. Serves 4.

Note: Double for 8 people.

Baked Whiting with Olives and Capers ••

4 whiting, weighing	4 oz. butter
8-12 oz. each	2 teaspoons dried
2 tablespoons capers	oregano, crumbled
8 black olives	black pepper
salt	2 tablespoons lemon
¼ cup olive oil	juice

Have fish cleaned and scaled but leave heads and tails on. Wash and drain capers. Cut each olive lengthwise into 3 slices, cutting around the stones.

Wash the fish thoroughly and dry with paper towels. Season the inside of the fish with salt. Heat olive oil with 1 oz. butter in a frying pan until it begins to sizzle. Add oregano and a little black pepper. Dip fish in the seasoned butter and oil. Place fish in a baking dish and bake in a moderately hot oven (375°F.) for 20-30 minutes, basting frequently or cover with aluminium foil for the first 15 minutes of cooking. Arrange fish on a heated serving plate. Heat remaining butter in a heavy frying pan over a low heat until it becomes nut brown but not burnt. Add capers and olives. Remove pan from heat. Add lemon juice and pour over fish. Serve accompanied by boiled new potatoes. Serves 4. Prepare two separate dishes for 8 people.

Cheese and Fruit Tray •

Select an assortment of cheeses including a soft cheese, a semi-soft and a firm cheese. Try also to choose cheese with distinctly different flavours and textures. A cheese tray for a luncheon or dinner can include as little as two cheeses or as many as five, depending on the number of guests or the variety available.

Suggested Cheese and Alternatives:

Brie: a soft, ripened cheese, delicate and indescribably delicious, if not available try **Camembert** which must be ripened à point, that is, when it is as soft and runny as butter.

Esrom: a mild flavour with butterlike texture with small holes or **Port Salut**, a creamy and yellow coloured cheese which is buttery in flavour.

Stilton: one of the greatest blue cheeses, English, an ivory full cream cheese well streaked with blue, or **Roquefort**, the most famous French blue cheese made from ewes milk, with a sharp salty flavour, or **Danish Blue** which, as the name suggests, is sharp in flavour, and is off-white in colour with blue mould veins and has a softish rather crumbly texture.

Fruits add interest to the cheese tray but it is as well to appreciate that certain fruit and cheese combinations are better than others. Serve single pieces on a separate tray or set out a bowl of mixed fruit.

Here is a guide to selecting fruit for the cheese tray:

Brie: fresh peaches or strawberries.
Camembert: fresh pineapple or grapes.
Port Salut: apples.
Stilton: ripe figs or plums.
Roquefort: oranges.
Danish Blue: red apples.
Crackers or water biscuits may be served on a separate plate, a choice of one or two biscuits may be offered.

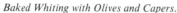
Baked Whiting with Olives and Capers.

Baked Whiting with Olives and Capers, in preparation

Sunday Luncheon or Supper
for eight people

Sunday is for leisure and leisurely meals. This meal was planned to serve out on the patio or even in the garden under the shade of a tree. Pork and Veal Terrine and Eggplant à la Turque can be made several days ahead and kept in the refrigerator. Allow guests to help themselves and be sure to provide a stack of small plates, a pile of paper napkins and forks. Crusty bread, melba toast or black bread go well with pâté and eggplant, known, incidentally, as 'poor man's caviar'.

Pasta with Beans is a hot main course. Bring it to the table in a large heated casserole with a lid. The casserole keeps the food warm if guests have taken the leisurely atmosphere seriously and do not want to eat immediately.

Jamaican Rum Cake has been included for those with a sweet tooth and no waistline problem to watch.

Wines: Allow a choice of chilled white wine or a light red wine. Flagon wines are ideal.

Pork and Veal Terrine
Eggplant à la Turque
Pasta with Beans
Greek Salad
Chocolate Log*

*Consult index for recipe.

Pork and Veal Terrine ••

1 lb. pork and 1 lb. veal, minced together
1 clove garlic, crushed
¼ teaspoon dried rosemary
pinch powdered cloves
2 teaspoons salt
freshly ground black pepper
1 egg

1 tablespoon (½ oz.) plain flour
grated rind of 1 lemon
½ cup dry vermouth
3 bay leaves
8 oz. bacon rashers
6 chicken livers, optional

Have butcher mince pork and veal very finely. Combine meat with garlic, rosemary, cloves, salt and pepper. Add beaten egg and flour and combine thoroughly. Stir in lemon rind and vermouth. Place 2 bay leaves on bottom of a 2-pint terrine or ovenproof mould and line with bacon rashers, slightly overlapping. Fill with the meat mixture, place 1 bay leaf on top and cover with bacon rashers. If using chicken livers, fill half mould with mixture, place chicken livers along the middle of the mixture and cover with rest of mixture and then the bacon rashers. Add enough vermouth to fill mould, cover, place on a baking tray and bake in a moderate oven (350°F.) for 1½ hours. Remove lid of mould, cover with a layer of aluminium foil and place a heavy weight on top. Allow to cool. Remove any excess fat and serve cut into slices accompanied by a little of the aspic jelly which forms around the terrine.

Pasta with Beans ••

1 lb. dried cannelini beans or 3-4 cups canned white beans
3 cloves garlic
2 large onions
2 carrots
6 oz. bacon
3 tablespoons olive oil
2 bay leaves
1 teaspoon dried oregano

3 large tomatoes, peeled and chopped
1 tablespoon salt
1 teaspoon pepper
1 lb. elbow macaroni
4 oz. butter
1 cup grated parmesan cheese
4 oz. salami, sliced
1 cup chopped parsley

If dried beans are used, soak overnight in water to cover. Drain. Cover with fresh water and simmer slowly 1-2 hours or until nearly tender. Drain. If canned beans are used drain off liquid.

Finely chop garlic, onions, carrots and bacon and sauté in hot oil in a pan. Add bay leaves, oregano, tomatoes, salt and pepper. Cover and simmer the mixture slowly for about 10 minutes or until all the vegetables are tender, stirring occasionally. Add cooked, drained beans. Simmer very slowly for 20-30 minutes. Meanwhile cook macaroni in boiling salted water for about 20 minutes, until tender, drain. Just before serving toss cooked macaroni lightly with melted butter and ½ cup of parmesan cheese. Cut salami into match strips, combine with bean mixture and macaroni. Serve sprinkled with chopped parsley and remaining parmesan cheese. Serves 8.

Eggplant à la Turque ••

2 medium size eggplants
1 onion, grated
2 teaspoons salt
¼ teaspoon freshly ground
   black pepper
approximately 2 table-
   spoons olive oil
1 tablespoon chopped
   parsley
1 tablespoon lemon juice

Remove the stem from eggplants and grill whole for 10 minutes or bake in a moderately hot oven (375°F.) for 30 minutes or until tender. Peel eggplants or cut into halves and scoop out the flesh. Put flesh through a mincer or mash in a bowl with a fork. Add the grated onion, salt, black pepper and beat until smooth. Add olive oil gradually and beat until the mixture is the consistency of mayonnaise, adding more oil if necessary. Stir in chopped parsley and lemon juice. Spoon into a serving bowl, chill and serve surrounded by rounds of black bread with which to scoop up and eat the purée. It also may be eaten with a fork with salad or used as a spread on crackers, toast or bread.

Greek Salad ••

1 large lettuce
1 bunch endive or other
   salad greens
2 tomatoes, cut into wedges
1 onion, finely chopped
2 dozen Greek olives
½ cup olive oil
2 tablespoons white
   vinegar
½ teaspoon salt
freshly ground black
   pepper
¼ teaspoon dry mustard
4 oz. feta cheese, diced
6 anchovy fillets

Tear the well washed and dried lettuce and endive into bite-size pieces and place in a large salad bowl. Add tomatoes, onion and olives. Beat together olive oil, vinegar, salt, pepper and mustard until blended. Toss dressing with the salad. Garnish with cheese and anchovy fillets. Serve immediately. Serves 6-8.

Pork and Veal Terrine.

Low Calorie Luncheon

for six people

Did you know that mushrooms have practically no calories? Did you suspect that lean chicken breasts can be baked in no fat at all and still remain juicy and full of flavour? This time the famous mustard from Dijon does the trick.

As salads are so often served to the calorie conscious,

Swedish Spinach Ring will be a welcome change, followed by Fresh Fruit with Yoghurt. Altogether a very pleasant Low Calorie Luncheon.

Wines: No wines for this lunch if dieting is very strict, otherwise a light hock or riesling type wine would be ideal.

Mushroom Prawn Salad
Chicken Dijon
Swedish Spinach Ring
Diet Rolls
Fresh Fruit with Yoghurt

Mushroom Prawn Salad •

1 lb. button mushrooms
2 tablespoons lemon
  juice
6 tablespoons olive oil
1-2 tablespoons vinegar
3 tablespoons finely
  chopped parsley
salt and pepper
2 lb. fresh prawns

Wash mushrooms, slice thinly and sprinkle with lemon juice. Beat together oil, vinegar, parsley and seasoning to taste. Sprinkle over mushrooms. Cover and chill for at least 2 hours. Serve piled on a dish and surround with peeled prawns. Serves 6.

Chicken Dijon • •

6 large chicken breasts
  or legs
salt and pepper
2 tablespoons Dijon
  mustard
approximately ½ cup
  mayonnaise
4 tablespoons grated
  Cheddar cheese

Season chicken with salt and pepper. Combine mustard with mayonnaise. Spread each piece with mustard mayonnaise and place in a shallow, lightly oiled baking dish. Sprinkle with cheese. Cover loosely with aluminium foil and bake in a hot oven (400°F.) for 30 minutes. (Allow 40 minutes if cooking legs). Remove foil, increase oven heat to very hot (450°F.) and bake a further 15 minutes until top is golden. Serves 6.

Swedish Spinach Ring • •

1 x 10 oz. packet frozen
  spinach
2 eggs
1 tablespoon (½ oz.) plain
  flour
1 cup milk
salt and pepper

Thaw spinach and drain off excess liquid. Chop spinach finely. Beat eggs with flour and add milk. Season well with salt and pepper to taste. Add spinach and stir well. Pour into a greased 7-inch ring tin or small bar tin and stand in a pan of water. Bake in a moderately slow oven (325°F.) for 40-50 minutes until set. Turn out onto a warm plate and serve.

Fresh Fruit with Yoghurt •

Select two varieties of fresh fruits in season (strawberries, Chinese gooseberries, peaches or any two suitable fruits) and serve chilled with the following topping.

1 cup skim milk
  yoghurt
1-2 tablespoons honey
1 teaspoon lemon juice
grated rind of
  ½ orange

Combine all ingredients. Serve chilled, spooned over prepared fresh fruits.

Jellied Avocado Consommé

Shower Teas
for twenty people

The custom of giving Shower parties for brides-to-be is a charming one and just as much fun for the hostess as for the guest of honour. It is usual to select a theme. The most popular is a Kitchen Tea, but usually one can be guided by the guest of honour who finds she is low on pantry stores, the cellar is bare, the bathroom needs brightening or she is mad about French cooking. If you are one of the hostesses planning a party for an old school chum about to be married, these party themes and menus will give you fresh thoughts on the kind of parties that are suitable for a Shower Tea.

A Kitchen Tea is probably the first choice for a Shower party. Guests bring pot holders, can openers, bowls, spoons, canisters—in fact anything that a new housewife is likely to need in the kitchen. But what to serve the guests? Here is a menu that is romantic and pretty, an afternoon tea shower.

Ham Canapés*
Cucumber Sandwiches
Asparagus Rolls
Semolina Cheesecake
Swedish Mazarines
Wedding Bells
Shower Cake

*Consult index for recipe.

Asparagus Rolls •

Follow recipe on page 66 using 1 small loaf of bread and 2 cans asparagus spears. The chicken spread may be omitted or thick mayonnaise may be used instead.

Semolina Cheesecake • •

Pastry:

1½ cups (6 oz.) plain flour	1 teaspoon castor sugar
pinch salt	1 egg yolk
3 oz. butter	

Filling:

2 oz. butter	¼ cup (1 oz.) ground almonds
½ cup (4 oz.) castor sugar	8 oz. cottage cheese
1 lemon	2 tablespoons semolina
2 eggs, separated	½ cup (3 oz.) raisins

Pastry: Sift flour and salt into a mixing bowl and rub in the butter until mixture resembles fine breadcrumbs. Add sugar and mix to a firm paste with beaten egg yolk. If necessary, add a little water. Chill. Roll out on a lightly floured board and line an 8-inch spring-form tin, pressing the pastry 1½-inches up side of tin. Press down well to remove any air bubbles and trim edges neatly.
For Filling: Cream butter and sugar until light and fluffy. Grate rind of lemon, squeeze and strain juice. Lightly beat egg yolks and mix with ground almonds, sieved cottage cheese, semolina, chopped raisins and the lemon rind and juice. Fold into creamed butter and sugar, then fold in stiffly beaten egg whites. Put filling into pastry lined tin and bake in a moderately slow oven (325°F.) for 50-60 minutes or until pastry is golden and filling is set. Remove side of tin, allow cake to cool on base. Chill before serving.

Swedish Mazarines • • •

Rich Short Crust Pastry:

1½ cups (6 oz.) plain flour	3 oz. softened butter
pinch salt	3 egg yolks
½ cup (4 oz.) castor sugar	

Cake Filling:

4 oz. butter	flavouring to taste (vanilla essence, lemon or orange juice or kirsch)
⅔ cup (5 oz.) castor sugar	
2 eggs, beaten	flaked almonds
1 cup (4 oz.) ground almonds	apricot jam or red currant jelly
¼ cup (1 oz.) plain flour	2 tablespoons ground almonds

Pastry: Sift flour with salt into a mixing bowl. Make a well in centre and in this, place sugar, butter and egg yolks. Using the fingertips pinch and work these ingredients together until well blended. Then draw in flour and knead lightly until smooth. Chill for 1 hour.

For Cake Filling: Cream butter and sugar until light and fluffy. Beat in eggs gradually and then stir in 4 oz. ground almonds, flour and flavouring.

For Mazarines: Set oven temperature at moderately hot (375°F.). Roll out pastry on a floured surface, cut into circles to fit greased tartlet tins, prick well and spoon in the cake mixture. Scatter flaked almonds over top and bake in a moderately hot oven (375°F.) for 12-15 minutes. As soon as they are cooked remove from tins and brush tops with hot sieved apricot jam or hot red currant jelly. Sprinkle with ground almonds which have been browned in a moderate oven (350°F.) for 8-10 minutes.

Cucumber Sandwiches •

1-2 cucumbers	4 oz. butter
1 loaf white bread, thinly sliced	salt and pepper

Peel cucumbers, slice thinly and put into a colander, sprinkle with 2 teaspoons salt. Press down with plate and leave to drain for 1 hour.

Spread slices of bread with butter. Drain cucumber thoroughly and place on half the bread slices. Season with salt and pepper. Cover with remaining bread slices. Remove the crusts from bread. Cut into quarters. Arrange on plates to serve. If preparing ahead of party, cover with clear plastic food wrap or aluminium foil and chill.

Note: These sandwiches may also be cut into heart shapes with a biscuit cutter.

Wedding Bells ••

3 oz. butter or margarine	1½ teaspoons baking powder
¾ cup (6 oz.) castor sugar	¼ teaspoon salt
1 egg	½ teaspoon each ginger, nutmeg and cinnamon
1 tablespoon milk	maraschino cherries to decorate
2½ cups (10 oz.) plain flour	

Nut Filling:

¼ cup (1½ oz.) firmly packed brown sugar	¾ cup (4 oz.) finely chopped hazelnuts or almonds
1 teaspoon butter	
3 teaspoons maraschino cherry syrup	

Cream butter and sugar until light and fluffy. Add egg and milk and beat well. Sift flour with baking powder, salt and spices and blend into creamed mixture. Form into a ball and chill for 1 hour.

Roll dough to ⅛-inch thickness on a floured surface and cut into rounds with a 2-inch cutter. Place on greased baking trays and put ½ teaspoon filling in the centre of each round. Chill if dough is too soft. Shape each into a 'bell' by folding sides over to meet filling, using a spatula. Make top of bell narrower than 'clapper' end. Place half a maraschino cherry at open end of each bell for the clapper. Bake in a moderate oven (350°F.) for 10-15 minutes.

For Nut Filling: Mix brown sugar, butter and cherry syrup. Stir in hazelnuts.

Shower Cake ••

4 oz. butter or margarine	2 cups (8 oz.) self-raising flour
¾ cup (6 oz.) castor sugar	pinch salt
finely grated rind of 1 lemon	½ teaspoon ground ginger
	½ cup milk
2 eggs	2 tablespoons chopped glacé ginger
1 tablespoon lemon juice	flaked almonds and silver cachous to decorate

Vienna Icing:

6 oz. butter	3 tablespoons lemon juice
4½ cups (1 lb. 6 oz.) icing sugar	few drops red food colouring

Grease two 8-inch sandwich tins. Set oven temperature at moderate (350°F.).

Cream butter, sugar and lemon rind until mixture is light and fluffy. Beat in eggs, one at a time, then stir in lemon juice. Sift flour, salt and ginger, fold into creamed mixture alternately with milk and glacé ginger. Spread into prepared tins and bake in a moderate oven (350°F.) for 25-30 minutes until a skewer inserted in the centre comes out clean. Cool on wire cooling racks.

Join cake with Vienna Icing. Reserve some of the icing and colour a deeper pink for piping the umbrella. Using a spatula and pale pink Vienna Icing cover side and top of cake. Lightly press flaked almonds around side of cake. With a ribbon pipe and the deep pink icing, pipe an umbrella design on top of cake (see picture). Pipe handle of umbrella using a small star pipe. For the rain-drops and bow use a writing pipe. Decorate the rain-drops with silver cachous.

For Vienna Icing: Cream butter, gradually add sifted icing sugar. Stir in lemon juice. Colour a pale pink with red food colouring.

Shower Cake.

Card Party
for eight men or four couples

When men are playing cards you would think they wouldn't know or care about eating. There comes a time in every card game, the hand is suddenly over and the outside world breaks through. Everyone is hungry. Sandwiches are always popular and, even if crab is too expensive, you could get away with corned beef and mustard providing there are no dry crusts. Moscow Piroshki, little bacon and onion pies, will be demolished in no time, they are easy to handle and definitely more-ish. Carpet bag sausages, as the name implies, is a variation of the famous steak. Provide plenty of paper napkins and a choice of mustards for dunking the sausages. Serve hot coffee and let everyone get back to the game, ready for a grand slam or royal flush.

Sesame Cheese Crisps
Crab Sandwiches*
Moscow Piroshki
Carpet Bag Sausages

*Consult index for recipe.

Sesame Cheese Crisps •

6 oz. butter	1 teaspoon salt
1½ cups finely grated tasty edam cheese	1 teaspoon paprika pepper pinch cayenne pepper
¼ cup grated parmesan cheese	2 tablespoons toasted sesame seeds
1½ cups (6 oz.) plain flour	

Cream butter and both cheeses together in a mixing bowl. Sift dry ingredients and stir into creamed butter with the sesame seeds. Form into a dough and roll into four logs, 1-inch in diameter. Chill at least 2 hours. Slice ¼-inch thick, place on baking trays and bake in a moderate oven (350°F.) for 12-15 minutes until golden. Cool on wire cooling racks and serve with drinks.

Moscow Piroshki • • •

Yeast Dough:

1 oz. compressed yeast	4 oz. butter
2½ tablespoons (2 oz.) sugar	2 teaspoons salt
3 cups (12 oz.) plain flour	1 egg yolk
½ pint milk	beaten egg to glaze

Filling:

3 large onions	8 oz. speck or bacon
2 oz. butter	1 teaspoon white pepper

In a small bowl combine yeast and ½ tablespoon sugar. Stir until yeast becomes liquid. Sprinkle with 1 teaspoon of the flour and leave in a warm place. Place milk, butter, salt and remaining sugar in a saucepan. Heat gently until lukewarm stirring occasionally. Sift remaining flour into a large mixing bowl. Make a well in the centre and pour in the milk mixture, yeast mixture and lightly beaten egg yolk. Stir with wooden spoon, gradually incorporating the flour. Beat dough with a wooden spoon or your hand for 3 minutes until smooth and elastic. Sprinkle a little flour on the top, cover and place in a warm place until double in bulk, about 1 hour.
For Filling: Chop onions and fry in butter until golden. Cool. Chop speck very finely and mix with onion and pepper.

Turn dough out onto a floured board, knead lightly and take large tablespoon-size pieces of dough. Place 1 teaspoon of the filling on dough, fold edge over to enclose filling and mould into little balls. Place on lightly greased baking trays and leave in a warm place to rise for 15 minutes. Brush with beaten egg and bake in a very hot oven (450°F.) for 10-15 minutes until golden and cooked. Slide rolls on to a clean tea towel to keep warm. Serve hot.
Note: Piroshki are best served hot. If necessary, reheat in an aluminium foil parcel in a moderate oven (350°F.) for 10-15 minutes.

Carpet Bag Sausages • •

2 lb. sausages	12 oz. bacon
3 dozen oysters	

Put sausages into a pan of cold water, bring to the boil and simmer for 5 minutes. Drain and cool slightly.

Halve sausages, slit down the centre, insert 1 oyster in each. Remove rind from bacon and wrap the bacon around sausages. Secure with toothpick. Place in one layer in a baking dish and bake in a moderate oven (350°F.) for 20-25 minutes until sausages are hot and bacon crisp. Drain and serve. Provide toothpicks or cocktail forks for easy eating.

Canneloni

Card Party

for eight people

There are different kinds of card parties. There's the one when a little gossip is exchanged and conversation flows as freely as the cards, all light hearted fun. There is also the card game that some dread and others thrive on, the serious game when wit and skill are involved, and money is at stake.

My mother loved card parties and catered for them to perfection. At an early age I was given special jobs and learnt that card players are very particular about the food they eat and if tempers are to remain even the food has to be good. Today there are many aids for keeping this kind of food in good condition—clear plastic food wraps and plastic airtight containers to keep crisp food crisp, warming ovens to keep hot food hot. Make good use of them to keep food in peak condition.

Allow for the savoury and sweet tooths. Provide variety, and make sure the coffee is hot, strong and plentiful. For making good coffee, see recipe page

Cheese Caraway Crisps*
Crab or Chicken Sandwiches
Swiss Ham Triangles
Walnut Sables
Avocado Sandwiches*
Cherry Walnut Ring

*Consult index for recipe.

Crab Sandwiches •

1 x 7 oz. can king crab	salt and pepper
2 tablespoons mayonnaise	8 slices bread
squeeze of lemon juice	butter
good pinch dry mustard	crisp shredded lettuce
few drops hot pepper sauce	

Flake crab and combine with mayonnaise. Flavour with a squeeze of lemon juice, mustard and hot pepper sauce. Season to taste with salt and pepper. Butter 8 slices of bread and top with shredded lettuce. Place crab mixture on top and cover with the remaining bread slices. Cut each sandwich diagonally into four to serve. Makes 16.

Chicken Sandwiches •

Make as for crab sandwiches, substituting 1 cup finely chopped cooked chicken for crab and omit mustard.

Swiss Ham Triangles ••

8 oz. ham	8 oz. commercial puff pastry
1 teaspoon dry mustard	
2-3 tablespoons mayonnaise	1 egg yolk beaten with 1 teaspoon water to glaze
salt and pepper	

Chop ham very finely. Blend mustard with 2 tablespoons mayonnaise and add to ham. Season with salt and pepper to taste. If mixture is dry, stir in remaining mayonnaise. Roll out pastry on a lightly floured board to a 16-inch square. Trim edges and cut the pastry into 4-inch squares. Brush edges with egg glaze. Place 2 generous teaspoons of ham filling on each square and fold over to form triangles. Place on lightly greased baking trays. Brush tops with egg glaze and bake in a hot oven (400°F.) for 20 minutes. Serve warm. Makes 16 triangles.

Walnut Sables ••

Follow recipe for Cheese Sables on page 86, brush top with beaten egg, then sprinkle with coarsely chopped walnuts and a little salt. Bake as described in recipe.

Cherry Walnut Ring ••

4 oz. butter	$\frac{1}{2}$ cup halved glacé cherries
$\frac{1}{2}$ cup (4 oz.) castor sugar	
2 eggs	$\frac{1}{2}$ cup chopped walnuts
1$\frac{1}{2}$ cups (6 oz.) self-raising flour	1-2 tablespoons milk
pinch salt	icing sugar

Grease an 8-inch ring tin and set oven temperature at moderate (350°F.).

Cream butter in a mixing bowl, add sugar and beat well until mixture is light and fluffy. Add lightly beaten eggs gradually, mixing well. Sift flour with salt and mix 2 tablespoons with the prepared cherries and walnuts. Fold flour, cherries and walnuts and milk into creamed mixture. Put mixture into prepared tin and bake in a moderate oven (350°F.) for 1-1$\frac{1}{4}$ hours. Cool. Sprinkle top with icing sugar if liked before serving.

Piroshki.

International Parties

Curry Party
for eight to ten people

Entertaining with curry is one way to be a relaxed hostess. The truth is that it is not only possible to prepare curries ahead, it is better to do so. Two or three days under refrigeration makes a good curry a superb one. Flavours mix and blend and mellow, with delicious results. Accompaniments may be made in advance too and kept well chilled. Poppadums, of course, should be stored in airtight containers to keep them perfectly crisp. If they do get a little soft they can be crisped up in a moderate oven for a few minutes.

For your curry party, let your pre-dinner nibbles hint at the meal to follow. Serve crunchy devilled nuts, crisp poppadum strips, fried prawn crisps. The recipe for devilled almonds (page 28) may be adapted to use cashews. Break poppadums into quarters or cut three or four at a time into strips. Fry only two or three of these strips at a time in ½-inch hot oil for just a second or two until they turn a pale golden colour. Drain on absorbent paper. Prawn crisps are delicious, airy morsels. You can buy them at some delicatessens or food halls or at Chinese grocery stores. They come in a variety of colours. These puff and swell and curl into fascinating shapes and become pastel shades of the colours they start out with. Again, they need only a few seconds frying in deep hot oil and may be prepared ahead and stored in airtight containers.

The best drink to serve with curry is a light lager, but if you want to have a choice, a wine-based drink like Sangria would be preferable to even the best wine. In fact, do not serve beautiful wines with curry. Both loose by the confrontation.

Wines: Not necessary but offer a light rosé wine or a light chilled dinner ale.

Gimlet*
Curried Walnuts, Devilled
Cashews
Fried Poppadum Strips and
Prawn Crisps
Spiced Chicken
Curried Rice
Accompaniments
Chilled Fruit Compote

*Consult index for recipe.

Spiced Chicken served on Curried Rice, garnished with peas and accompaniments

Spiced Chicken ••

8 whole chicken breasts
4 oz. ghee or butter
1 onion, finely chopped
Marinade:
2 cups plain yoghurt
2 cloves garlic, crushed
1 onion, grated
2 tablespoons ground
  coriander
2 tablespoons ground
  almonds

1 clove garlic, crushed
8 whole cardamom pods
3-inch stick cinnamon

2 teaspoons finely
  chopped fresh ginger
2 teaspoons salt
1 teaspoon turmeric
½ teaspoon black
  pepper

Allow 1 whole chicken breast per person. Remove all bones except the main breastbone. Combine all ingredients for the marinade, add chicken and allow to marinate for 2 hours.

Melt 2 oz. ghee in a frying pan and sauté onion, garlic, cardamom pods and cinnamon for 5 minutes. Transfer to a buttered baking dish. Spoon as much of the marinade as possible from the chicken. Place chicken in the baking dish, dot with ghee, place in a hot oven (400°F.) until golden. Pour the marinade over chicken. Cover and continue cooking until chicken is tender, about 30 minutes. Serve with curried rice. Serves 8. **Note:** If whole chicken breasts are not available, use 2 x 3 lb. chickens cut into serving pieces.

Curried Rice ••

4 oz. ghee or butter
2 onions, finely sliced
1 teaspoon turmeric
2 teaspoons curry powder
2 lb. long grain rice
6½ cups chicken stock or
  water and chicken
  stock cubes

12 peppercorns
4 cloves
8 bruised cardamom pods
1 tablespoon salt
1 stick cinnamon
2 cups cooked peas

Heat ghee in saucepan. Fry half onions until golden brown, add turmeric and curry powder and stir well for a minute. Add rice and fry a few minutes, stirring, until it is golden in colour. Add boiling stock, spices, salt and remaining onions.

Stir well, cover tightly and cook on a very low heat for 20 minutes. Turn off heat, keep covered until ready to serve. A few minutes before serving uncover the pan to allow steam to escape. Fluff up with fork. Garnish with peas. Serves 8-10.

Accompaniments •

Cucumbers in Sour Cream: Peel and slice 3 cucumbers very thinly, sprinkle with salt and let stand for at least 20-30 minutes. Pour off all the liquid that collects, pressing out as much as possible. Mix into 1 carton sour cream a clove of garlic, crushed, and ½ teaspoon finely grated fresh ginger. Stir in a few drops of lemon juice. Combine with the cucumbers and chill before serving. If liked, sprinkle with a little paprika pepper.
Coconut Sambol: In a bowl combine ¾ cup desiccated coconut, 2-3 tablespoons hot milk, 1 small onion,

chopped, and lemon juice and salt to taste. Add enough paprika pepper to give a bright pink colour and, if a hot sambol is desired, a pinch of chilli powder. Mix well together and pile in a small bowl.
Tomato and Mint Chutney: Scald and peel 4 firm red tomatoes. Dice them and mix with 4 tablespoons chopped mint, 2 tablespoons lemon juice, salt to taste and, if liked, a dash of hot pepper sauce or a pinch of chilli powder. Serve chilled.
Fresh Pineapple Pieces: Remove skin, core and 'eyes' from a ripe pineapple and cut flesh into large cubes. Sprinkle lightly with salt, mix and chill. If liked, dust lightly with cayenne pepper or paprika pepper.
Poppadums: These spicy lentil wafers are bought in packets and need only to be fried in ½-inch hot oil for 3-4 seconds. Fry them one at a time, using tongs to turn them over and lift them out. They increase in size and become crisp and golden. Drain on absorbent paper.

Commercial chutneys and pickles may also be served as accompaniments to a curry meal and may be presented in the original container (so they can be identified by their labels) with a long handled spoon.

Chilled Fruit Compote •

¼ cup (2 oz.) sugar
½ cup orange juice
1 tablespoon lemon juice
3-inch stick cinnamon
6 cardamom pods

½ cup water
4 lb. watermelon
1 canteloup melon
1 honeydew melon
2 lb. seedless grapes

Combine sugar, fruit juice, spices and water. Bring to the boil and simmer for 5 minutes. Chill syrup. Remove spices before adding to fruit.

Scoop balls from watermelon, discarding as many seeds as possible. Halve cantaloup and honeydew melon, remove seeds and scoop flesh into balls. Pick washed grapes from stems. Combine fruit and syrup and chill for several hours. Serve in individual glasses or large glass bowl. Serves 8-10.

Ingredients for Fried Rice can be prepared ahead and stored in the refrigerator in an airtight container, ready to put together before serving.

Italian Style Buffet Dinner

for six to eight people

Despite the fact that everyone knows there is more to Italian food than spaghetti, this meal is planned around the choice of two superb pasta dishes. There seems no use avoiding a dish for which Italy has become justly proud, and, as both suggestions have equal merit, I leave it to you to see which stuffing you use for the Cannelloni.

The desserts one finds in Italian restaurants are invariably a slice of some showy cake to display the skills of the confectioner and pastry-cook. Italian pastry-cooks are famous throughout the world. In the home, the sweet dishes are no less delectable, but much more restrained. Oranges in wine is an example of the best kind of home-style Italian dessert, using fruit in season and cooking it in the wine of the region, displaying economy with originality and character.

Wines: Dry vermouth or campari on the rocks with a twist of lemon as an appetizer. A chianti wine or chablis or hock with the Cannelloni, or offer a light claret. Port or muscat with the dessert.

Artichokes in Sour Cream
Canneloni
or
Canneloni alla Nerone
Green Salad*
Spiced Orange Slices in Red Wine*

*Consult index for recipe.

Canneloni ••

12 large canneloni tubes
2 tablespoons oil
2 cloves garlic, crushed
2 x 16 oz. cans whole
    tomatoes
2 teaspoons sugar
⅔ cup tomato purée
Filling:
1 tablespoon oil
2 lb. minced steak
¼ teaspoon thyme
salt and pepper
6 shallots, chopped

1 cup water
salt and pepper
½ teaspoon dried oregano
1 bay leaf
4 oz. thinly sliced
    mozzarella or Swiss
    cheese

2 tablespoons (1 oz.)
    plain flour
1 cup beef stock or water
    and beef stock cube
½ cup tomato purée

For Filling: Prepare the filling first. Heat oil in a saucepan and quickly brown minced steak. Add thyme, 2 teaspoons salt, ¼ teaspoon pepper, shallots, flour and finally the stock and tomato purée. Cook until blended, stirring occasionally, about 15 minutes. Cool.

Cook canneloni for 10 minutes in a large pan of rapidly boiling salted water to which 1 tablespoon of oil has been added. Drain and rinse with cold water. Spoon or pipe filling into canneloni.

Heat oil and lightly sauté crushed garlic without browning. Add tomatoes (with liquid from cans), sugar, tomato purée, water, 1 teaspoon salt, freshly ground pepper to taste, oregano and bay leaf. Simmer 15 minutes and, if necessary, add more salt, sugar or pepper to taste. Spoon a little sauce into a shallow baking dish. Arrange filled canneloni on top and cover with remaining sauce. Top with cheese and bake in a moderately hot oven (375°F.) for 30 minutes. Serves 6-8.

Canneloni alla Nerone •••

6 chicken breasts, boned
6 oz. butter
1 lb. chicken livers
10 slices ham
2 cups grated parmesan
    cheese
½ cup (2 oz.) plain flour

2 pints milk
1 cup cream
¼ teaspoon white pepper
salt
12 large canneloni tubes
extra butter

In a frying pan, sauté the chicken breasts in 2 oz. butter until they are lightly browned. Sauté chicken livers briefly in the same pan. Mince the chicken breasts, livers and ham, using finest blade, or chop very finely. Add 1 cup of the grated cheese and mix in.

Melt remaining butter in a saucepan, add flour and stir over heat 1-2 minutes. Heat milk until bubbles form on top and gradually whisk into the flour and butter, stirring vigorously. Cook over low heat, stirring until thickened. Add cream and season with white pepper and salt to taste. Add about 1 cup sauce to the chicken mixture and combine thoroughly.

113

Cook canneloni in a large pan of boiling salted water for 10 minutes. Spoon or pipe about 2 tablespoons chicken filling into each tube. Arrange canneloni in two layers in one or two buttered baking dishes. Sprinkle with some of the remaining cheese and cover with some of the reserved sauce. This preparation may be done ahead. Dot the top of dish with small pieces of additional butter and bake in a moderate oven (350°F.) until tops are lightly browned, about 30 minutes. Serves 6-8.
Note: If canneloni tubes are unavailable, place the filling into pancakes (see recipe for Basic Crêpes on page 96). Roll up and cook as described above. Serves 6-8.

Artichokes in Sour Cream •

3 x 16 oz. cans artichoke hearts	1 tablespoon paprika pepper
1 x 1½ oz. can flat anchovy fillets	4 oz. grated parmesan cheese

Drain artichoke hearts, put into a well greased baking dish. Drain anchovy fillets, soak in a little milk for 20 minutes. Arrange on top of artichokes. Cover with sour cream and sprinkle with paprika pepper and cheese. Bake in a moderate oven (350°F.) for 30 minutes. Serves 6-8.

(a) Prepare the filling for Canneloni and when cool, spoon or pipe into the cooked and cooled pasta tubes.

(b) Arrange the pasta in an ovenproof dish, and spoon the sauce over top, making sure the pasta is coated with the sauce to prevent it drying out in the oven.

(c) Thinly sliced Swiss cheese is placed on top before baking.

Chinese Meal

for eight people

There is no such thing as a 'main' dish in Chinese cooking, a meal consists of several dishes and all are equally important. The food should contrast both in texture and flavour. The number of dishes you prepare will depend on the number of guests, allow one dish for each guest. The menu given is for eight people. If you invite more, simply add one or two more dishes from your favourite recipes.

The food is arranged on serving dishes in the centre of the table and guests help themselves, using serving chopsticks (or a serving spoon may be provided). Offer Chinese tea throughout the meal. Alcoholic beverages may be served, although wine does not complement the food and vice versa. Beer is popular with the men.

Unless you have had a great deal of experience in Chinese cooking, practise on the family first, cooking two or three dishes at a time.

The Won Ton are not essential, but they are a good start to the party. They are ideal to serve with drinks.

These Won Ton can be prepared the evening before the party and stored in sealed containers, each layer separated with absorbent paper. Fry just before serving. Won Ton skins are available from some Chinese Restaurants.

Have the rice ready and begin cooking just before the guests are seated. The cold platter can be already in the refrigerator for serving. The Chicken with Olive Nuts and the beef dish can be prepared, ready to fry, both only take a matter of seconds. The abalone also can be prepared and cooked, ready to reheat and serve. Pork chops are easy, they simply cook in the oven in the aromatic marinade.

In Chinese cuisine, soup is generally served toward the end of the meal, it may be prepared early in the day. Dessert is not necessary, but the colourful canned Oriental fruits are an excellent finale to a meal. Serve chilled.

*Fried Won Ton with
Sweet and Sour Sauce*

or

*Appetiser Platter
Chicken and Olive Nuts
Abalone with Oyster Sauce
Braised Chinese Vegetables
Sliced Beef with Celery
Shredded Vegetable and
Noodle Soup
Barbecued Pork Chops
Steamed Rice
Fried Rice
Loquats and Longans
Chinese Tea*

Fried Won Ton ● ● ●

These crisp, savoury filled pastry squares may be served as an hors d'oeuvre with the sauce placed alongside for dipping.

4 oz. pork fillet	1 teaspoon sugar
4 oz. raw prawns	2 teaspoons dark soy
6 canned water chestnuts	sauce
4 shallots	½ teaspoon monosodium
3 dried mushrooms, soaked	glutamate
in warm water for	8 oz. won ton skins
20 minutes	beaten egg white
3 teaspoons salt	oil for frying

Finely chop pork, prawns, water chestnuts, shallots and mushrooms (stalks removed) until mixture resembles fine minced steak. Season with salt, sugar, soy sauce and monosodium glutamate, mixing thoroughly.

Using a chopstick place ½ teaspoon mixture on one corner of each square of pastry and, holding the square of pastry in the left hand, roll dough over filling with the aid of the chopstick until half way, then dampen opposite corners with egg white and join together. Keep unused pastry squares covered with a damp cloth while preparing the won ton. A simple way to fill pastry squares is to place ½ teaspoon filling in centre, dampen two sides with egg white and fold other side over to form a triangle.

Deep fry won ton in hot oil until golden and filling is cooked. Drain and serve hot with Sweet and Sour Sauce for dipping.

Note: Won Ton skins are available from Chinese food stores and some Chinese restaurants when ordered in advance.

Sweet and Sour Sauce ●

½ cup (4 oz.) sugar	2 tablespoons tomato sauce
4 tablespoons white vinegar	1 teaspoon salt
1 tablespoon light soy	approximately 1 table-
sauce	spoon cornflour

Put sugar, vinegar, soy sauce, tomato sauce and salt into a small saucepan. Bring to the boil and stir in 1 tablespoon cornflour blended with a little cold water. Stir until clear and thickened. If sauce is too thin stir in a little more blended cornflour.

Appetiser Platter ● ●

A colourful arrangement of finely sliced, well flavoured foods can be prepared well in advance, covered and stored in the refrigerator. Choose four or more of the following depending on the occasion.

Soy Eggs: Boil 4 eggs for 8 minutes. Soak in cold water and remove shells. Heat 2 tablespoons soy sauce, 1 teaspoon each sugar and concentrated sesame oil and 2 tablespoons water. Add eggs and simmer for 5 minutes over a low heat. Remove from heat and leave for 30 minutes, turning eggs in mixture occasionally. Cut into quarters to serve.

Barbecued Pork: Slice barbecued pork thinly and mix with 2 teaspoons light soy sauce and a few drops concentrated sesame oil. Barbecued pork can be purchased from Chinese food stores. Ham may be used instead of pork.

Celery: String 3 stalks celery and cut into 1½-inch lengths, then shred finely, lengthwise. Combine 2 teaspoons light soy sauce, 2 teaspoons vinegar, ½ teaspoon each salt and sugar and a few drops concentrated sesame oil. Add celery and mix. Cover and chill.

Chicken: Use 3 large breasts and poach for 20-30 minutes in barely simmering water to which 1 teaspoon salt, 3 shallots and 2 slices green ginger have been added. Cool chicken in liquid. Remove chicken, discard skin and bones and slice the flesh. Sprinkle with 4 tablespoons Chinese wine or dry sherry and leave for 30 minutes. Drain off sherry and add a few drops sesame oil, 2 teaspoons light soy sauce and ½ teaspoon grated ginger. Pour over chicken.

Mushrooms: Select 15-20 large dried mushrooms. Soak in warm water for 20 minutes. Drain, cut off stems. Heat 2 tablespoons peanut oil, add mushrooms and fry 1 minute. Add ½ teaspoon grated ginger, 2 teaspoons sugar, 2 teaspoons soy sauce, ½ teaspoon salt and ½ cup chicken stock or water. Cover and simmer for 25 minutes, until liquid has almost been absorbed. Cool and serve whole or in slices.

Other ingredients which may be added are: peeled prawns, canned baby leeks, sliced Chinese salami, sliced canned abalone, peeled and sliced cucumber and sliced canned bamboo shoots.

Chicken and Olive Nuts ● ●

4 oz. olive nuts	pinch salt
oil for deep frying	2 tablespoons water
2 lb. chicken breasts	2 teaspoons peanut oil
1 egg white	2 shallots
1½ tablespoons cornflour	1-inch piece green
pinch bicarbonate of soda	ginger
Sauce:	
1 teaspoon soy sauce	pinch pepper
½ teaspoon sugar	few drops concentrated
½ teaspoon cornflour	sesame oil
1 tablespoon chicken	1 teaspoon brandy
stock or water	

Boil olive nuts in water for 5 minutes, then drain. Heat 2 tablespoons oil in a wok or frying pan and fry nuts for about 1 minute or until nuts are a pale brown. Remove and keep aside.

Bone chicken and slice into pieces 2½-inches long, 1-inch wide and $\frac{1}{16}$-inch thick. Put into a bowl, add egg white and mix well with chopsticks or spoon, then add cornflour, bicarbonate of soda, salt, water and peanut oil. Mix thoroughly and allow to stand 15 minutes. Cut shallots into 1-inch lengths. Peel and thinly slice ginger.

For Sauce: Mix all the sauce ingredients well together in a small bowl. Heat ½ cup oil in wok or frying pan and add chicken. Cook for 2 minutes or until golden brown. Remove from wok and keep warm. Drain oil, leaving about 1 tablespoon in wok. Heat oil, add shallots and ginger. Add cooked chicken, sauce and mix thoroughly in wok for 1 minute. Add olive nuts, mix and serve immediately.

Note: Olive nuts are available from Chinese food stores in major cities. Blanched almonds, peeled walnuts or raw cashews may be used instead.

Abalone with Oyster Sauce •

1 x 16 oz. can abalone
1 tablespoon peanut oil
1 clove garlic, crushed
3 teaspoons Chinese
   oyster sauce

2 teaspoons cornflour
$\frac{1}{2}$ cup chicken stock
salt
lettuce leaves for
   serving

Drain abalone and slice thinly. Heat oil in a saucepan, add garlic and cook gently without browning. Add abalone slices and the oyster sauce. Stir for 5 minutes. Blend cornflour with chicken stock, add to pan and cook, stirring until mixture boils and thickens. Simmer for 2 minutes and add salt if necessary. Serve hot on a bed of lettuce.

Note: Chinese oyster sauce is a concentrate of oysters cooked in soy and brine. It is used to intensify the flavour of food and can be purchased from Chinese stores.

Braised Chinese Vegetables •

1 Chinese cabbage
1 small red and 1 green
   pepper
8 canned water chestnuts
3 tablespoons peanut oil
1-inch piece green ginger
3 tablespoons chicken
   stock or water and
   chicken stock cube

1 teaspoon salt
1 teaspoon sugar
2 teaspoons soy sauce
$\frac{1}{2}$ teaspoon monosodium
   glutamate

Wash cabbage and drain. Cut into 1-inch lengths. Cut peppers into strips and slice water chestnuts. Heat oil with sliced ginger in a large saucepan or frypan. Add cabbage, peppers and chestnuts and fry for 3 minutes. Add stock, then season with salt, sugar, soy sauce and monosodium glutamate. Mix well and simmer, covered, until vegetables are tender but still crisp. Remove ginger and serve hot.

Sliced Beef with Celery •

1 lb. rump steak
1$\frac{1}{2}$ teaspoons cornflour
2 teaspoons light soy
   sauce
1 egg white
pinch bicarbonate of soda
2 tablespoons peanut oil
Sauce:
1 teaspoon oyster sauce
1 teaspoon light soy sauce
$\frac{1}{4}$ teaspoon salt

1 teaspoon dark soy
   sauce
$\frac{1}{3}$ cup water
1-inch piece green ginger
1 shallot
2 stalks celery
peanut oil for frying

$\frac{1}{4}$ teaspoon sugar
1 tablespoon water

Trim fat off steak and cut the meat finely across the grain. Put into a bowl with cornflour, light soy sauce, egg white, bicarbonate of soda, 2 tablespoons peanut oil, dark soy sauce and water. Mix thoroughly, beating with chopsticks or spoon, until meat absorbs the liquid. Set aside for 30 minutes. Peel and thinly slice ginger, cut shallot into 1-inch lengths. String celery, cut into 2-inch lengths, then slice each lengthwise into fine strips.

For Sauce: Combine all ingredients for sauce in a

small bowl.

   Heat $\frac{1}{4}$ cup oil in wok or frying pan. Add beef and cook for 1$\frac{1}{2}$ minutes, stirring constantly. Remove beef and add ginger, shallot and celery to wok. Cook for 30 seconds, return beef and add the sauce. Cook for a further 30 seconds. Serve immediately.

Shredded Vegetables and Noodle Soup •

2 stalks celery
4 shallots
1 canned bamboo shoot
4-6 oz. ham
8 oz. fine egg noodles

6 cups chicken stock
   or water and chicken
   stock cubes
salt and pepper

String celery, cut into 2-inch lengths, then shred finely. Cut shallots, bamboo shoot and ham the same way. Cook bundles of noodles in a large saucepan of boiling salted water, separating with chopsticks or a fork, for 3-5 minutes until tender. Drain and spread on a tray to keep strands separate. Heat stock, add noodles, vegetables and ham and simmer for 2-3 minutes. Season to taste with salt and pepper.

Note: If liked, strips of raw chicken breast may be cooked in the soup. Add to the stock with the noodles.

Barbecued Pork Chops •

This pungent pork dish is simply made with pieces of pork chop marinated and then baked in a spicy sauce.

2 lb. pork loin chops
2 teaspoons Chinese wine
   or dry sherry
$\frac{1}{2}$ teaspoon salt
2 teaspoons light soy
   sauce
1-inch piece green ginger,
   finely chopped

2 shallots, finely
   chopped
1 tablespoon hoi sin
   sauce
pinch five spice powder
1 large onion, sliced
2 tablespoons peanut oil

Bone pork chops, trim away rind and cut each chop into four pieces. Put into a bowl and mix with wine, salt, soy sauce, ginger, shallots, hoi sin sauce and spice powder. Allow to marinate for 30 minutes. Put chops and mixture into a baking dish and bake in a moderate oven (350°F.) for 45 minutes, turning once. Fry sliced onion in oil, but do not colour. Drain well, spoon onto a serving plate and place pork chops on top. Serve immediately.

Steamed Rice Chinese Style •

Wash 1 lb. rice in cold water several times until water runs clear. Put rice in a heavy saucepan and add cold water to come approximately $\frac{3}{4}$-inch above level of rice. Bring to boil, then lower heat to medium and continue cooking until water has almost evaporated and holes form in the rice mass. Reduce heat to lowest point, cover with a tight fitting lid and steam for 15-20 minutes until rice is tender. Do not stir during cooking.

117

Fried Rice •

4 oz. barbecued pork
   or ham
6 dried mushrooms, soaked
   in warm water for 20
   minutes
6 tablespoons peanut oil
3 eggs, beaten
5-6 shallots, chopped
8 oz. small prawns, peeled
   (optional)

6 cups cold cooked rice
salt
1 cup cooked peas
¼ cup chicken stock or
   water
1 tablespoon sherry
2-3 teaspoons soy sauce

Cut pork and mushrooms into small squares. Heat 2 tablespoons oil in a wok or large frying pan and fry eggs in a flat pancake, turn over and cook other side. Remove and cut into shreds. Heat remaining oil and fry shallots, prawns, pork and mushrooms. Add rice and gently mix. Season to taste with salt and add fried egg and peas. Combine stock, sherry and soy sauce, sprinkle over rice, mix well and serve hot.

Loquats and Longans •

Canned Loquats and Longans are imported from China and can be purchased from good supermarkets and Chinese food stores. Serve chilled, topped with a few slices of glacé ginger.

Chinese Tea

The delicate fragrance of Chinese tea harmonises perfectly with the flavour of Chinese food and is the best beverage to serve with it. Tea may be drunk before, during and after the meal. It cleanses and refreshes the palate ready for the next course.

Chinese teas come in many different aromas, the three main types being green tea, black tea and oolong. Often teas are blended with fresh or dried flowers to make scented teas. Jasmine tea is the best known. When properly brewed Chinese tea is clear, very pale in colour, with a fine bouquet. Never add sugar, milk or cream to Chinese tea.

To make Chinese tea in a pot:
Pour boiling water into teapot, preferably a porcelain pot kept specially for Chinese tea. Empty pot, then measure ½-1 small teaspoon tea for every cup of water. Pour in the boiling water. Cover and steep for 3-5 minutes.

To brew tea in a teacup:
Scald teacups and drain. Use about ½ teaspoon tea, no more, for each cup. Pour in 1 tablespoon boiling water. Cover and infuse for 1 minute. Fill cup with boiling water and let steep about 2 minutes.

(a) To make Fried Won Ton, a little of the filling is placed on each won ton skin.
(b) Holding the square of pastry in the left hand roll the pastry over filling with the aid of a chopstick until half way, then dampen opposite corners with egg white and join. The won ton are then deep fried in hot oil.

French Dinner

for six to eight people

Wherever one travels in the world looking for something more than the mere satisfaction of hunger, the word 'France' is synonymous with perfection. If I am invited to a good French dinner, I find myself planning imaginary menus, mentally debating the merits of one dish against another and what wines will be served—all in anticipation!

Planning a French meal is tremendous fun. If you know how to cook and you love cooking, you will know that the aim in French cooking is perfection. Selecting a menu that will not tax your skills or your purse-strings is important. This is such a menu, simple food from the provinces and an elegant restaurant type dessert to finish the meal.

Wines: Serve a fruity red Burgundy with the Coq au Vin, also with the cheese or consider a good port wine, and Champagne with the Strawberries Romanoff.

Potage Parmentier

or

Cream of Watercress Soup

Coq au Vin

Parsley Potatoes

Green Peas with Cream

Cheese Board

Strawberries Romanoff

with

Almond Lace Biscuits

or

Pears in Burgundy

Potage Parmentier ••

4 leeks	1½ pints water
1 small onion, finely chopped	1 teaspoon salt
	white pepper
2 oz. butter	1 pint hot milk
4 large potatoes, peeled and cut into large cubes	2 egg yolks
	¼ pint cream

Halve leeks lengthwise, wash thoroughly to remove all grit, then finely chop the white parts of the leeks. Place in a large saucepan with the onion and butter. Cover and cook slowly until soft but not brown. Stir in the potatoes, then add water, salt and pepper. Bring to the boil and simmer gently for about 30 minutes or until potatoes are soft. Press through a fine sieve or purée in a blender. Add milk. Correct seasoning and heat gently. Mix egg yolks with the cream and combine with a little hot soup then add to soup, stirring all the time. Do not allow soup to boil after adding the egg yolk mixture. Serves 6-8.

Note: If preparing soup in advance do not add egg yolks and cream until just before serving.

Cream of Watercress Soup ••

1 lb. potatoes	1 oz. butter
1½ pints water	1 tablespoon finely chopped parsley
¾ pint milk, scalded	¼ pint cream
salt	
1 bunch watercress	

Peel potatoes and cut into small pieces. Place potatoes into a saucepan, cover with water and boil for 15-20 minutes. Do not drain but mash them in the saucepan with the cooking liquid. Add the milk and season with salt. Trim the stems from the watercress and wash the leaves well. Add the watercress leaves to the soup and cook for 10 minutes. Just before serving add the butter, parsley and cream. Serves 6-8.

Coq au Vin • • •

2 x 3 lb. chickens	salt and pepper
5 oz. butter	1½ pints red wine
2 large onions	bouquet garni
6 oz. bacon	8 oz. button mushrooms,
3 cloves garlic	(optional)
2 tablespoons tomato	cornflour
paste	

Cut chickens into serving portions. Heat butter in a
frying pan and fry chicken, turning with two spoons,
until golden on all sides. Put into a fireproof casserole or
heavy based saucepan. Slice onions and cut bacon into
small pieces. Add to frying pan and cook until golden.
Add chopped garlic, then stir in tomato paste. Add to
chicken in casserole and season with salt and pepper.
Add wine and bouquet garni. Cook gently, covered, for
30 minutes until chicken is tender.

Lift chicken out of pan and put on a serving plate.
Keep warm. Add washed mushrooms to liquid in pan
and boil gently until liquid has reduced a little. Thicken
with a little cornflour blended with cold water and add
more seasoning if necessary. Pour over chicken and serve
hot with Parsley Potatoes. Serves 6-8.

Parsley Potatoes •

Scrub 3 lb. tiny new potatoes and put into a saucepan
with boiling salted water to cover. Cook with lid on for 25
minutes or until tender. Drain and peel if liked. Add 3 oz.
butter, salt and freshly ground pepper to taste, 3 tablespoons chopped parsley and toss over medium heat until
potatoes are well coated with the butter. Serves 6-8.

Green Peas with Cream •

3 lb. peas, shelled	1 oz. butter
½ teaspoon salt	4 tablespoons cream
1 teaspoon sugar	

Cook peas in 3 cups of boiling salted water for 20 minutes
or until tender. Drain.

Place salt, sugar and butter into a saucepan and add
cooked peas and cream, shaking together until well
combined. Serves 6-8.

Note: Frozen peas may be substituted and cooked
according to direction on package.

Strawberries Romanoff •

8 pieces loaf sugar	6 tablespoons curaçao
2 oranges	½ pint Cream Chantilly
2 punnets strawberries	
Cream Chantilly:	
½ pint cream	vanilla essence to
sugar to taste	flavour

Rub lumps of sugar over the skins of oranges until they
are well impregnated with the flavour of the fruit. Crush
sugar. Wash and hull strawberries. Macerate them in
curaçao and sugar in a covered container in refrigerator
until serving time. Arrange in a serving bowl in a pyramid
shape. Put Cream Chantilly into a piping bag with a rose
or star piping tube and decorate the strawberries with
rosettes of cream. Serve immediately with Almond Lace
Biscuits. Serves 6-8.

For Cream Chantilly: Whip the chilled cream with sugar
to taste until firm. Fold in vanilla essence to taste.

Note: Alternatively, the strawberries may be spooned
into individual dishes with the cream in a separate bowl
for guests to help themselves.

Almond Lace Biscuits • • •
(Almond Tuiles)

These delicate little biscuits are marvellous to serve with
a dessert. They require practice in making but are worth
the trouble. The almonds must be cut into very fine slivers.

3 oz. butter	⅓ cup (1½ oz.) plain flour
⅓ cup (3 oz.) castor	2½ oz. very finely slivered
sugar	almonds

Brush baking trays liberally with melted butter. Set oven
temperature at hot (400°F.).

Cream butter and sugar until light and fluffy. Stir in the
sifted flour, then the almonds. Put teaspoonfuls of
mixture onto prepared baking trays allowing room for
spreading. Make only three biscuits at a time. Flatten top
with a fork dipped in water and bake in a hot oven
(400°F.) until just coloured around the edges, 3-5
minutes. Allow to stand for a second or two before
removing from tray with a spatula or knife. Curve onto a
rolling pin, leave until set, then carefully lift biscuits onto
a wire cooling rack to cool. Store in an airtight tin. Makes
about 2 dozen.

Note: Bake one biscuit first to test the mixture. If
difficult to handle, add a teaspoon of flour, or if mixture
is too hard, add 1 teaspoon melted butter. If the biscuit
does not spread and turn a caramel golden colour in the
specified time, increase oven temperature another 25°F.

Pears in Burgundy •

1½ cups (12 oz.) sugar	scant ½ pint red
1 cinnamon stick	burgundy
½ pint water	6 small firm pears

Place sugar, cinnamon stick and water in a saucepan
and simmer, covered, for 15 minutes. Add wine. In
casserole place pears which have been peeled and kept
whole, cover with wine syrup and bake in a moderate
oven (350°F.) for 1-1½ hours. Place pears in a shallow
serving dish and boil syrup until reduced to consistency
of honey. Pour syrup over pears and chill. Serve very
cold. Serves 6.

Mediterranean Dinner

for six to eight people

The Mediterranean sea washes the shores of fifteen countries, all of which abound in a wealth of fresh fruits, vegetables, seafood and sunshine. These countries have given us wonderful dishes with beautiful colour and a flavour unique to Mediterranean cooking. There is a characteristic use of golden olive oil, pungent garlic, aromatic saffron, fresh vegetables—tomatoes, peppers and eggplants—citrus fruit, figs and melons.

This meal is expandable. For six guests, you can omit the Tiropetes, which would be served with pre-dinner drinks, for eight guests, increase the mandarins to eight, but use smaller fruit. Serve with Italian savoy fingers or similar crisp biscuits.

Wines: Dry Vermouth on the rocks with a twist of orange as an appetiser. Serve a light rosé wine from the south of France, or Chianti.

Tiropetes*
Prosciutto and Melon
or
Melon with Wine
Lamb Kebabs
Turkish Pilaf
Mandarin Gelato
or
Orange Gelato

*Consult index for recipe.

Prosciutto and Melon •

2 small cantaloup melons	black pepper
8 oz. prosciutto, thinly sliced	

Chill melons, cut each into six small wedges and remove seeds. The melon may be detached from the skin, if liked. Serve with thin slices of prosciutto. The prosciutto may be arranged over the melon or rolled into neat cigarette shapes and served beside the melon. The only seasoning is coarsely ground black pepper, straight from a pepper mill.

If Italian prosciutto is not available, use one of the smoked pork hams, sold in some speciality delicatessen shops as ham de luxe. Prosciutto is a raw ham, cured in a special manner. Boiled ham should not be substituted for this dish. Failing any acceptable substitute for prosciutto serve the melon with wine, the recipe follows.

Melon with Wine •

1 medium cantaloup or rockmelon	1 cup wine, port or sherry

Cut a triangle in the melon and remove seeds with a spoon. Fill with wine and replace triangle. Wrap in plastic bag and refrigerate for 3-4 hours. Place in a bowl and make sure the triangle is at the top, taking care that no wine spills. At serving time, pour off wine, and serve melon cut in wedges.

Lamb Kebabs ••

1 x 4-5 lb. leg of lamb, boned	1 medium size onion
1 green pepper	bay leaves
Marinade:	
1 tablespoon lemon juice	2 teaspoons honey
½ cup dry white wine	1 teaspoon salt
½ cup olive oil	¼ teaspoon white pepper
2 cloves garlic, crushed	1 tablespoon fresh rosemary or 1 teaspoon dried rosemary

Cut lamb in 1-inch cubes. Combine all ingredients for the marinade in a glass bowl, add lamb. Cover and chill several hours or overnight, turning meat occasionally.

Cut pepper into 1-inch cubes, peel and halve onion lengthwise. Blanch vegetables in boiling water for 3-4 minutes. Separate layers of onion. Thread lamb alternately with pepper, onion and bay leaves onto skewers and cook under a hot grill, turning so that each side browns, for about 10 minutes, brushing meat from time to time with the marinade. Serve hot on Turkish Pilaf. Sufficient for 6-8 skewers.

Turkish Pilaf ••

2 cups long grain
   rice
4 oz. ghee or butter
2 onions, finely
   chopped
2 tablespoons pine
   nuts
salt and pepper
2 tablespoons currants

2 teaspoons sugar
1-inch stick cinnamon
pinch saffron
3½ cups chicken stock
   or water and chicken
   stock cubes
extra pine nuts or
   pistachio nuts to
   garnish

Place rice in a shallow dish and cover with boiling water. When water is cold, drain the rice and wash several times under cold running water. Drain rice well.

Heat ghee in a heavy pan. Fry onions until golden brown, add 2 tablespoons pine nuts and fry gently for 1 minute. Add the rice and fry for a few minutes, stirring until it is golden in colour. Season with salt and pepper, stir in the currants, sugar and cinnamon stick. Dissolve saffron in the boiling stock. Add to rice, stir once, then cover tightly and cook over a low heat for 20 minutes. Turn off heat, keep covered until ready to serve. A few minutes before serving uncover the pan to allow steam to escape. Fluff up with a fork. Garnish with extra toasted pine nuts or pistachio nuts. Serves 6.
Note: To toast pine nuts place on a baking tray and grill until light golden brown.

Lamb Kebabs on a bed of spicy Turkish Pilaf. For dessert, Mandarin Gelato served in mandarin shells.

Mandarin Gelato •

6 large mandarins
¾ cup (6 oz.) castor sugar
juice of 1 lemon
few drops red food colouring

1 tablespoon gelatine
1 tablespoon kirsch
1 egg white

Turn freezer control to high. Cut a lid from the top of each mandarin and carefully remove mandarin pulp with a teaspoon. Rub pulp through a sieve to give 3½ cups juice. Stir in sugar until dissolved. Add lemon juice and red colouring to give juice a slightly deeper colour. Place 2 tablespoons juice in a saucepan, sprinkle gelatine over and stir over a low heat until dissolved. Allow to cool slightly and then whisk into remaining juice. Flavour with kirsch. Pour into shallow trays, cover with aluminium foil and freeze. After 1 hour remove gelato and stir well. Cover and return to freezer until frozen. Remove once more, put into a bowl, stir well and fold in stiffly beaten egg white. Return to shallow trays, cover, return to freezer and allow to set. This should take about 5 hours. Fill mandarin shells with gelato. Cover with lid and garnish with a small mandarin or orange leaf. Serves 6.
Note: If mandarin pulp does not measure 3½ cups liquid, make up the difference with water.

Orange Gelato •

Prepare as for Mandarin Gelato using 6 medium sized oranges in place of the mandarins.

Russian Casserole Dinner

for six people

Snow, fur hats, caviar, vodka, twirling dancers, romantic melancholic music, fiery music—Russia conjures up many contrasting pictures. Russian cuisine is just as varied. It blends sweet and sour and there is a clear cut sharpness about many dishes. It is almost always lusty and virile. Although Russian dishes differ vastly from ours, most people find the flavours interesting at first and better as the meal progresses.

There are other Russian recipes included in this book, Moscow Piroshki—small savoury pastries, Paskha—an Easter feast dish, and Moscow Mule—a drink with a kick. Compare them with the dinner menu, even include them if your appetite is lusty and Russian. Veal and Cherry Casserole shows the influence of bordering countries. Cherries, cardamom and raisins are the unusual flavourings. Yoghurt and cucumber salad will clear the palate for the rich, delectable chocolate mousse, and don't forget the sour cream, this is authentic Russian. **Wine:** A dry sherry for the borsch and a light bodied fruity red wine to accompany the veal.

Eggplant à la Turque*
Jellied Borsch
Russian Veal and Cherry
Casserole
Steamed Rice*
Yoghurt and Cucumber Salad
Chocolate Mousse Smetana

*Consult index for recipe.

Russian Veal and Cherry Casserole ••

2½ lb. veal from shoulder
  or leg
4 shallots
2 oz. butter
2 tablespoons (1 oz.) plain
  flour
1 cup drained, canned
  sour cherries, stoned
⅓ cup (2 oz.) raisins
⅔ cup chicken stock or
  water and chicken
  stock cubes

½ cup port
1 teaspoon ground
  cardamom
1 teaspoon salt
freshly ground black
  pepper
2 x 10 oz. cans kidney
  beans, drained

Cut veal into 1-inch cubes. Chop shallots, including some of the green tops. Heat butter in a large fireproof casserole or heavy saucepan and brown veal on all sides over high heat. Turn heat down as low as possible and sprinkle meat with flour. Stir until meat is evenly coated. Add shallots, cherries, raisins, stock, port, cardamom, salt and pepper. Mix thoroughly. Cover and simmer, stirring occasionally, for 1-1½ hours or until veal is tender. Add a little more stock if needed. Add the beans 10 minutes before serving time and heat through. Serves 6.
Note: If cherries used make casserole taste too sour, a little sugar may be added to taste at the end of cooking time. Morello cherries will give casserole a rich red colour. Sour cherries may make it look too pale, in which case a little beetroot juice, added at the last minute, improves colour of the sauce.

Jellied Borsch ••

1 x 15 oz. can shoestring
  beetroot
1 tablespoon gelatine
3 cups beef stock or water
  and beef stock cubes
3-inch strip orange rind

3 tablespoons dry sherry
1 tablespoon lemon juice
6 tablespoons sour cream
caviar, parsley or chives
  to garnish

Drain beetroot reserving ½ cup liquid. Soften gelatine in 3 tablespoons stock in top part of a double boiler. Put over simmering water, add reserved beetroot juice and orange rind and stir until the gelatine has dissolved. Remove orange rind.

Put beetroot into a blender container with gelatine mixture and blend until smooth, or press beetroot through a sieve. Combine beetroot with beef stock and sherry, then stir in lemon juice. Pour into six soup cups and chill until firm. To serve place a tablespoon of sour cream on each cup and garnish with black or red caviar, chopped parsley or chives. Serves 6.
Note: If shoestring beetroot is not available use 4 large cooked beetroot, chop finely, then use as above, replacing beetroot juice with stock.

Chocolate Mousse Smetana •

3 savoy fingers
1 tablespoon rum
1 teaspoon vanilla essence
3 oz. dark cooking
   chocolate

¼ cup (1½ oz.) icing
   sugar, sifted
½ pint thick sour cream
toasted slivered almonds
   to decorate

Crumble savoy fingers finely, place in a bowl and sprinkle
with rum and vanilla. Chop chocolate and melt in a bowl
over hot water. Stir in icing sugar, savoy fingers and sour
cream. Blend well and spoon into small mousse pots or
individual serving dishes. Chill at least 4 hours or overnight. Serve decorated with toasted slivered almonds.
If liked, the mousse may be topped with whipped cream,
then almonds. Serves 6.

Note: Ratafia biscuits which are available at speciality

*Chocolate Mousse Smetana may be served topped with swirls of
whipped cream and decorated with toasted, slivered almonds.*

Continental shops are best for this recipe. If you can find
them, use 6-8 ratafias in place of savoy fingers.

Yoghurt and Cucumber Salad •

3 cucumbers
1½ teaspoons salt
1 clove garlic, crushed
1 tablespoon lemon juice
1 cup yoghurt

1 tablespoon finely
   chopped dill or 1
   teaspoon dried dill
¼ cup olive oil
2 teaspoons finely
   chopped fresh mint

Peel cucumbers, cut in halves lengthwise, remove seeds,
then slice cucumbers thinly. Sprinkle with the salt and let
stand 15 minutes. Drain well. Mix together the garlic,
lemon juice, yoghurt and dill. Combine with cucumbers.
Pour oil over the top and sprinkle with mint. Serves 6.

Fondue Bourguignonne
for six to eight people

Fondue parties are great fun and perfect in winter. There is something about cooking your own meat around a community pot that goes so well with frosty weather. It makes for easy entertaining as guests cook their own dinner. All the hostess has to do about food is cube the beef and prepare the sauces.

For cooking the beef use a good vegetable oil and butter. It may be cooked to individual tastes, lightly by those who prefer it rare, or left in the pot for a longer time if well done meat is desired. The cubes are placed on the long fondue forks for cooking, then transferred to the dinner plate and dipped in sauce with the eating fork, while the next piece of meat is cooking on the fondue fork. If fondue forks are not available, butcher's skewers do just as well.

When setting the table, place the fondue pot in the centre. Dinner plates, knives and forks are set at each place. Food to be cooked may be arranged on two large serving dishes or on individual small plates. Bowls of sauce and accompaniments are put on the table too, and the cooked meat is dipped before eating. A fondue dinner calls for simple country style table settings—bright table mats or cloth, stout earthenware plates, baskets for bread and wooden salad bowls, salt and pepper mills. Special fondue plates are available, divided into five different sections to keep sauces separate. The food to be cooked may be arranged in one section.

With Fondue Bourguignonne serve a tossed salad and hot, crusty garlic or herb bread. Use a French or Vienna loaf, slice almost through to bottom crust and spread with garlic or herb flavoured butter before heating in a moderate oven (350°F.) for 15 minutes.

As the table will be set for the Fondue, serve Piroshki with pre-dinner drinks. For dessert nothing could be more delectable than Savarin au Rhum. Spiced Orange Slices in Red Wine would be the next choice.

Wines: Serve a full bodied red wine with the Fondue Bourguignonne.

Piroshki
Fondue Bourguignonne
with Sauces
Hot Garlic or Herb Bread*
Green Salad*
Savarin au Rhum*
or
Spiced Orange Slices in Red Wine*

*Consult index for recipe.

Piroshki ••

Pastry:

4 oz. packaged cream cheese	1 cup (4 oz.) plain flour
4 oz. butter	beaten egg to glaze

Filling:

2 oz. butter	4-6 rashers bacon or
1 onion, chopped	3 oz. speck, chopped
	salt and pepper

Pastry: Beat cream cheese and butter in a mixing bowl, add sifted flour and mix into a dough. Wrap in grease-proof paper and chill overnight or for several hours. (If left overnight, allow to stand at room temperature for an hour or so before rolling out).
Roll pastry out thinly and cut into 2-inch rounds with a pastry cutter. Put a teaspoonful of filling onto each round, moisten edges with a little beaten egg and fold pastry over to form a crescent shape. Seal well. Place on baking trays. Brush with beaten egg and bake in a hot oven (400°F.) for 10 minutes or until golden brown. Makes about 2 dozen.
For Filling: Melt butter, add onion and bacon and cook until onion is transparent and bacon is crisp. Season with salt and pepper.

Fondue Bourguignonne ••

2-2½ lb. fillet of beef	4 oz. butter
salt and pepper	piece of raw potato dried
cooking oil	in a clean tea towel

Cut beef into 1-inch cubes and season lightly with salt and pepper. Arrange on a platter and accompany by an assortment of sauces, relishes and condiments.

Pour cooking oil into fondue pot to a depth of 1½-2 inches and add butter. Place on stand, light burner, heat oil and butter until very hot (375°F. on a sugar thermometer) and add a piece of raw potato to prevent fat from spitting. Each guest spears a piece of meat on fondue fork and cooks it in the hot oil. The meat is then transferred to the eating fork before being dipped into sauces or seasoned to taste. Serves 6-8.

Note: Fillet of veal and sliced sheep's kidneys may also be used. Thin strips of rump steak may be used instead of fillet steak.

Fondue Sauces

Sauces for fondue meals should provide guests with a choice, creamy and bland or sharp and piquant. Following are recipes for sauces of both types and suggestions for commercial sauces suitable for a fondue. Commercial sauces and accompaniments to serve include: prepared French mustard, sweet mustard sauce, chilli sauce, plum sauce, Worcestershire sauce. Among suitable pickles are Italian assorted fruit in mustard flavoured syrup, mustard pickles, pickled onions and cauliflower, sweet mango chutney and mixed fruit chutney.

Horseradish Cream •

Combine ⅔ cup sour cream, 1 tablespoon grated horseradish and ½ clove crushed garlic.

Swiss Sauce Piquant •

Combine ⅔ cup sour cream, ⅓ cup French dressing (see page 16) and 1 tablespoon chopped capers.

Fondue Bourguignonne is served with various sauces and crusty Garlic or Herb Bread.

Sauce Smitane •

1 oz. butter	salt and pepper
1 small onion	1 teaspoon strained
½ cup dry white wine	lemon juice
1 cup sour cream, scalded	

Heat butter and sauté finely chopped onion until soft but not brown. Add wine, stir well and reduce liquid over high heat until almost evaporated, stirring occasionally. Pour in the scalded cream, stirring constantly, and continue to stir until thoroughly blended. Simmer gently for 5 minutes, strain through a fine sieve and season to taste with salt and pepper. Add lemon juice just before serving.

Ravigote Sauce •

1 cup mayonnaise	½ teaspoon dried chervil
½ teaspoon anchovy sauce	1 tablespoon chopped
1 hard-boiled egg white	shallots
1 tablespoon chopped	1 tablespoon chopped
capers	onion
1 tablespoon chopped	¼ cup tarragon vinegar
parsley	

Mix mayonnaise with anchovy sauce and finely chopped egg white. Cook together capers, parsley, chervil, shallots and onion in vinegar for 15 minutes. Cool and combine with mayonnaise. Chill well.

Quick Hollandaise ••

3 oz. butter	pinch salt
2 egg yolks	dash cayenne pepper
1 tablespoon lemon juice	2 teaspoons water

In a small saucepan melt butter and allow to cool slightly. Combine with egg yolks, lemon juice, salt, cayenne pepper and water. Place over medium heat and stir briskly with a wooden spoon or a whisk until thick. Do not allow to boil.

Cheese Fondue

for six to eight people

Cheese Fondue, perhaps the most popular fondue of all, has almost become the national dish of Switzerland, and undoubtedly it is ideal for parties in ski country. But no matter where you live, a Cheese Fondue party is thoroughly informal and lots of fun. The friendliness of people all dipping into the same pot makes for a happy atmosphere.

The key to perfect Cheese Fondue is in constant stirring and adjusting the heat to just the right degree to keep the mixture barely bubbling. To follow tradition, always stir in the same direction. Each guest takes a turn to stir as they dip their bread.

Here's a tip on how to keep the bread firmly attached to the fork. Push the tines of the fork through the soft part of the bread first, then through the crust. Dip it in the melted cheese and wine mixture and keep the fondue in motion until the next guest is ready to take over. Twirl the fork as you lift it out. If the fondue needs thinning, add a little more wine to the pot and stir with a wooden spoon.

Halfway through the fondue, it is traditional to offer kirsch (cherry brandy) which is said to promote digestion and stimulate the appetite.

If you do drop your bread in the pot, tradition demands that you pay a forfeit of a bottle of wine or a kiss. When the fondue is almost finished, the cheese at the bottom of the pot will be brown and crusty, this is considered the best part, so divide it among the guests.

Cheese fondue forms the whole meal. You need nothing else, except a green salad with an oil and vinegar dressing or a light fruit salad.

Wines: It is usual to drink the same white wine as is used in the fondue. Kirsch may be offered halfway through the fondue.

Cheese Fondue

Kirsch

Green Salad*

Fresh Fruit

Cheese Fondue ••

1 clove garlic
1½ cups dry white wine
1 lb. Swiss gruyère or
    emmenthaler cheese
2 teaspoons cornflour
2 tablespoons kirsch
freshly ground black
    pepper or nutmeg
crusty French bread,
    cubed

Rub inside of fondue dish or earthenware casserole with a cut clove of garlic. Pour in wine, heat over an alcohol burner, keeping flame low. Do not boil. Sprinkle cheese lightly with cornflour, add cheese and bring mixture just to boiling point, stirring constantly with a wooden spoon until cheese is melted and creamy. Stir in kirsch and season with freshly ground black pepper or freshly grated nutmeg. Serve immediately, keeping flame turned as low as possible. Pieces of French bread are speared on long fondue forks and dipped into the fondue as desired by each guest. Some recipes for fondue include a grating of nutmeg for extra flavour. This is a matter of personal preference and may be omitted if wished.

Points to watch if Cheese Fondue is to be kept smooth and uncurdled and with no risk of the cheese going stringy are: Cheese must be melted over low heat; the fondue must be stirred gently but constantly; it must be kept over the lowest possible heat when cooked and ready to eat. Add more wine if cheese thickens too much.

Dinner Parties

Luxury Dinner Party
for eight people

The Iron Duke left his mark in the world in more ways than one. To gastronomes, Wellington indicates a tender fillet of beef encased first in fine pâté and then in crisp, light-as-air pastry. It is indeed a most exquisite meat pie, worthy of a name that won battles and conquered nations and hearts.

This star studded menu commences with Lady Curzon Soup. The story goes that Lady Curzon, wife of one of the last great viceroys of India, had been advised by her physician to cut down on liquor. Cunningly, this soup was devised from clear turtle soup. The pinch of curry powder disguised the generous addition of brandy and the cream enriched the combined flavours to add to the deception. Were Lord Curzon and the physician aware of the secret ingredient in this superlative soup? One can never be sure.

In spite of the luxury touch in this menu, most of the preparation can be done beforehand. The soup is superbly simple. The Asparagus Mousse should be made well ahead and refrigerated. Prepare Tournedos Wellington on the day of the dinner and bake as guests are sitting down to the first course. The beans go on a little earlier.

Soufflé Grand Marnier is considered by many as too difficult for a lone hostess to attempt. I would suggest a trial run on the family even if you replace the liqueur with a little vanilla essence. Once you get the hang of making the sauce in advance and preparing the soufflé dish leaving only the whipped egg whites to be added at the very last minute, the rest is simple. You won't be the first hostess to feel convinced that the soufflé conspiracy has been devised to stop other people from realising just how easy it is to make this most delectable of all desserts. My only word of warning—accurate timing is essential, so allow at least ten minutes when guests can chatter while the soufflé finishes cooking. We all know it is better for guests to wait for the soufflé than the other way around.

Wine: A chablis style wine to accompany the Asparagus Mousse and a full bodied red wine to accompany the tournedos. A chilled semi-sweet Champagne would be delicious with the Soufflé Grand Marnier.

Lady Curzon Soup*
Asparagus Mousse*
Tournedos Wellington
with Madeira Sauce
Faggots of French Beans
Soufflé Grand Marnier
or
Crème Eugene
*Consult index for recipe.

Chicken In Wine served with olives.

Tournedos Wellington •••

Tournedos Wellington may be prepared well in advance. Have beef cooked and covered with pastry, ready to glaze and decorate before baking. Refrigerate if keeping overnight.

8 fillet steaks, cut 1½-inches thick	1 tablespoon brandy
salt and pepper	1 lb. commercial puff pastry
2 oz. butter	1 egg, separated
4 oz. small mushrooms	
6 oz. good liver pâté or Latvian liverwurst	

Madeira Sauce:

mushroom stems	2 cups beef stock or water and beef stock cubes
1 oz. butter	
1 shallot	½ cup Madeira or dry sherry
salt and pepper	
1 tablespoon (½ oz.) plain flour	

Trim fillet steaks of all fat and gristle. Tie string around each steak to keep a neat shape. Season with salt and pepper. Heat 1 oz. butter in a frying pan and sauté steaks for 3 minutes each side. Cool. Remove string.

Wash mushrooms, remove stems and reserve for sauce. Slice the caps thinly. Add to pan with remaining butter and cook gently until lightly browned. Add pâté and heat thoroughly, stirring. Season with salt and pepper to taste, then blend in brandy. Spread on top of each steak.

Roll out half the pastry thinly on a lightly floured surface. Cut into eight circles, 1-inch larger than meat. Using a fluted round cutter cut crescent shapes out of pastry scraps and set aside for decoration. Place steaks on the circles of pastry. Brush edges with slightly beaten egg white. Roll out remaining pastry thinly and cut into eight circles, 1½-inches larger than meat. Gently mould over the meat, pressing edges to seal. Trim edges. Brush pastry with slightly beaten egg yolk and arrange pastry crescents in a pattern on top. Bake in a very hot oven (450°F.) for 15 minutes until pastry is golden. Serve with Madeira Sauce and Faggots of French Beans.

For Madeira Sauce: Finely chop mushroom stems and cook gently in melted butter in a saucepan for 5 minutes until softened. Add finely chopped shallot and season to taste. Stir in flour, cook, stirring, for 2 minutes longer. Stir in beef stock, bring to the boil stirring, and add Madeira. Bring to the boil again and simmer for 5-6 minutes, stirring occasionally. Strain sauce and, if necessary, add more salt and pepper. Serve hot. Serves 8.

Faggots of French Beans ••

2 lb. green beans	1 teaspoon sugar
8 shallots	1 cup water
2 oz. butter	1 bay leaf
salt	2 sprigs parsley

Top and tail beans, then remove strings. Trim whites off shallots and plunge green tops into boiling salted water, then drain and rinse under cold running water. Separate beans into eight even-sized bundles. Tie with the shallots.

Heat 1 oz. butter in a large pan, place bundles of beans in butter and add salt, sugar, water, bay leaf and parsley Bring to the boil, lower heat and cook gently, covered, for 45 minutes until beans are tender, shaking pan occasionally. Add more water during cooking if it evaporates too quickly. Remove bay leaf and parsley. Lift bundles of beans onto a heated serving platter. If necessary, boil liquid in pan until reduced to 3 tablespoons, add remaining butter and season with more salt if required. Pour over beans and serve immediately. Serves 6-8.

Soufflé Grand Marnier •••

Ingredients for 8:

3 oz. butter	½ teaspoon vanilla essence
2 tablespoons (1 oz.) plain flour	7 egg yolks
1½ cups milk	4 tablespoons grand marnier
½ teaspoon salt	8 egg whites
1 cup (8 oz.) sugar	

Ingredients for 4-6:

1½ oz. butter	½ teaspoon vanilla essence
1 tablespoon (½ oz.) plain flour	4 egg yolks
1 cup milk	2 tablespoons grand marnier
¼ teaspoon salt	5 egg whites
½ cup (4 oz.) sugar	

Butter inside of a 1½ pint soufflé dish. Use two dishes for serving 8 people. Sprinkle with a little castor sugar. Remove excess sugar by turning the dish upside down and tapping gently. For a high soufflé, tie a band of double greased greaseproof paper or aluminium foil around the dish.

Melt butter in a saucepan, stir in flour, cook 1 minute. Remove from heat, gradually add milk, stirring constantly. Add salt, sugar and vanilla. Return to heat and bring to the boil, stirring continuously. Beat well and when sauce is thick and smooth remove from heat and cool. Add lightly beaten egg yolks and grand marnier. Lastly, fold in stiffly beaten egg whites. Pour into prepared soufflé dish (divide between two if preparing for 8 people) and bake in a moderate oven (350°F.) for 35 minutes or until soufflé is well puffed and golden. Serve immediately.

Crème Eugene ••

8 peaches or 4 lb. grapes	1 pint cream
sugar to taste	brown sugar
4-6 tablespoons grand marnier or cointreau	

Peel and stone peaches or grapes. Cut into ¼-inch slices and divide mixture between two soufflé dishes. Sprinkle with sugar to taste. Sprinkle with liqueur. Whip cream until thick and spread all over fruit. Leave in the refrigerator 3 hours or preferably overnight.

Shortly before serving, sprinkle brown sugar over the cream to the depth of ½-inch. When ready to serve, place under a medium grill until sugar is bubbling and lightly caramelised, about 3-4 minutes.

Note: Any fruit may be prepared in the same way.

Tournedos Wellington with Madeira Sauce, Faggots of French Beans

Springtime Roast Lamb Dinner
for six people

The mark of a good cook is the ability to use foods that are plentiful, in season and probably inexpensive, and turn them into an important superlative meal.

A leg of lamb is all too often kept as a family meal. Everyone always enjoys it but it is considered too plain for guests. In Greece, it could never be considered anything but fit for the gods, flavoured with rosemary, garlic and anchovy, lamb has a taste that could only have been inspired by the gods.

Oranges, too, take on new life when chilled in a spicy wine syrup. Our picture of this deceptively simple dish speaks for itself.

Wines: Accompany soup with same wine as used in soup. A light bodied, full flavoured red wine would be ideal for accompanying the lamb with its full flavoured sauce.

Jellied Wine Consommé*
Leg of Lamb
Anchovy Sauce
Potato and Onion Scallop
Spinach Rosemary
Green Salad
Spiced Orange Slices in Red Wine

*Consult index for recipe.

Leg of Lamb with Anchovy Sauce ••

1 x 4 lb. leg of lamb	juice of 1 lemon
2 cloves garlic	½ cup olive oil
1 teaspoon dried rosemary or sprig of fresh rosemary	salt and pepper
Anchovy Sauce:	
6 anchovy fillets	1 teaspoon lemon juice
1 clove garlic, finely chopped	1 teaspoon grated lemon rind
12 black olives, stoned and chopped	½ cup beef stock
	dash hot pepper sauce

Score lamb in diamond shapes making sure not to cut through fat too deeply. Make six or eight small incisions in lamb with a small pointed knife. Cut garlic into thin slices, push a toothpick through each slice and place in incisions in lamb. Combine rosemary with lemon juice, oil, salt and black pepper to taste. Spread leg of lamb with this mixture and place on a rack in a roasting pan. Bake in a moderately slow oven (325°F.) allowing 30 minutes per pound. Baste from time to time with pan juices. Transfer lamb to a heated dish and allow to stand for 15 minutes in a warm place before carving. Serve Anchovy Sauce separately. Serves 6.
For Anchovy Sauce: Soak anchovies in a little milk for 15 minutes. Drain and chop finely. Combine all ingredients and stir over a medium heat until sauce is heated through. Pour into sauceboat and serve hot.

Potato and Onion Scallop ••

6 medium size potatoes	salt and pepper
2 large onions, thinly sliced	3 oz. butter
	¾ cup water

Peel potatoes and slice about ⅛-inch thick. Butter an 8-inch ovenproof baking dish, put in a third of the potato slices and cover with half the onions. Sprinkle with salt and pepper, dot with 1 oz. butter. Spread with another third of the potatoes, then with remaining onions and another 1 oz. butter. Sprinkle with more salt and pepper. Top with remaining potatoes, pour in the water and dot with more butter. Cover and bake in a moderately slow oven (325°F.) for 1½ hours until potatoes are tender. Remove lid about 20 minutes before end of cooking time, to brown top. Serves 6.

Green Salad •

To 1 lettuce or a combination of several salad greens, well washed and dried, add 1 tablespoon chopped parsley, 1 tablespoon chopped chives, 1 tablespoon vinegar, 3 tablespoons olive oil, salt and freshly ground black pepper. Toss well in a salad bowl and serve immediately. Serves 6.

132

Spinach Rosemary •

1 lb. spinach
1 tablespoon finely
  chopped parsley
4 shallots, finely
  chopped

2 oz. butter
salt
½ teaspoon dried
  rosemary

Wash spinach in cold water. Place spinach in a large
saucepan and combine with parsley and shallots. Add
butter, salt and rosemary. Cover the pan and cook over
a low heat for 5-10 minutes. Shake pan from time to time
while spinach is cooking. Serves 6.

Spiced Orange Slices in Red Wine •

¾ cup (6 oz.) sugar
1 cup water
1 cup dry red wine
2 cloves
1 x 3-inch stick
  cinnamon

2 slices mandarin,
  optional
2 slices lemon
6-8 oranges

Dissolve sugar in water and add wine. Add cloves,
cinnamon, mandarin and lemon. Bring to the boil and
cook until mixture is thick and syrupy. Cool slightly.
Peel oranges with a sharp knife removing all white pith.
Cut into ¼-inch slices. Add to wine syrup and chill. Serve
cold with a jug of thin pouring cream. Serves 6-8.

Devilled Tomatoes.

Cook-ahead Dinner

for eight people

If you are lucky enough to have a planned, orderly life with plenty of time to shop, cook, go to the hairdressers, fix the house just the way you want it, then you probably won't need this menu.

Let's face it, for the majority, an important dinner can happen on the wrong day, and a foolproof cook-ahead dinner plan is something to have up your sleeve. This menu is designed to make your guests very happy and relaxed. The consommé has just enough wine to ensure a genial atmosphere. The veal is lightly laced with sherry, just enough to add intrigue and, along with the dessert,

can be made days ahead of the dinner. The salad can be made well before dinner, keeping crisp in the refrigerator with a covering of aluminium foil or plastic wrap. Have a big pan of water on the boil to take the noodles which will cook as you have the soup—it is always nice to have one part of the meal just freshly cooked!

Wines: A full bodied sherry would be a suitable wine for the soup or serve the wine used in the soup. Accompany the veal with a full bodied white Burgundy.

Wine Consommé
Sherried Veal with Cream
Buttered Noodles Verdi
Tossed Salad with Avocado
Iced Coffee Soufflés

Wine Consommé •

6 cups beef consommé	dash of lemon juice
1 cup dry red wine	thinly sliced lemon and
1 teaspoon sugar	chopped chives to
salt and pepper	garnish

Bring beef consommé to boil and stir in red wine, sugar, salt and pepper to taste and lemon juice. Serve the soup hot or cold, garnished with lemon slices and chives. Serves 8.

Note: Very good canned consommé is now available and may be used for this recipe. Dilute if using concentrated consommé, three cans will be more than adequate to serve 8 people.

Sherried Veal with Cream • •

3 lb. veal from shoulder or leg	1 tablespoon tomato paste
3 oz. butter	1 cup veal or chicken
3 tablespoons dry sherry	stock or water and
2 onions, finely chopped	chicken stock cubes
3 tablespoons (1½ oz.) plain flour	¾ cup thin sour cream
1 clove garlic, crushed	salt and pepper
4 tomatoes, peeled and sliced	1 bay leaf
	chopped chives

Cut veal into large squares, brown on all sides in the hot butter in a large heavy based saucepan, then pour in the

warmed sherry. Remove the veal. Add onions to pan and cook for 2 minutes. Sprinkle with flour, stir over heat. Add garlic and tomatoes and cook for a further 3 minutes. Remove from heat and stir in tomato paste, then stock. Cook over a gentle heat until mixture comes to the boil. Carefully blend in the sour cream and seasoning to taste. Add bay leaf and return veal to the pan. Cook over a very gentle heat for 45 minutes or place in a casserole and bake in a moderate oven (350°F.) for 1-1½ hours. Serve in casserole. If sauce is too thin, thicken with a little beurre manié (1 oz. butter blended with 1 tablespoon (½ oz.) plain flour). Sprinkle with chives. Serve with buttered noodles. Serves 8.

Buttered Noodles Verdi •

2 lb. ½-inch wide noodles verdi (green noodles)	4 oz. butter

Cook noodles in two large saucepans of boiling, salted water for about 8 minutes. Do not cover. Stir at the start of cooking to prevent sticking. When noodles are tender but still firm enough to bite comfortably, remove from heat and pour a pint of cold water into the pan to stop boiling and drain immediately. Place noodles into a large serving dish and toss with butter. Serves 8.

Spiced Orange Slices in Red Wine

Tossed Salad with Avocado •

2 lettuce
1 cup watercress sprigs
1 clove garlic
2 teaspoons finely
   chopped chives
½ cup French dressing
   (see page 16)
1 avocado, peeled,
   stoned and sliced
lemon juice

Wash and prepare lettuce and watercress. Shake dry in a salad basket, or dry each leaf carefully in a clean tea towel. Wrap in tea towel and allow to crisp in refrigerator until ready for use.

Arrange lettuce and watercress in a salad bowl. Chop garlic finely and sprinkle with chives over greens in bowl. If preparing salad ahead of time, cover and chill at this point. Just before serving sprinkle with French dressing. Garnish with wedges of avocado sprinkled with lemon juice to prevent discolouring. Toss salad until each leaf is glistening. Serves 8.

Note: When avocados are out of season, replace with a combination of chopped fresh herbs such as basil, marjoram and parsley.

Iced Coffee Soufflés ••

6 eggs, separated
6 oz. (¾ cup) sugar
1½ tablespoons instant
   coffee powder
3 oz. dark cooking
   chocolate, chopped
2 tablespoons water
1 tablespoon rum
¾ pint cream
grated chocolate to
   decorate

Beat egg yolks with sugar and instant coffee over hot water until mixture is thick and creamy. Melt chocolate and water in a small saucepan. Add rum and stir into egg and coffee mixture. Whip cream and fold into soufflé mixture. Whisk egg whites and fold into mixture. Pour into individual soufflé dishes or custard cups and freeze for 4 hours. The mixture may be frozen in ice cream trays and served in chunks in a coupe dish. Decorate with grated chocolate and serve with a macaroon type biscuit or wafer. Serves 8.

Note: If using individual soufflé dishes, tie a double strip of aluminium foil around each dish to come 1-inch above rim of the dish. Remove the foil collars just before serving.

Iced Coffee Souffles.

Chicken Pilaf Dinner
for eight people

Mango Chicken may have come as a surprise to Mrs. Beeton, but there is no doubt she would have taken it in her stride and included the recipe in her famous works, for Mrs. Beeton could at least recognise a good idea.

The combination of chicken and mango has long been known to Pacific Islanders and in the Middle East. Now that the exotic mango is available fresh for a few months of every year, and canned all the year round, this com-patable twosome can be enjoyed by the whole world. It is a spectacular looking dish as our picture shows. The dessert that follows such a filling dish is, as it should be, rich but light. Serve this meal buffet style or as a sit-down dinner, it lends itself to either service.

Wines: Accompany the soup with a fruity moselle type wine. This type of wine could also accompany the chicken dish.

Zucchini Soup
Mango Chicken Pilaf
Caramel Mousse
with Fresh Strawberries

Mango Chicken Pilaf •••

2 x 3 lb. chickens or 4 lb. chicken pieces
3 oz. butter
2 large onions, thinly sliced
pinch grated nutmeg
1 lemon
½ pint chicken stock or water
Pilaf:
1 large onion
3 oz. butter
3 cups long grain rice
2 teaspoons turmeric

salt and freshly ground black pepper
10-12 slices fresh or canned mango (or 3-4 oranges, peeled and sliced)
¼ pint cream

1½ pints chicken stock
salt and freshly ground black pepper

Cut chickens into joints. Use the back and trimmings for stock. Fry chicken pieces slowly in butter in a large heavy saucepan or fireproof casserole until golden brown, turning with two spoons. Remove chicken. If necessary, add a little more butter to pan and fry onions slowly until transparent. Raise heat and continue frying for a few more minutes. Return chicken to pan. Add nutmeg with 2 strips of thinly peeled lemon rind. Add the stock and seasoning. Top with mango slices. Cover the pan tightly and cook slowly, preferably in a moderate oven (350°F.) for about 1 hour. When the chicken is tender, remove from pan and keep warm. Discard lemon rind. Boil sauce, adding lemon juice to taste. Stir in the cream and cook rapidly until sauce thickens slightly. Add more salt and pepper to taste if necessary.

Place chicken in serving dish, pour over the sauce and serve rice separately.

For Pilaf: Chop onion and fry gently in butter in a large pan until transparent. Add rice and fry, stirring for 1 minute, add turmeric. Pour in the stock, season well, bring to the boil, cover and cook over a low heat for about 25 minutes until rice is tender and liquid absorbed. Serves 6-8.

Zucchini Soup ••

1 onion
1 medium-sized potato
6 medium-sized zucchini
1 tablespoon oil
1 teaspoon salt
pepper

1 teaspoon dried tarragon leaves
4 cups chicken stock or water and chicken stock cubes

Peel and chop onion. Peel potato and slice thinly. Cut zucchini into thick slices. Heat oil gently in pan, add vegetables and sprinkle with salt, freshly ground pepper and tarragon. Cover and cook over a low heat for 10 minutes, shaking pan from time to time. Do not allow vegetables to colour. Add stock and simmer, covered, for 20 minutes. Cool soup, then sieve or purée in a blender. Reheat soup, taste and add more seasoning if necessary. May be served hot or cold. Accompany soup with Melba toast or crackers. Serves 6-8.

Note: A little cream may be added to each serving.

To make Melba Toast: Slice white bread very thinly, remove crusts, then halve each slice diagonally. Place on baking trays in one layer and bake in a slow oven (300°F.) until crisp and a pale golden colour. Cool. If preparing in advance, store in an airtight container.

Caramel Mousse with Fresh Strawberries •••

4 whole eggs
3 egg yolks
½ cup (4 oz.) sugar
2 tablespoons gelatine
Caramel:
¼ cup (2 oz.) sugar
¼ cup cold water

grated rind of 1 lemon
1 cup cream, whipped
red currant jelly
1 box fresh strawberries

4 tablespoons hot
  water

Beat whole eggs, egg yolks and sugar in an electric mixer at high speed (or with a rotary beater) until very stiff. Soak the gelatine in a little water and dissolve by standing in a saucepan of boiling water. Mix gelatine into egg mixture with grated lemon rind, beating well. Add the caramel made as follows, this can be made while the mousse is in the electric mixer.

For Caramel: Put sugar and cold water in a pan and cook quickly without stirring until dark caramel. Then add the hot water. Stir until smooth.

Add the caramel to the mousse, stirring vigorously. Pour in a serving bowl. Chill until set. Before serving, spread with whipped cream. Decorate with criss-cross lines of red currant jelly. Pipe rosettes of cream all around edge and place a strawberry on each rosette. Serves 8.

Peach Sherbet.

Avocado with Crab, Tournedos, Turned Mushrooms, Faggots of French Beans, Buttered New Potatoes

Low Calorie Dinner

for six people

Whether we like it or not, we often find that at least one of the guests we have invited to dinner is on a diet. They are either just starting and full of enthusiasm, right in the middle of one and rather tired of it, or have reached the point of finding their diet so monotonous that they are quite willing to break out and be wicked, but how they will hate you for it the next day.

However festive the occasion, there is really no need to break any diet. What dieters need is a change for they are feeling deprived. They need cheering up. Surprising as it may seem, many of the best dishes are very low in calories. The artful use of herbs, careful selection of vegetables and a little extra care in the preparation of each dish will give your dieting friends the best meal they ever ate on a calorie counting diet. As a special bonus, this is a low cholesterol menu too.

Wines: A crisp aromatic Rhine riesling throughout the meal. A dry Champagne with dessert if it is a festive meal. Remember wines have calories!

Jellied Wine Consommé*
Tarragon Chicken in a Pot
Devilled Tomatoes
Almond Broccoli
Green Salad*
Peach Sherbet

*Consult index for recipe.

Tarragon Chicken in a Pot •

1 x 3-4 lb. chicken
3 oz. butter
1½ teaspoons dried
   tarragon
½ clove garlic, chopped
½ teaspoon freshly
   ground pepper
1 teaspoon salt

Soak a clay pot and lid for 2 hours in very hot water. Wipe chicken with paper towels. Blend remaining ingredients together. Place half the butter mixture into cavity of chicken. Tie legs together. Rub remaining butter mixture over chicken and put into rinsed pot. Cover with lid and put into oven. Turn temperature control to hot (400°F.) and roast for 1½ hours. Serves 6.
Note: The clay pots can be purchased from specialty kitchenware shops.

Devilled Tomatoes •

3 large or 6 small tomatoes
salt and pepper
3 tablespoons mayonnaise
½ teaspoon dry mustard
few drops hot pepper
   sauce
squeeze lemon juice

Cut large tomatoes in two or cut tops off small tomatoes. Scoop out a little of the pulp. Season tomatoes with salt and pepper. Bake in a hot oven (400°F.) for 10 minutes.

Meanwhile blend together mayonnaise, mustard, hot pepper sauce and lemon juice. Remove tomatoes from oven and spoon the mayonnaise mixture into each.

Return to oven for 10 minutes until tomatoes are soft and tops bubble and are brown. Serves 6.

Almond Broccoli •

1½ lb. broccoli
salt and pepper
2 teaspoons lemon juice
2 oz. toasted slivered
   almonds

Trim broccoli and scrape stalks. Place in a pan of boiling salted water to cover and cook for 12-15 minutes until broccoli is tender. Drain. Sprinkle with lemon juice and season to taste with freshly ground pepper. Serve garnished with almonds. Serves 6.

Peach Sherbet •

6 medium sized fresh
   peaches or 3 x 8 oz. cans
   unsweetened peaches
⅓ cup lemon juice
finely grated rind of 1
   large lemon
2½ cups buttermilk
pinch salt
¾ teaspoon liquid
   sweetener
extra peaches to
   decorate

Turn freezer control to highest setting. Peel fresh peaches and remove stones. Mash peaches with a fork (or purée in blender), add lemon juice and rind. Stir in buttermilk, salt and liquid sweetener. Pour into freezer trays and freeze until almost solid. Turn into bowl and whip until light. Return to trays and freeze until set. Spoon into serving glasses and decorate with peach slices. Serves 6-8.

Romantic Dinner I

for two people

You love him. You want to cook the most divine dinner for him because you suspect that the way to his heart just might be through his stomach. Nothing is too much trouble but you want to be your most radiant self when he sets foot on your doorstep.

The trick is to keep the first and last courses simple, the sort of food that can be prepared beforehand. The main course should be reasonably hearty, and even if it needs last minute preparation this is not a bad thing—proof, if he needs any, that you did it all with your own fair hands and didn't sneak it in from the corner delicatessen. Let him help you in the kitchen, tossing the salad, warming the plates.

Here are two menus that are extra special. Just the sort of food you will want to set before that extra special man in your life.

What could be more romantic than this menu and it is quite easy to prepare, too.

Crisp devilled almonds to crunch with pre-dinner drinks may be made days before and stored in an airtight container. The filling for the first course is made ahead and chilled. Chill the whole avocado, too, cut and fill it just before serving.

Those elegant fluted mushrooms garnishing the tournedos are the sort of thing you will do only for a very special person. It is not difficult if you don't try to hurry, and why hurry when you can dream such beautiful dreams as you learn the art of making 'turned' mushrooms.

If he has not yet popped the question, surely the delectable dessert, Coeur à la Crème, will be all the prompting that is necessary. Good luck and good eating!

Wines: A light riesling or white Burgundy could be served throughout the meal and maybe a full flavoured cabernet sauvignon or aromatic claret style wine with the beef.

Devilled Almonds
Avocado with Crab
Tournedos
Turned Mushrooms
Faggots of French Beans
Buttered New Potatoes
Coeur à la Crème
Café Royale

Devilled Almonds •

Blanch 8 oz. almonds in boiling water, drain, remove skins and dry thoroughly. Heat 2-3 tablespoons olive oil in a frying pan, add almonds and cook, stirring constantly, until golden. Drain on absorbent paper and sprinkle with a little salt and chilli powder, about $\frac{1}{8}$ teaspoon to 1 teaspoon salt. Dust off excess salt and chilli powder and serve in small bowls.

Avocado with Crab •

1 x 6½ oz. can king crab	dash of hot pepper
2 tablespoons oil	sauce
2 teaspoons vinegar	1 ripe avocado pear
salt and pepper	lemon wedges

Pick over crabmeat, removing all cartilage, cut into bite-size chunks. Pour oil into a bowl, beat in vinegar and seasonings. Add crab and chill for at least 1 hour.

To serve, cut the avocado in half, remove seed and fill cavity with crab mixture. Garnish each with a lemon wedge. Serves 2.

Tournedos •

Tournedos are cut from the heart of the eye fillet of beef, 1-1½-inches thick.

2 tournedos	2 oz. butter
salt and pepper	turned mushrooms

Season tournedos with salt and pepper. Heat butter in a heavy pan and add tournedos when butter is sizzling. Sauté 4-5 minutes each side. Remove from pan and keep hot. Sauté mushrooms lightly in pan juices. Serve tournedos on a hot platter garnished with mushrooms. Serves 2.

Turned Mushrooms ••

Select 4 oz. firm white button mushrooms, wipe with damp cloth and cut off stem level with cap. Hold cap at an angle and with a small sharp knife held at a slant, cut from top to base of mushroom while rotating cap with other hand. Flute all around the mushroom, then remove any pieces of peel attached to lower edge. Gently sauté mushrooms until golden and tender in pan in which tournedos were cooked. Serves 2.

Faggots of French Beans ••

Follow recipe on page 130 using 8 oz. beans, 2 shallots, 1 oz. butter, $\frac{1}{2}$ teaspoon sugar, salt, 1 cup water, 1 bay leaf and 1 sprig parsley. Make 2 bundles of beans.

Buttered New Potatoes •

8 oz. baby new   2 oz. butter
**   potatoes   chopped parsley**

Scrub potatoes and cook in boiling salted water until tender, about 25 minutes. Drain, add butter and toss over heat a few seconds. Serve hot sprinkled with chopped parsley. Serves 2.

Coeur à la Crème ••

This is an enchanting dessert for Valentine's Day or people in love at any time. The white ceramic moulds are available at specialty kitchen shops. The quantity makes enough for two with return helpings.

4 oz. fresh cottage cheese $\frac{1}{4}$ pint cream
4 oz. cream cheese   1 punnet fresh
1 tablespoon icing sugar   strawberries
pinch salt   extra icing sugar

Combine both cheeses, 1 tablespoon icing sugar and salt, and beat well. Gradually add cream, beating constantly until the mixture is smooth. Press the mixture into three or four individual heart shaped moulds with perforated bottoms. Place in a deep dish and refrigerate overnight allowing the mixture to drain.

When ready to serve, unmould the hearts onto chilled plates and serve surrounded with strawberries which have been sprinkled with icing sugar. Half the strawberries may be crushed, lightly sweetened and spooned over the hearts. Serves 2 or 4.

Café Royale •

Float 1-2 teaspoons cognac on a cup of hot black coffee. Put a sugar cube in a teaspoon and fill spoon with cognac or brandy. Hold the spoon just above the coffee or near a lighted candle to warm. Light the liquor in the spoon and, as it burns, lower it gently into the coffee, holding it barely below the surface of the liquid, thereby igniting the cognac. Swish spoon gently until flame dies out.

(a) For fluted mushrooms, select firm white button mushrooms, wipe over with cloth dipped in water with squeeze of lemon juice to clean and trim off stem. With a small sharp knife, held on a slant, cut from top of mushroom to base, rotating the cap with left hand.

(b) Flute all around the mushroom, then remove any pieces of peel attached to lower edge.

Chicken Liver Pâté served moulded or in a crock, Crusted Veal Pie, Country Style Pâté and Veal Saumone

Romantic Dinner II

A dinner like this would make any man feel like a lover and act like one. That goes for husbands too. Start with well chilled Seafood Cocktail, progress to Chicken Kiev (if ever there was a dish to show what a clever cook you are, this is it) and end the meal in a blaze of glory with Bananas au Rhum flamed right at the table.

Wines: Accompany chicken with a traminer wine and the dessert with a chilled moselle.

Seafood Cocktail
Chicken Kiev
Sautéed Mushrooms
Watercress Salad
Bananas au Rhum

Seafood Cocktail •

4 fl. oz. sour cream
2 teaspoons tomato paste
2 teaspoons lemon juice
½ teaspoon bottled
   horseradish
pinch salt
few drops hot pepper
   sauce
1 cup shellfish (prawns,
   lobster, crab,
   oysters)
shredded lettuce

Combine sour cream, tomato paste, lemon juice, horseradish, salt and hot pepper sauce. Stir in seafood. Cover and chill. Serve in cocktail glasses on top of shredded lettuce, with thinly sliced brown bread and butter. Serves 2.

Chicken Kiev • • •

This famous Russian dish of chicken breasts rolled in butter requires care and attention when cooking. The oil must be hot enough to brown the chicken, but not so hot it will colour before the exact time is up. With a little practice you will be able to cook perfect Chicken Kiev.

1 whole chicken breast
1 oz. butter
salt
freshly ground black
   pepper
2 tablespoons chopped
   chives
plain flour
1 egg, lightly beaten
1 cup soft white
   breadcrumbs
oil for deep frying

Halve chicken breast. Using a sharp pointed knife remove all bones from breast, leaving the wing joint attached. Peel away skin. Place chicken breast between pieces of waxed paper and pound until thin with a mallet or the flat side of a heavy knife. Do not split the flesh. Remove the waxed paper.

Cut butter into two parts and roll each into a cork shape. Chill. Place a cork of butter at base of each chicken breast, diagonally in line with wing bone. Sprinkle with salt, pepper and chives. Fold the chicken flesh over the butter, then roll up towards the bone, folding the sides in as you go so the butter is completely enclosed in the chicken. The flesh will adhere without skewers. Coat each breast lightly with flour, brush with egg and roll in breadcrumbs (you will not use all the crumbs). Refrigerate 1 hour or more.

Heat oil in a saucepan (there must be enough oil to completely cover the chicken breasts). Gently lower chicken into oil and fry for 4½-5 minutes. Drain on absorbent paper and serve immediately. Serves 2.
Note: The breast of a medium sized chicken is required for this dish.

Sautéed Mushrooms •

8 oz. button mushrooms
4 oz. butter
salt and freshly ground
   pepper
good squeeze lemon juice
finely chopped parsley
   to garnish

Turn the mushrooms if desired, (see page 142), otherwise clean them and cut stems even with the base of the caps. Melt butter in a large frying pan and gently cook the mushrooms about 2 minutes on each side, or until they are golden. Sprinkle with salt and pepper to taste and the lemon juice. Serve mushrooms with the pan juices over them. Sprinkle with parsley. Serves 2-3.

Watercress Salad •

1 bunch watercress
salt
3 tablespoons olive oil
1 tablespoon tarragon
   vinegar
juice of ½ lemon

Wash watercress, discard stems, dry leaves thoroughly. Put the watercress in a salad bowl and sprinkle lightly with salt. Cover and chill well. Just before serving, sprinkle oil, vinegar and lemon juice over salad. Toss lightly. Serves 2.

Bananas au Rhum •

1 oz. butter
2 bananas
2 teaspoons brown sugar

pinch cinnamon
1 tablespoon rum

Melt butter in frying pan. When hot, add bananas, peeled and halved lengthwise. Sprinkle with brown sugar and cinnamon. Sauté until lightly browned. Turn and fry other side, sprinkling again with brown sugar and cinnamon. When bananas are soft but not mushy, warm rum, ignite and pour over bananas. When flame has burnt out, serve with cream or ice cream. Serves 2.

To make Chicken Kiev, a cork-shaped piece of chilled butter is placed on the boned chicken breast and the breast is then rolled up, crumbed and chilled for at least 1 hour. Deep fry for 4-5 minutes, drain and serve.

Dinner straight from the Pot

Take a tip from the French, not the fabulous chefs who create complicated time-consuming concoctions, but the French housewife, under whose care good but simple meals become culinary masterpieces.

What is the secret of good French home cooking? If you ask a French housewife to let you in on some of her culinary secrets you will find it often begins with 'Mettez dans la cocotte . . .'. Without a cocotte or heavy iron pot a French housewife would be lost. This wonderful piece of equipment does the multiple job of a frying pan, casserole and roaster. You can brown food in it without it sticking and, with a low heat and the heavy lid, foods cook evenly in their own flavoursome juices.

Casserole or cocotte cookery is economical and easy, important if you are a working woman who likes to entertain, for casseroles actually taste better for being made a day or two before required. A great boon when you get home at 6.00 p.m. and have to face up to guests at 7.30 p.m., the casserole gently heats through as you relax with pre-dinner drinks.

What type of pot to buy

Many types of casserole pans are available, but it is wise to select one which is large, heavy, has a tight-fitting lid and which cooks well and looks well enough to take to the table. A casserole that may be used to cook on top of the stove and in the oven is the most practical as many foods are browned on top of the stove first. A flameproof casserole saves having to use two vessels. A 4-4½ quart casserole serves 4-6, for a larger family or for party cooking invest in a larger one.

Cast Iron with Enamel Coating

These are fireproof and ovenproof and come in attractive colours, also in white with black teflon lining. Cast iron is a good conductor of heat and the enamel is easy to clean. A good quality enamel minimises the risk of chipping, so it is worth the extra money you have to pay. It will last a lifetime.

Flameproof

There are flameproof ceramic casseroles, suitable for direct use on an electric plate, flame or in the oven. Look for the flameproof label.

Earthenware

Attractive pots in brown and terracotta shades, sometimes with a dull finish and glazed inside or glazed inside and out. Most of these cook only in the oven, food is browned in another pan and transferred to earthenware for oven cooking.

Pottery and Stoneware

This oven-to-table ware comes in dark colours or pure white with decorations, it has a smooth, easy to clean lining and can be used only in oven.

Pyroceram

A very durable material that will never break from extremes of temperature. It can be taken straight from the freezer to the oven.

Copper

An excellent conductor of heat and can be used for stove top or oven cookery. It is worth buying heavy quality copper as it wears well.

Casserole of Beef in Wine ● ●

2 lb. chuck steak	2 teaspoons tomato paste
salt and pepper	¾ cup dry red wine
2 tablespoons (1 oz.) plain flour	¾ cup beef stock or water and beef stock cube
6 small white onions	1 bay leaf
3 carrots	1 sprig rosemary
2 tablespoons oil	few celery leaves
2 tablespoons brandy	8 oz. mushrooms

Cut steak into 1½-inch cubes. Season with salt and pepper and toss in flour. Peel onions. Peel carrots and halve lengthwise. Heat oil in a heavy casserole and lightly brown onions and carrots. Remove vegetables and sauté meat in pan until brown on all sides, then return onions and carrots. Warm brandy, ignite and pour over meat and vegetables. Shake pan until flame subsides, then stir in tomato paste blended with wine and stock. Add bay leaf, rosemary and celery leaves. Cover and simmer for 1-1½ hours, until meat is tender. Wash mushrooms, trim stems and add to casserole for last 15 minutes of cooking. Taste and, if necessary, add more salt and pepper. Discard bay leaf, rosemary and celery. If the gravy is too thin, lift meat and vegetables out of casserole and add a little cornflour blended in cold water to the liquid, stirring until it boils and thickens. Return meat and vegetables. Serve with Boiled New Potatoes or Creamy Mashed Potatoes and Zucchini or Green Peas. Serves 4-6.

Sauerbraten ● ● ●

1 x 4 lb. corner of topside	1 teaspoon paprika pepper
salt and pepper	2 teaspoons sugar
1 clove garlic, sliced	1 large tomato, peeled and chopped
3 onions	1 oz. softened butter
plain flour	
3 tablespoons oil	
Marinade:	
2 pints water	2 slices of lemon
¼ pint white vinegar	1 bay leaf
6 peppercorns	2 cloves

Rub meat with salt and pepper. Cut ½-inch deep slits in meat and insert the slices of garlic. Put into a heatproof bowl and top with 1 onion, sliced. Boil all ingredients for the marinade together and pour, while boiling, over the meat. Cover and cool. Allow to stand in the refrigerator for 24 hours.

Next day, lift meat out of marinade, wipe dry and rub lightly with flour. Reserve 2 tablespoons marinade. Heat 2 tablespoons of the oil in a large fireproof casserole or a heavy saucepan and sear the meat over a high heat until brown on all sides. Lift out of pan, add remaining oil and fry the remaining onions which have been chopped. When the onions are a light golden colour, return meat and add the paprika pepper, sugar and tomato. Stir in the reserved marinade. Cover pan and simmer very gently over a low heat for about 3 hours until the meat is tender when tested with a fine skewer. Shake pan from time to time to prevent sticking. Transfer meat to a heated platter. Blend 1 tablespoon plain flour with the softened butter and stir into gravy to thicken. Taste and, if necessary, add more salt and pepper. Spoon some of the gravy over meat and serve remainder in a sauceboat. Serve with Bavarian Cabbage and Boiled New Potatoes. Serves 8.

Note: The Sauerbraten may be cooked in a moderate oven (350°F.). Allow approximately 30 minutes more cooking time. Sour cream may be stirred into gravy before serving.

Veal Paprika with Capers ••

3 large onions	2 tablespoons tomato
3 oz. butter	paste
2½ lb. stewing veal	1 small green pepper
(shoulder or neck)	2 tablespoons water
3 teaspoons paprika	1 tablespoon capers
pepper	½ pint sour cream
salt and pepper	

Chop onions finely and gently cook in butter in a heavy pan until beginning to turn golden. Cut veal into small squares and add to pan with paprika pepper, salt and pepper to season. Cook quickly until meat browns, stirring constantly. Add tomato paste, chopped green pepper and water. Cover and simmer slowly for 45 minutes or longer until meat is tender. It may be necessary to add a little more water during cooking. Stir in capers and sour cream. Serve with buttered noodles. Follow recipe for Buttered Noodles Verdi (see index) but use plain ribbon noodles instead of the green. Serves 6.

Note: 8 oz. washed button mushrooms may be added to casserole 15 minutes before serving.

Norwegian Lamb Shanks with Sour Cream Sauce ••

6 lamb shanks	2 tablespoons (1 oz.)
salt and pepper	plain flour
3 oz. butter	3 tablespoons chopped
1 large onion, chopped	fresh dill or 2
1½ cups dry white wine	teaspoons dried
½ cup beef stock or water	green dill
and beef stock cube	1 cup thick sour cream
1 bay leaf	

Trim excess fat from lamb shanks, and season shanks with salt and freshly ground pepper. Heat 2 oz. butter in a frying pan and brown lamb shanks on all sides. Transfer to a fireproof casserole. Gently cook onion in pan drippings until onion is transparent, pour in wine and stock, bring to the boil and add to lamb shanks with bay leaf. Simmer, covered, for about 1½ hours or until shanks are tender. Cool, then chill and remove any fat that sets on top. Heat again. Remove shanks to a hot plate and keep warm. Strain stock. Melt remaining butter in the casserole, add flour and stir over moderate heat for 2 minutes. Gradually add stock. Stir until mixture boils and thickens. Add dill and sour cream. Season to taste

with salt and pepper. Return lamb shanks. Heat thoroughly, but do not boil. Serve with Boiled New Potatoes and Cucumber Salad. Serves 6.

Chicken Provençal en Casserole •••

1 x 3½-4 lb. chicken	1 clove garlic, crushed
4 oz. butter	2 tablespoons olive oil
salt and pepper	1 x 16 oz. can tomatoes,
few stalks parsley	drained
3 strips orange rind	8 oz. button mushrooms
½ cup chicken stock	chopped parsley to
½ cup dry white wine	garnish
1 onion, finely chopped	

Put 1 oz. butter, a little salt and pepper, parsley stalks and orange rind inside chicken. Tie legs together with string. Rub bird with 3 oz. butter and put on its side in a roasting pan with ¼ cup each stock and wine. Put into a hot oven (400°F.) for 20 minutes, turn on other side and baste well with stock and wine. Reduce heat to moderately hot (375°F.) and continue cooking, turning and basting every 15 minutes and adding more stock and wine as necessary. There should be just enough stock to keep the juice in pan from scorching. Cook for 1-1½ hours or until chicken is done, turning on its back for the last 15 minutes to brown the breast.

When chicken has cooled slightly, cut into joints. In a fireproof casserole, gently fry onion and garlic in oil until onion is transparent. Add tomatoes and cook for 1 minute. Strain the wine and stock mixture in which chicken was roasted into a measuring cup and, if necessary, add more stock or wine to measure ¾ cup. Add to tomatoes in pan. When boiling, top with chicken and washed mushrooms. Cover and place in a moderately hot oven (375°F.) for 20-30 minutes until thoroughly heated. Sprinkle with parsley. Serve with Steamed Rice or Baked Potatoes and Green Beans or a Green Salad (see index for recipes). Serves 5-6.

Chicken in Wine ••

1 x 3 lb. chicken	1 cup dry white wine
salt and pepper	1 sprig parsley
1 oz. butter	1 sprig rosemary
1 tablespoon olive oil	8 oz. button mushrooms
2-3 cloves garlic, finely	4 tomatoes
chopped	6 oz. large green olives
1 tablespoon (½ oz.)	(optional)
plain flour	
1 cup chicken stock or	
water and chicken	
stock cube	

Cut chicken into serving pieces and wipe dry. Season with salt and pepper. Heat butter and oil in a fireproof casserole and sauté chicken gently until golden on all sides. Sauté one layer at a time. Remove chicken and set aside. To pan add garlic and flour. Stir over a low heat 1 minute without colouring. Add stock and wine. Season with salt and pepper and bring to the boil, stirring. Lower heat, return chicken pieces and add parsley and rosemary. Simmer gently for 1 hour.

Wash mushrooms, trim stems. Peel and halve tomatoes and remove stones from olives. Add prepared mushrooms, tomatoes and olives to pan and simmer a further 30 minutes. Taste and, if necessary, add more salt and pepper. Serve with Steamed Rice. (See index for recipe). Serves 4-6.

Note: 2½ lb. chicken pieces, which can be purchased from most large stores, may be used instead of the whole chicken.

Lapin Moutarde ••

This casserole has the flavour of mustard and bacon. Gentle cooking and a subtle combination of flavours make it a delicately delicious dish.

1 rabbit	salt and pepper
2 teaspoons vinegar	2 tablespoons French
1 tablespoon (½ oz.)	mustard
plain flour	bouquet garni (bunch of
1 tablespoon oil	fresh herbs)
1 oz. butter	¼ pint cream
4-6 onions, peeled	2 teaspoons chopped
4 oz. streaky bacon, diced	parsley
1¼ pints stock or water	
and bacon or chicken	
stock cubes	

Joint the rabbit and soak overnight in salted water, with vinegar, to cover. Drain and dry rabbit thoroughly, then coat with the flour. Heat oil and butter in a fireproof casserole or heavy saucepan, add onions, cut into quarters lengthwise and cook for 3 minutes, remove. Add rabbit and bacon and cook to a golden brown. Pour in stock, add salt, pepper, mustard and bouquet garni. Bring slowly to the boil and simmer, covered, for 1½ hours until tender. If sauce is too thin, lift rabbit out of pan and boil liquid rapidly, until slightly thickened. Add cream and chopped parsley. If necessary, add more seasoning to taste. Pour over rabbit and serve with Boiled New Potatoes or Creamy Mashed Potatoes. (See index for recipes). Serves 4.

Rabbit in Beer ••

Beer goes exceptionally well with rabbit and seems to give it a rather gamey taste. For those who like a robust flavour, this is an ideal choice.

1 rabbit	½ pint beer
salt and pepper	2 teaspoons sugar
3 small onions	bouquet garni (bunch
4 oz. streaky bacon	of fresh herbs)
2 oz. butter	1 teaspoon French
1 tablespoon (½ oz.)	mustard
plain flour	

Soak rabbit in cold salted water to cover for 1 hour. Dry well, cut into joints and season with salt and pepper. Slice onions and chop bacon. Melt 1 oz. butter in fireproof casserole or a heavy saucepan, add onion and bacon and fry until golden. Remove. Add remaining butter to casserole and fry rabbit, turning constantly until a pale golden colour. Add to onion and bacon. Stir flour into pan, blend well and add beer, scraping to loosen all the pan juices. Return rabbit, onion and bacon to casserole, add sugar, bouquet garni and mustard. Cover and bring to the boil, lower heat and simmer, for 1½ hours or until the rabbit is tender. Or bake in a moderate oven (350°F.) for about 2 hours. Serve with Creamy Mashed Potatoes or Boiled New Potatoes. (See index for recipes). Serves 4.

Cucumber Salad •

2 green cucumbers	⅓ cup water
2 teaspoons snipped fresh	2 teaspoons sugar
dill or ½ teaspoon	½ teaspoon salt or more
dried dill	to taste
⅓ cup white vinegar	1 tablespoon salad oil

Slice cucumbers very thinly and arrange in bowl. Sprinkle layers with dill. Mix together vinegar, water, sugar, salt and salad oil. Taste and add more salt if necessary. Pour over cucumber slices. Cover and chill about 2 hours. Serves 6.

Boiled New Potatoes •

Scrub 2 lb. new potatoes and boil in their skins in salted water to cover, with a sprig of mint, for 15-20 minutes, or until tender. Drain. Serve with a pat of butter and garnish, if liked, with chopped mint or parsley. Serves 6.

Bavarian Cabbage ••

½ large cabbage	2 teaspoons brown sugar
1 onion, finely chopped	¼ pint white wine (or ½
1 oz. butter	cup water and 1
salt	tablespoon white
freshly ground pepper	vinegar)

Shred cabbage finely, discarding thick ribs. Gently fry onion in butter until tender, top with cabbage, seasoning and brown sugar. Add wine. Bring to the boil, lower heat and simmer for about 8 minutes until cabbage is tender, shaking pan occasionally. Add more salt and pepper if necessary.

Tarragon Chicken cooked in a Pot.

148

Lapin Moutarde.

Drinks

One of the most thumbed books in our house is the 'Esquire Drink Book'.* It is inscribed,

> 'To Margaret
> Don't let this go to your head.
> Denis'.

My husband was not to know when he included it in my Christmas stocking that I was not always going to heed his advice. Like our marriage vows taken for better or worse, it has given us and our friends so much pleasure, for drinks are surely as important as food to most parties.

Remember that making a good drink is like making a good dish. Start with a reliable recipe, measure and follow instructions. If the recipe says stir, stir lightly, if it says shake, shake hard.

Some suggestions that help run a party smoothly:
Invite only as many guests as you can comfortably accommodate, just as important when catering for drinks as for food.
Check that you have sufficient glasses, china, and cutlery and set all out ready for use. The day before, wash and polish glasses to a sparkle. For large parties consider hiring glasses.
See that ice buckets, dishes for savouries and all bar equipment such as bottle openers, can openers, knife, ice-pick, cocktail picks, stirrers, coasters, tongs and dishes for garnishes and nibbles are ready at hand.
Replenish your soda siphon and keep it chilled.
Order plenty of party ice in plastic bags. If your refrigerator cannot accommodate all the food and drink needed for the party, fill a large sink or small tub with ice and bury bottles in it. Cover with an old blanket to prevent quick melting.
For a large party, as a first drink, have ready a welcoming punch bowl. Serve a punch to each guest as they arrive.
For a cocktail party serve two cocktails, one sweet and one dry. These can often be mixed early in a big jug, poured back into the bottles and chilled in the refrigerator (never more than overnight).
If not serving cocktails offer sweet and dry sherry, whisky and gin with the appropriate bottled carbonated drinks. Also have plenty of cold beer on hand.
When serving 'nips' use a jigger measure for the liquor and fill up to taste.
Well chilled glasses make all drinks more appetising. Chill as many as possible in the refrigerator or bury in party ice. Put fresh ice into glasses before pouring the drink.

Wine and Cheese Party.

*Published by Shakespeare Head, in Australia, 1957.

Cocktails and Short Drinks

A cocktail served before a meal should not be more than $2\frac{1}{2}$ fl. oz. It is a very short drink to whet the appetite and two cocktails are generally enough, as they are quite potent. Of course, if dinner is not ready, serve a third but not more. Cocktails consist of a liquor base with added flavours and are always served ice cold.

Short drinks are also popular and lend themselves to more variety. Some include fruit juices and are suitable for those who prefer a sweet drink.

Banana Rum Flip •

8 ice cubes	$\frac{1}{2}$ cup canned pineapple
1 can daiquiri mix	juice
1 tablespoon icing	$\frac{1}{2}$ cup light rum
sugar	2 small ripe bananas

Put all ingredients into the container of an electric blender. Blend 1 minute at high speed, or until ice is completely crushed and mixture is very smooth. Pour into cocktail glasses and serve immediately. Serves 6.

Champagne Cocktail •

In a chilled Champagne glass, saturate a lump of sugar with Angostura bitters. Add a cube of ice and fill the glass with Champagne. Twist a strip of lemon peel over the glass and drop it in.

Crème de Menthe Frappé •

Fill cocktail glass with crushed ice and pour over crème de menthe or your favourite liqueur. Top with a sprig of mint.

Gimlet •

Put 3 parts dry gin and 1 part lime or lemon juice in a cocktail shaker or pitcher. Shake or stir with ice and strain into a large 4 fl. oz. cocktail glass. Add a dash of soda water.

Martini •

Put 6 parts gin and 1 part vermouth into a cocktail jug over ice. Stir and strain into cocktail glasses. Serve with an olive.

Sweet Martini •

Half fill a mixing glass with ice and pour over it 1 part each of sweet and dry vermouth. Add 6 parts gin, stir the mixture thoroughly, and strain it into chilled cocktail glasses, each containing a green olive.

Margarita •

salt

1½ fl. oz. white tequila

½ fl. oz. triple sec

1 fl. oz. lemon juice

cracked ice

Moisten the glass rim with fruit rind and then dip in salt. Shake the tequila, triple sec and lemon juice with cracked ice, strain. Sip over the salty glass rim.

Mai Tai •

The unofficial drink of the state of Hawaii.

1½ fl. oz. light rum

3 fl. oz. pineapple juice

3 fl. oz. orange juice

3 fl. oz. lemon juice

½ fl. oz. orange Curaçao

1½ fl. oz. dark rum

Mix together all the ingredients except dark rum. Pour over crushed ice. Float dark rum on top of drink. Decorate with an orchid, gardenia, maraschino cherry or a spear of fresh pineapple. Makes 2 drinks.

Scotch on the Rocks •

Half fill an old fashioned glass with ice. Pour over the ice 2 fl. oz. of your favourite Scotch whisky.

Vermouth Half and Half •

Half fill a mixing glass with ice and pour over it equal parts of sweet and dry vermouth. Stir the mixture thoroughly and strain into chilled cocktail glasses. Twist a strip of lemon peel over each drink and drop it in.

Vermouth on the Rocks •

Half fill an old fashioned glass with ice. Fill the glass with either sweet or dry vermouth and add a strip of lemon peel, twisted.

Whisky Sour •

Put into a cocktail shaker 1½ fl. oz. whisky, ½ fl. oz. lemon juice, ½ fl. oz. sugar syrup and a dash of egg white. Shake with crushed ice and pour into a 7 fl. oz. glass. Decorate with a cherry and orange slice.

Long Drinks

Long drinks, served ice cold in tall, frosted glasses, are most suitable for summer. The very act of holding the glass cools you down. They usually consist of spirits mixed with fruit juices, carbonated drinks or diluted fruit cordials. Fruit, sprigs of mint or slices of cucumber may be added.

Hot long drinks have the opposite effect, they are ideal for winter drinking.

Pimm's Cup with Riesling •

3 fl. oz. Pimm's No. 1 cup

3 fl. oz. sweet vermouth

3 fl. oz. riesling

1 cup soda water

crushed ice

cucumber rind

Just before serving, combine all ingredients (except cucumber) with crushed ice and stir well. Pour into tall glasses and decorate each with a strip of cucumber rind.

Bloody Mary •

3 fl. oz. tomato juice

½ fl. oz. lemon juice

dash Worcestershire sauce

1½ fl. oz. vodka

salt and pepper

cracked ice

Shake all ingredients well together until thoroughly chilled and strain into a 6 fl. oz. glass. Or, omit cracked ice and mix all other ingredients well together. Pour over crushed ice in a highball glass.

Brandy Fizz •

Put 2 fl. oz. brandy in a tall glass with crushed ice. Fill up with ginger ale, add a piece of orange peel and 4 leaves of fresh mint.

Brandy Tropical •

Half fill a mixing glass with cracked ice and pour over it 1 part lemon juice, 2 parts Curaçao, 8 parts brandy and 1 dash of bitters for each drink. Shake the mixture vigorously and pour into glasses. Add a strip of lemon peel.

Cherry Flip •

Half fill a 5-7 fl. oz. glass with ice. Add 1 fl. oz. Amsterdam (cherry and egg brandy) and then add enough soda water to fill.

English Bishop ••

1 orange

whole cloves

brown sugar

1 bottle port

3 fl. oz. cognac, heated

Stud the orange generously with the cloves, coat with brown sugar and cook in a moderately hot oven (375°F.) until sugar lightly caramelizes. Cut the candied orange into quarters, put into a glass or porcelain saucepan with port and simmer the mixture for 20 minutes. Remove from heat and add cognac. Serve drink in heated mugs or punch cups. Makes 6 x 4 fl. oz. servings.

Crème de Menthe Soda •

Spoon crushed ice into a 5-7 fl. oz. glass, add 1 oz. crème de menthe and enough soda to almost fill glass. Top with a spoonful of vanilla ice cream.

Hot Buttered Rum and Cider •

For each drink you need:

2-inch strip orange peel

1 teaspoon brown sugar

1½ jiggers rum

1 heaped teaspoon

    unsalted butter

small piece cinnamon

    stick

3 pinches ground cloves

3 pinches ground allspice

cider, scalding hot

Put orange peel, sugar and ½ jigger warmed rum into a flameproof silver or pewter cup. Ignite the rum and let it burn out. Add remaining rum, butter, cinnamon, cloves and allspice. Fill cup with hot cider and stir vigorously. **Note:** A jigger is 1½ fluid ounces.

Long Brandy Crusta •

2½ tablespoons water
1 tablespoon castor
  sugar
2-3 sprigs of mint

4 fl. oz. brandy
crushed ice
strawberries
slices of orange

Put into a large glass the water, castor sugar and sprigs of mint. Press mint into sugar and water to extract the flavour, then add the brandy. Fill up with crushed ice and stir well. A few strawberries and a slice of orange add attraction.

Moscow Mule •

Place 2 ice cubes in long glasses or mugs. Add 2 fl. oz. vodka, the juice of ½ small lemon and fill up with ginger beer. Decorate with a slice of lemon.

Screwdriver •

Put ice cubes into a 6 fl. oz. glass. Add 1½ fl. oz. vodka and enough orange juice to fill. Stir well and serve.

The Collinses •

Half fill a cocktail shaker with ice and pour over it 1 teaspoon castor sugar, juice of ½ lemon and 1 jigger liquor. The liquor may be gin, vodka, bourbon, rye, rum or Irish or Scotch whisky. Shake the mixture thoroughly, and strain it into a large highball glass over ice. Fill the glass with soda water and garnish with a cherry, orange or lemon slice as desired.

The most familiar Collins is the Tom Collins made with gin.

Whisky Highball •

Put ice cubes into a highball glass and pour 1½ fl. oz. whisky over. Add a twist of lemon peel. Add enough soda from siphon to fill glass. Stir.

Punches and Wine Cups

Punches and wine cups are the best way to quench the thirst of a crowd. Use a traditional punch bowl or any large container available, such as a large glass jug or a glass or pottery bowl. It makes for easy serving as it needs only to be ladled out.

The traditional serving used is a 4-5 fl. oz. claret or a 6 fl. oz. Champagne saucer or the small glass cups sometimes made to go with punch bowls.

Punch should be served cold, so keep the bowl in the refrigerator until serving time.

Most of the punch ingredients can be combined in the serving bowl in advance and chilled. Add chilled sparkling wine or carbonated drinks only at serving time.

Use a large block of ice rather than smaller pieces or cubes as it melts much more slowly.

A stock of canned and fresh frozen fruit juices is invaluable for giving fruit flavour to punch in the most convenient way.

Decorative additions for punch may include thinly sliced cucumber rind, sprigs of fresh mint, fresh pineapple spears, cherries with the stems left on, peeled white grapes, thin slices of orange or lemon and spirals of orange or lemon rind.

Bubbly on the Block •

1 small unpeeled
  cucumber
16 fl. oz. vodka

8 fl. oz. Curaçao
large block ice
4 bottles Champagne

Remove seeds from unpeeled cucumber and cut flesh into strips. Mix vodka and Curaçao together and add to cucumber. Leave for at least 1 hour to ripen. Place ice in punch bowl, pour over mixture and gently stir in well chilled Champagne.

Claret Punch •

If a stronger flavour is preferred, add another bottle of claret. Fresh or canned fruit salad may be added to garnish.

1 bottle claret or dry
  red wine
2 large bottles lemonade
  or soda water

½ cup brandy or Curaçao
  (optional)
mint
orange and lemon slices

Just before serving, combine wine, lemonade or soda (or a combination of both) and brandy. Serve in glasses decorated with mint and orange and lemon slices. Serves 8-10.

Gin Mint Punch •

24 sprigs mint
1 cup (8 oz.) castor sugar
1 cup lemon juice

ice
1 bottle gin
2 large bottles ginger ale

Bruise mint sprigs and place in a bowl. Add sugar and lemon juice, cover and chill several hours or overnight. Strain over a block of ice, then stir in gin. Leave until required. Just before serving, add ginger ale and blend well. Serve in chilled punch glasses with a sprig of mint.

Iced Tea Punch •

2 pints boiling water
3 tablespoons tea leaves
4 cups sweet white wine
  (sauterne or moselle)
½ cup lemon juice

crushed ice
whole strawberries or
  cherries
pineapple pieces
lemon and orange slices

Pour briskly boiling water over tea leaves. Allow to stand 5 minutes. Strain into a bowl. Cool, add chilled wine and lemon juice. Pour into serving bowl with crushed ice. Decorate with fruit. Serves 8-10.

Negus •

1 bottle port
1 tablespoon sugar
2 lemons
¼ teaspoon ground
  nutmeg

¼ teaspoon ground
  cinnamon
¼ teaspoon ground cloves
1¼ pints boiling water

Heat port, but do not let boil. Stir in sugar, juice of lemons, grated rind of 1 lemon, nutmeg, cinnamon and cloves. Let mixture stand in a warm place for about 15 minutes. Add boiling water and serve immediately, garnished with grated lemon rind. Makes 16 x 4 fl. oz. servings.

Peach Bowle •

6 ripe peaches	ice
1 cup (8 oz.) sugar	extra peaches
4 bottles riesling	

Peel 6 peaches and slice into a small bowl. Sprinkle fruit with sugar and pour over ½ bottle riesling. Cover and chill overnight.

Just before serving, pour over a large block of ice and add remaining wine. Decorate with 1 or 2 peaches.

Sliced apricots, nectarines, or pineapple or whole strawberries may also be used.

Pineapple Punch •

This punch may be lightened by addition of soda water if desired, or soda water may replace the Champagne or white wine.

1 pineapple	1½ cups (10 oz.) castor
1 bottle port	sugar
1 bottle dry red wine	2 bottles sparkling white
1 bottle dry white wine	wine or Champagne
	mint

Peel and slice pineapple, put into a bowl. Add all remaining ingredients except the sparkling wine and mint. Chill well and just before serving add the sparkling wine. Decorate with mint. Serves 25-30.

Pink Champagne Bowl •

1 punnet strawberries	½ cup cognac
⅓ cup (3 oz.) sugar	large block ice
½ bottle sauterne	3 bottles pink Champagne

Place strawberries in a bowl and sprinkle with sugar. Add sauterne and cognac and chill for at least 1 hour. Place ice in a punch bowl and pour mixture over. Slowly add pink Champagne and mix punch gently.

Sangria •

2 lemons	1 flagon dry red wine
3 oranges	about 2 bottles soda
crushed ice	water
Syrup:	
½ pint water	1 cinnamon stick
1 cup (8 oz.) sugar	

Slice lemons and oranges. Put into a punch bowl or large jug. Pour the cooled syrup over fruit and chill. When ready to serve add plenty of crushed ice and the wine. Stir well and add enough chilled soda to taste. Serves about 25.

For Syrup: Boil water and sugar with cinnamon stick for 5 minutes. Allow to cool.

Note: Peach slices, strawberries or other fruit in season may replace oranges and lemons.

Trader Vic's Punch •

As well known for drinks as for food, Trader Vic serves Polynesian drinks made from recipes he gathered around the Islands and others that he concocted himself. Here is an easy one especially suited for hot weather.

For each drink you will need:

½ orange	1 slice pineapple,
½ lemon	chopped
shaved ice	1 teaspoon sugar
1 fl. oz. each dark and	½ teaspoon almond
white rum	essence

Squeeze orange and lemon, put juice into a glass, add a spoonful of shaved ice, the rum, pineapple, sugar and flavouring. Shake well and serve, unstrained in a glass or coconut shell.

For a Crowd

½ pint orange juice	2 tablespoons sugar
¼ pint lemon juice	1 tablespoon almond
1 pint each white and	essence
dark rum	crushed ice
1 x 29 oz. can crushed	2 pints soda water
pineapple	

Combine orange juice, lemon juice, rum, pineapple, sugar and almond essence in a punch bowl. Add soda water just before serving. Serves 20.

Note: This is an adaptation of the original Trader Vic's Punch, not as strong but more suitable as a punch to serve throughout a long evening of feasting.

Wedding Punch •

1 punnet strawberries,	1 orange, thinly sliced
washed and hulled	2 large bottles soda
½ cup Curaçao	water
3 bottles dry red wine	sprigs of mint

Marinate the strawberries in the Curaçao for 2 hours, then pour in the red wine. Garnish with oranges slices, add soda and sprigs of mint, chill. This punch may be extended with the addition of extra bottles of soda water or 2 full siphon bottles of soda water. Serves 25.

Wine Cup •

1 flagon wine	mint sprigs
½-1 cup brandy (optional)	orange and lemon slices
4 pints chilled soda water	
or lemonade	

For the wine use hock, sauterne, rosé or claret. About 2 hours before serving combine wine and brandy (if used). Chill. Add soda just before serving and decorate with mint and fruit slices. Serve in small glasses, or, for a tall cool drink, pour the Wine Cup over ice cubes.

Non-alcoholic Drinks

Non-alcoholic or 'soft' drinks have a very definite place in entertaining. Your liquor cabinet may be well stocked but there are often guests who prefer soft drinks. Meet their needs in an imaginative way with these delicious cool combinations of fruit juices and carbonated drinks.

Beverages with a coffee, tea or chocolate base will prove popular with the younger crowd.

Citrus Grape Cooler •

3 tablespoons sugar
1 cup orange juice
½ cup lemon juice
½ cup canned grape juice
2 cups water
1 tray ice cubes

Combine sugar and fruit juices. Stir until sugar dissolves. Add water and ice. Stir well to mix.

Fresh Lemonade •

4-6 lemons
6 cups water
1½ cups (12 oz.) sugar
ice cubes
lemon slices to garnish

Peel the rind from 4 lemons as thinly as possible, discarding any white pith. Put rinds into a saucepan with 2 cups water and sugar. Simmer gently for 20 minutes. Strain and allow to cool. Squeeze enough lemons to make 1 cup juice and strain into a large jug.

Add remaining 4 cups water, then stir in the cold syrup. Put ice into tall glasses and pour lemon mixture over. Decorate with lemon slices. Serves about 8.

50/50 Punch •

8 cups (4 lb.) sugar
3 pints water
grated rind of 2 oranges
    and 1 lemon
juice of 6 oranges
juice of 3 lemons
1 oz. citric acid
1 packet (¾ oz.) Epsom
    salts

Boil sugar and water together for 5 minutes, then pour over the rind and juice of the oranges and lemons, the citric acid and Epsom salts. Stir until dissolved, strain and bottle. Store in the refrigerator. Put 1-2 tablespoons of the syrup in each glass, fill with ice and water. Decorate with orange or lemon slices.

Note: If serving the punch in a large bowl, add plenty of ice to the bowl, pour on the syrup and water to taste. Decorate the bowl with sliced fruits. For a bubbly punch, add soda water before serving.

Iced Coffee •

For each serving, dissolve 1½ teaspoons instant coffee powder in a little boiling water. Add ice and cold water to make about ¾ cup. In tall glass stir 1 tablespoon vanilla ice cream with ½ teaspoon vanilla essence. Gradually add coffee, stirring. If liked top with a spoonful of whipped cream. Sprinkle with drinking chocolate. For a special flavour 2 teaspoons of crème de cacao may be added.

Iced Tea •

This makes a most refreshing drink on hot summer days. Allow 1½-2 teaspoons tea to each ¾ cup boiling water. Allow to stand for 3 minutes. Strain and add three times the quantity of cold tap water. (If chilled in refrigerator the tea will become cloudy). Add ice and serve in glasses with slices of lemon and, if liked, sprigs of mint.

Pineappleade •

1 pineapple
8 cups water
¼ cup lemon juice
1 cup (8 oz.) sugar
ice
sprigs of mint

Cut top from pineapple, then remove skin in strips. Cut pineapple into quarters lengthwise with a large sharp knife, then remove core from each quarter. Put skin and core into a saucepan with water. Bring to the boil and simmer, covered, for 1½-2 hours. Strain liquid into another pan, add lemon juice and sugar. Boil 5 minutes. Cover and cool. Serve icy cold in tall glasses with ice cubes and mint. Serves about 10.

Note: This is an ideal way of using up pineapple skins when pineapple is used as a dessert, however pineapple spears may be added to the drink.

Pink Lemonade •

Into each tall glass squeeze the juice of 1 lemon, add 2 teaspoons sugar and blend well. Add ice cubes and fill with soda water. Add enough strawberry or raspberry cordial to colour.

Wine to serve during dinner

You don't have to be a connoisseur of fine wine to know what types of wine go with certain foods. If you are uncertain, rely on a good wine merchant for almost anyone who sells wine has a good idea of what they are selling. They usually have small informative booklets from the wine companies which give suggestions on serving the wines.

There are no real rules about serving white wines with white meats, red wines with red meats. Most wine men will tell you to drink what you like best, but it will be noted that the same men are most selective in their choice of wines with food. Most agree that dinner wines should be dry or semi-dry, whether they are red or white.

On page 17, pointers are given on what to look for in a wine. Learn as you go. It is amazing how soon wine characteristics are recognised and remembered.

A guide to wine types to serve with different foods:

Appetiser Wines: Pale (dry) sherries are ideal, sweet sherry tends to have a depressing affect on the appetite. Pale sherry also goes well with many soups. They may be chilled or not.

Dry White Wines: There are light delicate white wines and more robust ones. The more delicate the dish the more delicate the wine. Dry whites go with fish, poultry, lamb and veal.

Dry Red Wines: Serve with beef, seasoned poultry, lamb, veal, beef, fruit and cheese. Like white wines, reds may be light or more robust. The more highly seasoned dishes will be complemented by the more robust wines.

Rosé Wines: For hot, summery days rosé wines are ideal and have the advantage of going with almost anything. A rosé is especially good with cold summer buffet food, and it looks beautiful in the glass.

Sweet White Wines: Serve with desserts and fruit.

Champagne: Can be served throughout the meal. Do not serve a dry Champagne with desserts for it makes them taste sour. However dry a Champagne, it still goes with cheese and fruit.

Weights and measures

All the recipes in this book use these measures which simplify cooking and can be depended upon to give perfect results.

"How to measure correctly"

Dry ingredients

Measurements are given in cups or pounds and ounces. The cup measurements are based on the 8 fluid ounce measuring cup. Metal measuring cups are ideal for dry ingredients. Look for a graduated set that includes $\frac{1}{4}$ cup, $\frac{1}{3}$ cup, $\frac{1}{2}$ cup and 1 cup. A good set of scales is also useful.

In measuring dry ingredients (flour, icing sugar etc.) heap the cup or spoon then level off excess with a straight edged knife or spatula.

Spoon measures

Spoon measurements are *level* unless otherwise stated. Sets of Australian measuring spoons are available but are smaller than most household spoons. *We have used household spoons throughout*, however, all recipes have been tested and are successful using both the new standard measuring spoons or the household spoons.

Liquid measures

The most important fact to know is that the British Imperial Pint is 20 fluid ounces, (this is used in Australia and in this book) and the American and Canadian pint is 16 fluid ounces. For accuracy, a glass measuring cup with a lip is recommended when measuring liquid ingredients. These cups are available in several sizes:

1 cup or 8 fluid ounces
2 cups or 16 fluid ounces
$\frac{1}{2}$ pint or 10 fluid ounces

All of these cups are divided into ounce measures, also cups and fractions of cups, i.e. $\frac{1}{4}$ cup, $\frac{1}{3}$ cup, $\frac{1}{2}$ cup, etc. These may also be used for measuring dry ingredients.

Common food weights and measures

For accurate measuring, spoon dry ingredients into cups, level off or shake gently unless otherwise stated.

8 fluid ounce measuring cup:	Weight in ounces
1 cup butter or margarine	8 oz
1 cup flour	4 oz
1 cup crystal sugar	8 oz
1 cup brown sugar (lightly packed)	5 oz
1 cup brown sugar (firmly packed)	6 oz
1 cup icing sugar (free from lumps)	5 oz
1 cup castor sugar	8 oz
1 cup desiccated coconut	3 oz
1 cup uncooked rice	8 oz
1 cup raisins	6 oz
1 cup currants	5 oz
1 cup sultanas	6 oz
1 cup liquid (e.g. milk, water)	8 fl oz

Household tablespoon

2 tablespoons flour	1 oz
1 tablespoon sugar (slightly rounded)	1 oz
2 tablespoons icing sugar (sifted)	1 oz
3 tablespoons cornflour	1 oz
2 tablespoons gelatine	1 oz
1 tablespoon jam	1 oz
$1\frac{1}{2}$ tablespoons uncooked rice	1 oz
1 tablespoon golden syrup	1 oz
1 tablespoon butter	1 oz
1-$1\frac{1}{2}$ tablespoons dried fruit	1 oz
5 tablespoons instant coffee powder	1 oz
2 tablespoons cocoa	1 oz

In this book the Imperial Pint is used

1 pint	20 fl oz
$\frac{1}{2}$ pint	10 fl oz
$\frac{1}{4}$ pint	5 fl oz
1 cup	8 fl oz
$\frac{1}{2}$ cup	4 fl oz
1 gill	5 fl oz or $\frac{1}{4}$ pint

Oven temperatures

1. Follow instructions for your own particular make of stove or cooker to set the temperature indicated.
2. The oven temperatures given in the recipes in this book refer to a gas oven. Adjust the temperature accordingly, with reference to the guide below for electric ovens.
3. Here is a general guide to the main oven settings.

Description of Oven	Automatic Electric	Gas Thermostat Setting °F
Cool or low	200	200
Very slow	250	250
Slow	300–325	300
Moderately slow	325–350	325
Moderate	350–375	350
Moderately hot	375–400	375
Hot	400–450	400
Very hot	450–500	450

Index

159